STREET FOODS

STREET FOODS

Urban Food and Employment
in Developing Countries

IRENE TINKER

New York   Oxford   •   Oxford University Press   1997

Oxford University Press

Oxford   New York

Athens   Auckland   Bangkok   Bogota   Bombay   Buenos Aires
Calcutta   Cape Town   Dar es Salaam   Delhi   Florence   Hong Kong
Istanbul   Karachi   Kuala Lumpur   Madras   Madrid   Melbourne
Mexico City   Nairobi   Paris   Singapore   Taipei   Tokyo   Toronto

and associated companies in
Berlin   Ibadan

Published by Oxford University Press, Inc.
198 Madison Avenue, New York, New York 10016

Oxford is a registered trademark of Oxford University Press

Library of Congress Cataloging-in-Publication Data
Tinker, Irene.
   Street Foods : urban food and employment in developing
countries / by Irene Tinker.
      p.   cm.
   Includes bibliographic references and index.
   ISBN 0-19-510435-8; ISBN 0-19-511711-5 (pbk)
   1. Food industry and trade—Developing countries—Case studies.
2. Vending stands—Developing countries—Case studies.
3. Women—Employment—Developing countries—Case studies.   I. Title.
HD9018.D44T56   1996
381'.456413'0091724—dc20   96-23909

9 8 7 6 5 4 3 2 1

Printed in the United States of America
on acid free paper

Preface

The Street Food Project on which this book is based encompasses a decade; revisiting the sites and writing the book took another five years. Thanking everyone who supported and encouraged this ground-breaking project is not possible: it would take another book. Further, the usual way of acknowledging assistance presumes that the author created the book alone.

Such is definitely not the case with the Street Food Project, which was a collaborative effort from the start. Based at the Equity Policy Center (EPOC), a research policy center established in Washington, D.C., to insert the differential concerns of women and men into the international development discourse, the entire enterprise was geared to principles of feminist research. Colleagues in each of the countries are featured in the appropriate chapters and in the bibliography, but deserve to be mentioned here as well: Naomi Owens and Naseem Hussain in Bangladesh; Sarah Loza in Egypt; Barbara Anne Chapman in Indonesia; Olufemi O. Kujore, Tola Olu Pearce, and V. Aina Agboh-Bankole in Nigeria; Gerald Barth and Mei-Jean Kuo in the Philippines; Jill Posner in Senegal; and Cristina Blanc Szanton, Amara Pongsapich, and Napat Sirisambhand in Thailand. The excellence of their initial studies can only be partly captured in this book; their assistance in reading over draft chapters, sending photographs and maps, and clarifying conclusions, after many years doing other work, cannot be overestimated.

Here I wish to credit the broader circles of support. Congressional hearings initiated by Congressman Donald Fraser in 1973 gave legitimacy to the arguments undergirding the Women in Development movement. Arvonne Fraser, as director of the WID Office in the U.S. Agency for International Development, supported this burgeoning effort with funds and enthusiasm; EPOC was only one of the centers and groups that benefited from her leadership, but the cumulation of activity launched the WID movement. Paula Goddard provided agency support, through which Jean Ellickson, Jane Jaquette, and John Hourihand served as program officers and good friends. In the field, Tom Timberg and Bob Barnes in Bangladesh, Gary Cook in the Philippines, and Bill Fuller in Indonesia championed the project.

The Ford Foundation had more bureaucratic difficulty fitting this urban-based study of women and men into their hierarchy: Katherine McKee, our program officer, was situated in the rural section. In Jakarta, Tom Kessinger was instrumental in both the Indonesian and Thai studies; Ann Sutoro supported the Bogor study. Cynthia Mynitti in Cairo and Lillian Trager in Lagos made those respective studies possible. The long-term interest of Susan Berresford in street foods facilitated my return visits; regional staff opened their files and offices to me: Natalia Kanem in Lagos, Akwasi Aidoo in Dakar, and Heba El-Kholy in Cairo.

Crucial to these return study trips were colleagues who were themselves associated with projects or policies related to street vending. In Lagos, Clara Osinulu of the African-American Institute helped immeasurably by setting up meetings and arranging accommodations and travel; her careful reading of the Nigeria chapter was much appreciated. Interviewing Isaac Olaolu Akinyele in Ibadan about his extensive street foods studies in Nigeria was a delight; I thank him, too, for recognizing that I needed more than tea at mid-morning, having eaten nothing before leaving Lagos. Lillian Trager connected me with Clara Osinulu and offered salient comments on the chapter.

In Iloilo, my return visit was programmed by Mayor Malabor, who met me at the airport with his retinue and wreaths. Most helpful in filling gaps in the 10 years between visits were former Mayor Herrera and Alex Umadhay, who also read over the draft of my chapter on the Philippines. In Bogor, Joep J. M. Bijlmer provided me with extensive materials on the follow-up study and on his earlier research. In Thailand, young scholar Gisele Yasmin brought me up to date on Bangkok's burgeoning street food trade. In Dhaka, Aroma Goon had moved from USAID to PACT (Private Agencies Collaborating Together) and provided recent information on the Manikganj Association for Social Service (MASS). It was Sarah Loza's enthusiasm for the Street Food Project in Minia, and its amazing impact, that propelled me to study the long-term impact of the project in all the countries; her current street food project in Cairo deserves worldwide attention.

The two street food studies supported by the International Development Research Centre utilized the methodology and resources of EPOC. But without the determination of Meera Bapat and Christopher Benninger in Pune, that study would not have happened. Elsa Chaney, a member of the EPOC board, stimulated Dorian Powell in Jamaica to undertake the project in Kingston and served as volunteer advisor.

The Food and Agriculture Organization in Rome observed the Street Food Project from its inception and incorporated many aspects in their voluminous studies of the sector. Many staff provided research materials and arranged meetings over the years. After I interviewed him in Rome in 1994, Alan Randell rounded up an almost complete collection of FAO street food studies and sent them to me. Zak Sabry is now my valued colleague at Berkeley.

EPOC board member Laure Sharp reviewed survey instruments. Esther Ocloo,

Nkulenu Industries, Accra, Ghana; Per Pinstrup-Andersen, International Food Policy Research Institute; Gelia Castillo, University of the Philippines at Los Baños; John Bardach, East-West Center, Honolulu; and Terrence McGee, University of British Columbia have all maintained interest in the project long after the completion of their tour on the project's International Advisory Committee. Monique Cohen, director of the Street Food Project during its most intensive period, continues her research on nutrition and street foods and reminds her Washington colleagues of the importance of this microentreprenuerial activity. Pamela Hunte and Coralie Turbitt worked diligently on the project while at EPOC; Naresh "Kuku" Johri performed miracles in the budget office and provided us all with a model of courage before her untimely death. Many other staff and interns added their support and enthusiasm to this major effort.

The University of California, Berkeley, has provided research grants to encourage the completion of this book. Many students have utilized the country studies in their own research, and provided insights into the findings. Susanne Freidberg took my first class on the topic and, along with William Mazzarella, assisted in the final editing. Their searching questions and comments contributed significantly to the framing of the debates relating the project to contemporary theory. Jennie Freeman utilized state-of-the-art computer technology to design the maps, and Kate Blood tested and adapted some recipes; Pat Kimball translated French materials on Senegal and compared those street foods with his favorites in Niger.

Rose Grant wrote a recipe book entitled *Street Foods* in 1988. Seeing this book encouraged me to include a few recipes in this otherwise scholarly publication: after all, everyone eats. She was delighted to contribute four recipes to this volume.

The Bellagio Study and Conference Center of the Rockefeller Foundation insulated me from my usual frenetic schedule long enough to concentrate on the final draft of the book. At the center, Louisa Green and Bessie Carrington commented on several chapters; Gianna Celli and Pasquale Pesce were gracious hosts.

The willingness of Oxford University Press to produce this unusual, many-faceted book is much appreciated. I am especially grateful to Herb Addison for agreeing to a simultaneous publication of a paperback edition and to Cynthia Garver for her thoughtful editing.

Throughout this journey and many preceding it, I have been nurtured mentally and physically by my husband, Millidge Walker, whose contribution to my life and this book are inestimable.

Berkeley, California   I. T.
November 1996

Contents

STREET FOODS

Introduction

Street foods are sold in almost every country in the world; they are so familiar that there is a tendency to look past the vendors without registering their existence, unless of course you are hungry. Then you see vendors selling foods for quick meals or snacks from daybreak until night. In Senegal, women sit on the ground outside the market place to sell *monie*, porridge made from millet, from large calabashes. In Peru, fried fish is a cheap and satisfying meal; women cook it before the customer so it is crisp and fresh. Men push carts to major intersections and sell kebabs of different types with different spices in different countries: in Indonesia, the small chunks of meat or chicken or rows of shrimp are served with peppery peanut sauce and called *sate*; meat chunks, usually beef, are larger in Senegal; ground lamb is encased in dough for *samosas* served in Bangladesh. Fried bean curd is a favorite lunch food for school-children in Indonesia; flatbread sandwiches of *foul* and *tamia,* both made from dried beans, are preferred in Egypt. Soup meals are ubiquitous throughout Southeast Asia: the stock is kept hot, with noodles and meat added to order. Soup is really a thick sauce served over farina or corn pudding in Nigeria; it is sold from gaily painted road-side stalls called *buka* that provide shaded tables for customers.

Looking at this entrepreneurial activity through a development lens, I wondered: Do the women and men selling the foods make a good living? Why do women dominate the trade in Nigeria or Thailand, but hardly a woman can be seen selling food in Bangladesh? Why, if street food is so popular, do many governments embark on street cleaning exercises, destroying stalls and confiscating supplies?

These questions eventually led to a series of comparable studies in seven provincial towns in Asia and Africa, which form Part I of this book. The studies were a means to the objective of improving the income of the vendors or the safety of the food they sold. They were designed and carried out by the Equity Policy Center (EPOC), a small think tank in Washington, D.C., which I founded in 1978 to document the differential impact of development on women and to design interventions that might assist women to attain greater equity with men.

3

The origins of the EPOC Street Foods Project cannot be comprehended without situating the ideas and the organization in its historical context. The idea of studying a microenterprise in which women in some countries were making money was a response to the well-meant but poorly conceived spate of "knitting and sewing" projects proliferating among organizations trying to help poor women in developing countries survive. The pertinence of studying a sector, not just women's roles, was grounded in the appreciation of the role of family and its precedence over individual aspirations. The relevance of working with municipal authorities was a move away from confrontational approaches of earlier women in development formulations in recognition of the bureaucratic minefields that await any shift in institutional direction. The significance of identifying interventions that would improve the income or enhance the quality and safety of the food sold was fundamental to an applied project.

EPOC was not embarked on an academic project challenging concepts of the informal sector. After all, most studies of this ephemeral sector focused on enterprises large enough to hire employees, and thus effectively erased from consideration most women who were primarily self-employed or who ran or participated in family enterprises. The ultimate project goal was to chip away at the walls of assumptions embedded in development theory that assigned women to maternal and passive roles, discounted their economic contributions, and dismissed their altruistic notions of feeding their children as behavior that was neither rational nor economic.

The success of the project can be measured in many tangible ways. Most significant is the influence of EPOC's viewpoint on working with vendors, which has influenced the position of the Food and Agriculture Organization (FAO). Moving away from a focus on the enforcement of unrealistically high food safety standards on street food vendors, FAO has instituted an impressive series of studies of street foods around the world for which they have even adopted the term "street foods", which EPOC coined. These studies detail the trade and its epidemiological problems in order to identify the most serious health issues in each city so that municipal governments can work with the vendors to change the most dangerous practices. The FAO-funded follow-up study in Bogor is extensively reported to illustrate the symbiotic relationship of the two studies. In Nigeria, studies done in three cities, but not including the EPOC site in Ife, add immeasurably to the understanding of the regional variations of the street food trade and consequently of the interventions needed to improve safety standards.

EPOC studies emphasized the critical nature that water played either in spreading disease or in avoiding contamination; many cities sought ways of providing improved access at the same time that they issued tighter regulations. Renewed efforts to train vendors in water use and food handling were a consequence of the attention locally garnered by the staff and its work with municipal and health officials. In Ife, training initiatives by faculty at the local university actually led to the EPOC project; this model was so persuasive that EPOC promoted it elsewhere. Interventions for improving the income of the vendors that were suggested by project teams in different cities have had important impacts. Insights about the interplay of vendors with government, about methods of organizing vendors, and about the types of services the vendors needed emerged in many cities. Perhaps the most impressive is the formation of the Street Food Vendors Organization in Minia, Egypt. This organization for vendors is distinct from other organizations, established or encouraged in other EPOC cities, in the composition of its government board, which includes both vendors and local decision makers. The issues raised about middle-class intermediaries and their role vis-à-vis their intended beneficiaries speaks to the concerns of the development community about ways to work with and help the world's urban poor, and adds to the literature about the growing importance of nongovernmental organizations globally.

The rich data that was produced by the EPOC study has pertinence in the academic community as well. Policy and consulting groups in Washington feed on academic research; unfortunately the reverse is seldom true. Too often, hasty writing and absence of arcane footnotes in government documents leads academics to discredit the insightful findings and robust data that are produced, which often challenges the assumptions and conclusions in scholarly discourse. The result is the production of separate streams of knowledge that would become more powerful if joined.

Many distinct discourses converge in this book: development policy, practice, and theory regarding women, poverty, training, and microenterprise; government, anthropology and economics; nutrition and epidemiology. No one, certainly not the author, can claim expert knowledge within such an array. But because the Street Food Project contributes to all of these discourses, I have sketched the range of interactions and suggested both how the findings of this project contribute to these focused debates and how these various discourses might weave among themselves to add reality to the scholarly view.

Organization of the Book

This book reflects the stages of the project and the styles of the research teams who carried out the studies. The remaining sections of the introduction trace the origin of the project in the heady atmosphere of Washington, D.C., during the early days of the second wave of the women's movement. Women were organizing to influence national legislation and international policy. "Women in development" was becoming an acceptable concept to international agencies. EPOC was a major player at the time, documenting women's economic role in development and critiquing development policies regarding energy and technology, which ignored constraints on women's time. The Street Food Project exemplifies this research at its most innovative.

The seven EPOC studies of street foods are presented in Part I: Bogor, Indonesia; Iloilo, Philippines; Chonburi, Thailand; Manikganj, Bangladesh; Minia, Egypt; Ziguinchor, Senegal; and Ile-Ife, Nigeria. Based on the original and much longer country reports that were written predominantly by anthropologists, each study provides a geographic and gastronomic tour of the city, its vendors, and the food they sell. A brief economic and political sketch of the country helps explain the particular problems faced by vendors in each city. A few typical recipes are provided to allow readers to experience the variety of tastes. Events since the studies were completed detail the local impact of each study and the interventions suggested.

The analytical chapters in Part II are grounded in scholarly discourses from many academic disciplines and address debates drawn from both theory and practice. Chapter 8 presents and analyzes the findings of the seven studies, including as appropriate the studies of Kingston, Jamaica, and Pune, India, that utilized the EPOC design. The comparative data are robust. Nine case studies conducted in highly variable areas but based on a common design and methodology produced impressively consistent results.

The food aspects of the trade are presented in chapter 9, which explores first what foods people eat on the street, and where the foods are produced and prepared. A section on demand looks at the importance of prepared food in total household food consumption across the countries, and then compares types of street food customers, when they eat, and how often. The discussion of the nutritional value of street foods focuses on the role of street foods in the diet of schoolchildren and how vendors are welcomed into schools in several countries. The chapter concludes with a section on the current food handling problems typical of the trade, and on the various training programs launched to improve vendors' practice.

The impact of the study at the micro and macro levels is explored in chapter 10, which describes the interventions recommended by the country projects and their effectiveness. The two conflicting approaches to small entrepreneurs—the microenterprise perspective of the development community and the informal sector debate that characterized scholarly research—are discussed in reference to the findings of the EPOC study. Neither approach reached to the individual or family enterprise that characterizes the street food trade, and consequently overlooked the gender aspects of their theories. The convergence of these approaches in the last decade has brought the debate to the household level, where gender analysis is imperative, especially in light of the current debate about home-based work.

In the afterword I have summarized the importance of the street food trade and speculated about its future in the next century.

Policy Origins of the EPOC Project

The Street Food Project was conceived specifically to challenge the assumptions in the development community about how best to help poor women earn an income. It was also designed as an action research project: findings from the study were meant to be utilized by members on local advisory committees for the benefit of the street food vendors themselves. The project was a logical expansion of a series of reports by Equity Policy Center staff identifying critical needs of women as rapid development often adversely affected their lives. The immediate stimulus was the failure of many early attempts to provide poor women with a means of earning an income by producing garments or knitted goods without first ascertaining a market for them.

Even when sweaters or dresses made in these "income-generating" projects for women (projects for men produced income) were sold, they provided only minimal returns for the women's work. Seeking some way to identify and support an economic activity in which women had for years been active, I brought up the idea of snack food vendors in Southeast Asia. The metamorphosis of this idea into a research design, and the challenges of securing funding and study sites, are recounted in the next section of the introduction.

Women Affecting Public Policy

Washington, D.C., in the 1970s provided many opportunities for women to change public policy. Feminists had discovered organizing; the Women's Yellow Pages, published in 1978, listed over 250 organizations, centers, and groups in the metropolitan area alone. The purpose of all this organizing was to change the way government and business and associations had been doing business. At the time of strong federal government, the key to change was found in government legislation and regulations. At first the focus was on domestic issues; but the realization that the United States was replicating abroad those same gender systems that we were trying to change at home led a group of us to focus on the impact of international development on women.

But we needed research to support our views when testifying before congressional committees and when recommending alternative programs. At the time, studies about women in the United States were minimal and were based on tiny samples; research on women in developing countries was buried in anthropological essays or in obscure government documents. To remedy this situation, many of us sought research grants, first through our professional organizations and later through research centers: I was a co-founder of the Wellesley Center for Research on Women in 1974 and a founder of the International Center for Research on Women in 1976.[1]

As a result of our testimony before Congress and at the State Department, combined with phone calls, meetings, and reports, Congress passed an amendment to the U.S. Foreign Assistance Act of 1973 that required the integration of women into development programs. Called the Percy amendment, its passage precipitated similar directives for U.N. agencies and bilateral organizations around the world (Tinker 1976, 1983). This policy shift generated a new field of research that explored women's multifaceted roles in societies around the world. Informed by the standpoint of American feminists, these studies tended to emphasize women's economic roles and to view women as independent actors; because previous development programs viewed women as adjuncts to motherhood, we downplayed and often ignored their interrelationships with family, kin, and community. The Street Food study corrects this imbalance by revealing street food vending as a family strategy (Tinker 1993a, 1995.)

A stint in the government as an appointee of President Jimmy Carter undermined my naive view that if policy makers were presented with facts about the negative impacts on women of present or proposed programs or legislation, they would accept the accuracy of the findings and change their policies. I became acutely aware of the resistance and inertia of bureaucracy. Despite my convictions, my suggestions and changes were often stymied; no wonder that others, for whom women's rights was their third or fourth priority, could not effect change. I also learned that even with excellent programs in place and enthusiastic staff, implementation was often frustrated by indigenous male-dominated groups in recipient countries, and that projects designed to assist women that did not take into account their position within the family and community were likely to fail. After resigning from ACTION, the U.S. government agency then comprising both international programs including the Peace Corps and domestic programs including VISTA (Volunteers in Service to America), I set up the Equity Policy Center in 1978 specifically to analyze the roles of both women and men relating to the sector under study, and then to work with appropriate agencies on the problems of design and implementation of development projects.

Women and Work

Efforts to understand the reality of women's existence in near subsistence societies centered first on time-use studies or on detailed research on women's work in agriculture (Acharya and Bennett 1981; Dixon-Mueller 1985; Kandiyoti 1985; Tinker 1976, 1984). By documenting the extent of women's work in rural areas, these findings questioned data on which development programs were based, and instigated pressure to revise statistical collection and analyses. Further research demonstrated that rapid social change often leads to a one-sided breakdown of the sexual division of labor, with women assuming male tasks in addition to their own while men often gain additional leisure. The growing feminization of poverty was caused in large measure by men, who left their families to search for jobs elsewhere, and sometimes failed to return.

What became clear was that poor women worked, had always worked, and needed to continue to work. What had changed was the economy: subsistence exchange was not enough, as women needed money to survive. Many traditional products that women had made to earn income, such as pottery or basket weaving, were often replaced by plastic products; beer making was declared illegal in many countries. It seemed incumbent upon planning agencies to identify and support new job opportunities. Early "income-generating" activities were largely unsuccessful, not only because women living in subsistence societies knew how to farm, not sew, but also because products were developed with no attention either to demand or marketing. Many good intentions resulted in heightened expectations and minimal returns.

Why not study an activity in which women were already earning money, and find out what might be done to improve their income? While West African agricultural produce and cloth traders had been well studied, there were indications that both politics and competitive modern delivery systems were undercutting their economic power.[2] Street vending of prepared food snacks, on the other hand, seemed to be increasing in developing countries as urban populations rose. Available literature raised as many questions at it answered; EPOC would itself have to conduct the primary research.

To obtain funding we needed a project with a title that was instantly recognizable and which reflected the importance of the topic. The term "snack" itself diminished the economic importance of the foods sold. After considerable brainstorming, envisioning the *sate* vendor in Indonesia or recalling the pungent smells of a Bangkok street, we realized that what we were talking about was food being sold on the street. "Street foods" became not only the name of the EPOC project; today it defines the study of all the meals and snacks and sweets sold on the street, and it is used by many who do not know its origin.

Designing the Study

EPOC's project design was dictated, first, by the lack of previous data. Since no data existed on street food vendors, the sector had to be studied before women's roles within it could be understood. Secondly, the project was informed by our philosophical commitment to action research, undertaken in collaboration with local research staff and benefiting the people studied. Because EPOC was a small center with no long-term funding, any suggested interventions would have to be continued by residents in the cities to be studied. To stimulate involvement in the project and its results, and to advise the research staff about everything from translations of local food products to provincial politics, participation of local decision-makers was essential at every stage of the project. As a product of the U.S. women's movement, EPOC was determined to include as many women scholars and NGO (nongovernmental organization) leaders as possible; we correctly predicted that most municipal officials would be men.

Given these parameters, we designed a generic approach that could serve as the template for each of the city studies. Actual data collection was planned to take place over the course of a year to allow for seasonal variations in food sold and any regular fluctuations in the number of vendors. Another three months were allocated for preliminary activities such as selecting sites, hiring staff, and setting up contacts in each city, and for completing the project, writing the report, and presenting the findings at local seminars.

Collecting Data

The popular image of street vendors finds them clustering around the market and clogging downtown sidewalks. But vendors also sell to travelers at bus stops, along highways, and near boat landings. They sell to celebrants at festivals and weddings, and outside temples and movie theaters. Hospitals and schools in developing countries often rely on vendors to supply food for patients, staff, and visitors.

To capture all these potential sites where vendors might sell, the first step in each study was to map the city, creating a census of street food vendors by sex and type:

mobile, semi-itinerant, and permanent. Depending on the pattern of food consumption in each town, this initial survey was taken two or three times a day to pick up those vendors selling only one meal as well as those who sold from more than one site during each day. To compensate for seasonal variations, the census was repeated several times during the year of study. As it turned out, these variations were based as often on religious holidays as on climatic or agricultural cycles.

Part of the purpose of the census-taking was to identify and list the foods that were being sold on the street. Details were recorded about when and where each food was sold, and who sold it: men or women, and specific ethnic groups. In every city, the plethora of available food astounded the research staff. Since one of the criteria for the vendor sample was to be based the type of food they sold, staff in each city had to group the foods into manageable categories that reflected local sensibilities. Some categorized the foods by their dominant ingredient, such as cassava, millet, wheat, or rice; others grouped foods by type: breakfast foods, full meals, sweets, or snacks. Others selected the most popular foods as the basis of their sample.

A 10% sample of vendors was drawn from the initial census, based on the vendors' locations and the type of food they sold. Subsequent interviews collected information about their socioeconomic background and the economics of running their enterprise. The questionnaire also inquired about relations with government officials and the existence and objectives of networks or organizations among vendors. Recognizing both the difficulty many vendors might have in reporting profits, as well as the predilection of many entrepreneurs to over- or underestimate income based on their assessment of how such information might be used, staff were asked to calculate profits of each enterprise based on their own knowledge of the costs of ingredients, fixed expenditures, and sale price of each item. In addition to the formal interview, just spending time around the selling sites provided information and insights about the vendors, their helpers, and their methods.

Staff were asked to record the food handling practices of the vendors as well as any other habits, either of vendors or customers, that might affect the sanitary conditions of the immediate environs. Was food cooked to order? How was cooked food handled before sale? Were left-overs recycled, thrown out, or eaten at home? Was water available to wash dishes or hands? Was the stall set up along a dusty road or open sewer, or in a protected area? Were children playing underfoot? Were toilets available nearby?

In addition, food samples of at least five of the most popular foods were tested for contamination. Local nutritionists were consulted on the food value of popular foods and asked for suggestions on ways to enhance nutrient value, especially for food consumed by schoolchildren. Of course, most of the researchers sampled the food they were studying, but the staff in Iloilo decided on their own to sample each type of food themselves to test its wholesomeness; only ceviche, raw fish cured with vinegar, caused any unpleasantness.

A customer survey was administered to clients of the sample vendors to elicit socioeconomic information about who eats street foods. For instance, do well-off people eat street food, or only the poor? Are consumption patterns based on occupation? Do women eat street foods as often as men? We were also curious about the frequency of consumption and whether customers were loyal to a particular vendor. Where funding allowed, household surveys were also carried out in neighborhoods representing different economic levels to find out how important street foods were to a family's diet.

The final study component in the design involved the daily observation of fifteen vendors for an extended period to examine how they allocated their time for buying, preparing, cooking, and selling their wares. The objectives of this close observation were not only to confirm earlier data, but to investigate more closely the gender divisions of labor within the street food trade. How long did it take from purchase to produce edible food? Was the food preparation area clean, and were the utensils well washed? Did wives make the food their husbands sold? Did husbands help their vendor wives in any way? Did other adult women in the household assist in food preparation or take over household and childcare duties for the vendor? Did children help with any of the enterprise activities?

Engaging the Community

From the first visit to the city, the study director was expected to call on appropriate municipal authorities both to request permission to work in their town and to involve them in the project. Usually the mayor was asked to join a project advisory committee or to appoint a member of his staff to attend. Professors in social sciences or nutrition at local universities were sought out for advice on references and potential staff; the most enthusiastic were also invited to join the advisory committee. Wherever nongovernmental organizations were active in the community, their leaders, too, were invited to participate. Some committees met monthly, helped test translation of the questionnaires into the local languages, and commented on results at every phase of the study. Other groups met only once or twice during the project; advisors in some cities were consulted individually when group meetings did not appear feasible. Whatever the form, these local contacts were invaluable to legitimize the research, provide local contacts and assistance, interpret survey results, and help identify realistic interventions that could be introduced by government or NGOs to assist the vendors and their enterprises.

At the end of each city project, advisory committee members, vendors, and anyone else with interest in street foods were invited to a final seminar held at the municipal office or local university. A draft summary of project data was available both in English and the local language. In keeping with local custom, these seminars were formally opened by local dignitaries; summary findings were immediately presented so that the governor or district officer or university rector would learn something about the study results before he left. Often these dignitaries were so intrigued by the employment or income figures presented that they stayed for the ensuing discussions about policy changes and program implementation. The magnitude of the trade was everywhere unanticipated. And the local street foods we always served were enjoyed by all.

This seminar in the city studied was followed by a similar presentation in the capital of the country. These seminars provided a superb way of ensuring that appropriate ministers or planners heard the results: we asked them to speak. The audience was always a mixture of academics and practitioners of development, both local and foreign. At the time, urban projects were not common. Our information on income, credit, and organizations was of great interest to community organizers. Challenges to the conventional wisdom concerning the informal sector intrigued the scholars. UN Agencies such as UNICEF (U.N. Children's Fund) and FAO focused their attention on the data about nutrition and food safety. Local planners found the employment and income statistics most valuable. Questions and ideas from these meetings helped sharpen recommendations for subsequent interventions and occasionally provided the mechanism for implementing these suggestions.

Getting into the Field

We now had a distinctive title and an innovative research design. Our next step was funding. At the time, our proposal to study the roles of both men and women was a departure from the women-focused projects usually funded with Women in Development (WID) grants. However, the topic intrigued two of our previous funders: the Women in Development Office of the U.S. Agency for International Development (USAID), and the Ford Foundation. Funding was ultimately dependent on lining up support from staff of these agencies in field offices, finding cooperative organizations to sponsor and conduct the research, and obtaining permission from the host government to carry out the project.

During this planning phase, the International Development Research Centre of Canada (IDRC) supplied EPOC with copies of early studies of hawkers and vendors that it had funded (McGee and Yeung 1977). IDRC does not fund U.S. organizations directly, but at our suggestion they eventually funded centers in Kingston, Jamaica, and in Pune, India. These studies utilized the EPOC methodology, background materials, and reports from the first EPOC studies. During the Jamaica study, EPOC affiliate Elsa Chaney worked with the project staff in an informal arrangement.

Overall, nine comparable studies on street foods were completed between 1983 and 1992. Each project published its report separately in English, and in the local language where appropriate. The country reports and subsequent publications that utilized the project data are listed by author in the bibliography. A comparative analysis of all nine countries is presented in Chapters 8 and 9. Because I visited Jamaica and Pune only once, and met only briefly with the project staff, I have chosen to present case studies in Part I only of the seven EPOC cities.

Situating the Indonesian Project   Indonesia exemplifies the difficulties in putting a project in place and the convolutions through which EPOC staff had to go to complete the study. Barbara Chapman, a medical anthropologist, had recently completed her doctorate at the University of Hawaii on market women in Indonesia and was anxious to return to that country. We had met in 1979; her comments on the Indonesian food system helped trigger the idea of studying women vendors.

Indonesia was one of the largest USAID missions, and finding project officers willing to take on this small, centrally funded project in addition to their regular work was difficult. The mission director, Bill Fuller, had just joined the agency, having previously headed the Bangladesh office for the Ford Foundation. This background made him sympathetic toward small research projects, and he eventually proposed a hybrid project: the USAID mission would agree to accept central USAID funding if the local Ford office would provide oversight for the study. Tom Kessinger, Ford's country director, was enthusiastic and later funded the EPOC Thai study. The Ford Foundation was already funding Lembaga Studi Pembangunan, or LSP, a local NGO that was helping to organize street vendors in several Javanese cities, and thought the two projects might complement and inform each other. Further, a newly established women's research center at the University of Indonesia was anxious to utilize the study to train their graduate students in research methods.

Chapman arrived in Indonesia in February 1983 and spent the next three months simultaneously trying to secure Indonesian government permission to conduct the study, talking to national and international organizations who might utilize the findings, and traveling around Java evaluating various cities as possible sites for the project. For governmental permission, an Indonesian sponsor was needed that would then request ministerial support. While such permission was in process, Chapman could continue her work on a three-month tourist visa given automatically to incoming visitors. But Indonesian politics and bureaucratic blunders on all sides required several shifts in sponsorship. By the end of the project, she had seen a lot more of Singapore than was either intended or budgeted for; she completed her work before official permission was granted.

While in Jakarta, Chapman met with representatives of national and international agencies both to learn about current projects in the country dealing with issues related to the EPOC project and to inform them about our project in the hope that some of them might wish to utilize our findings or to pursue interventions with vendor groups. For example, UNICEF was starting a credit program in Solo for small traders; the International Labour Organization (ILO) was sponsoring a project on women, nutrition, and firewood; the Ministry of Trade and Commerce was producing a publication on the informal sector; the Women's Study Center at the University of Indonesia was involved in a variety of studies about contemporary roles of women; and the National Body for Family Planning (BKKBN) had received U.N. funds to provide credit and technical assistance to women's groups active in the informal sector. All these contacts received invitations to the final seminar in Jakarta so that they could have copies of the country report and discuss possible follow-up projects.

In her *Indonesian Site Report* of May 1983, Chapman summarized her trips by train, bus, and *becak* (pedicab) to the six cities that were potential study sites, where she "met with social scientists interested in the informal sector," city officials, street vendors, and consumers; and visited *pasars* (markets), schools, hospitals, and residential neighborhoods to assess the level and patterns of street food selling. In the two smallest towns, Salatiga in Central Java and Cianjur in West Java, she found most sellers around the market keeping the same short hours; in contrast, in the larger cities, street food activity spilled out into the neighborhoods and congregated around the modern institutions, from bus stops and movie theaters to hospitals and universities. Bandung was particularly attractive, with its strong research institutions and the recent founding of vendor cooperatives by LSP, but the 1.5 million population seemed daunting. The other large town considered, the Central Javanese port city of Semarang, revealed a distinct pattern of vending in the poorer sections, but it had few street food sellers in commercial areas, and so was of less interest to one who had studied markets. Yogjakarta, the precolonial court city and now a separate province located on the south-central coast of Java, would have been a logical choice, not only because of its lively street food activity and strong university, but because student NGOs had already organized several vendor cooperatives in town. However, a sidewalk construction project had temporarily pushed a quarter of the vendors out of the city, disrupting both vendors and customers. Bogor was selected for its vital street food trade, its medium size, and the offer of institutional support from both the sociology and nutrition departments of its university, Institute Pertanian Bogor.

Differences between West and Central Java were immediately evident. In Central Java about half the vendors were women who worked alone, using fairly simple traditional equipment for preparation, and who sold very small portions of inexpensive food, often containing ingredients such as eels, pits, cassava, and seeds, that are no longer craved by the Westernized elite. In contrast, only one in three vendors in West Java was a woman; family operations were more conspicuous; well-made pushcarts and tents suggested greater capital investment in the operation; and the food sold was more Westernized, including more bread and dishes containing meat.

These analyses of regional differences, added to Chapman's comments on the variations in the street food trade by city size, emphasize how dissimilar the food system could be in cities within a few hundred miles of each other, and provide a cautionary reminder about the perils of generalization based on limited studies. Throughout the book I have tried to use data as indicative of trends and as challenges to contemporary wisdom rather than as hard immutable facts.

Refining the Design

With sites selected, an advisory committee in place, and interviewers hired, the mapping of cities and the enumeration of street food vendors began. Suddenly the plethora of foods and the complexity of the street food trade became obvious. Questions about definitions and procedures, too complicated to solve by letter, began to surface. Basically, the generic design of the project had to be adapted to a series of very different real-life situations. In October 1982, EPOC convened a small methodological workshop that included the first three country study directors. Three concepts were particularly troublesome since they formed the basis of the research design: the definition of street foods, the description of a street food enterprise, and the delineation of city boundaries.

1. *Street foods* in our original definition is any minimally processed food sold on the street for immediate consumption. In practice, the definition of certain foods was not clear-cut. When was fresh fruit a street food? A large bunch of bananas was considered a market commodity but a woman selling servings of one or two bananas along the street was selling street foods. What of food that was not nutritious and not meant to be swallowed, like chewing gum, or *pan* (betel nut with lime and spices) in Bangladesh, or kola nuts in Nigeria? We certainly were not including cigarettes, so we excluded these chewing foods.

Purchased food, that could be eaten on the spot but that was carried home or to the office, was classified as street food. Ready-to-eat food that was carried through the streets by the preparer rather than the purchaser, for eating at home or office, and was not for sale *on* the street, we labeled "invisible street foods." This category designates street foods supplied regularly to workers, usually on contract, and prepared in or served from the basement of the office building or from a nearby home. The foods were termed "invisible" because they were not sold from a visible shop or cart.

Catering—food prepared sporadically on contract—seems to be a microentrepreneurial activity in most places; women prepare special treats and traditional dishes for weddings and wakes, graduation celebrations, and birthday parties. More unusual are contract meals, usually prepared by women, consisting of many different foods, each in its own metal container, that are stacked five high and held in place by a handle. Called *rantangan* in Indonesia, *pin-to* in Thailand, or *tiffin* boxes in India, the meals are delivered to the buyer's desk at midday or at home in the evening. In Bangkok I observed a wealthy customer picking up several pin-to in her Mercedes, to heat the food for her family in her microwave at home: an upper-class version of the "plastic ladies," described in the Thai study, who carry dinner home in plastic bags. Bombay was famous for an elaborate distribution system of these tiffin boxes: women cooked food mid-morning at home, after which it was picked up and taken by railroad, bus, or bicycle into town, to arrive on the right desk for the midday meal. However, urbanization seems to have diminished this practice.

Textile workers in Bombay often contract for lunch in this manner, but take the evening meal in the home of the cook who, like these workers, lives in the squatter settlement; often the meal payments were irregular, so these *kaniwallah* were encouraged to organize (Savara 1981). Such home catering on contract is called *pension* in many Latin America cities, where a two-hour meal break is customary, but where public transport systems are too costly and the distances too far for most white-collar workers to return home to eat. While none of these systems of serving food are classed as street foods, neither are they included as formal sector food service activities. Only a total census of all types of food services available to urban residents will provide the refined data necessary for planning how to feed the burgeoning populations of urban agglomerations.

In many cities, food sold by vendors was made by women in their homes, often in rural areas, an important backward linkage that deserves greater attention than it has received to date. While the vendors often bought these foods, such as the crunchy snack *canacur* in Bangladesh, they also sold the foods on commission. This custom is so typical in Indonesia that there is a special word for this type of food: *titipan*.

With these refinements, we thought the definition was clear. But several country directors, wishing to focus on locally produced, nutritious foods, excluded various types of "industrially processed" Westernized snack foods and bottled sodas. In Nigeria, imported sweets such as chocolates and toffees were not included, but packaged biscuits and soda were because they were locally made. The Minia study excludes all such foods. In fact, bottled sodas are an important street drink and have replaced local drinks in many countries because of safety reasons; in contrast, packaged snack foods did not seem to challenge local favorites. In Bogor, I observed that the small packages of potato chips clipped to a mobile cart were covered with dust while the containers of *krupuk* were constantly being refilled.

2. *Street food enterprises* The array of street food vendors is immediately obvious once you start looking for them. "Mobile vendors" include women with baskets, men bearing balance poles on their shoulders, and tricycle vendors of bread or ice cream; but what of an ice cream truck roaming the residential streets?

"Semi-mobile" vendors are those with carts that become their stationary place of sale. In Egypt the carts are frequently parked in one place and have water and light connections, suggesting permanence; others are moved from the market area in the winter to the promenade in the summer months. In Indonesia the *kaki lima* (five feet, two on the vendor and three on the cart) are more easily rolled from a morning location, perhaps near a school, to places where crowds congregate at night, such as near the movie theater or park. And should we include mobile vans like those that service construction workers in the United States?

Vendors in markets may rent regular stall space, as in Nigeria, or pay a daily fee to set up a table or squat on the path, as in Senegal. Because such vendors are regulated, are they no longer in the informal sector? If they sold street foods, we included them in our census; I discuss the theoretical debate over the definition of the informal sector in chapter 10. Outside the market, women erect stalls and may attract more customers by providing a table and bench where they can eat. Next, to shade both buyer and seller, comes some sort of roofing of bamboo or straw or canvas or wood. In Nigeria these *buka* are often rented; some are fancy concrete structures built by a bank or university to improve the conditions of the vendors who sell to their employees or students. Throughout Southeast Asia, soup simmers on burners at the entrance of shop houses; you order the boiling liquid poured over a selection of noodles or rice, bits of meat or fish, raw vegetables, and eat within the cool shop. Are these still street food establishments?

After lively debate, we defined a street food business as one selling ready-to-eat foods from a place having no more than three permanent walls. Thus the few mobile vans that appeared in Nigerian cities were enumerated. The variety of types within the three categories led most country staff to code their data in such a way that income differences could be ascertained and compared. In addition, during the initial mapping phase, most feeding establishments of any sort were noted so that restaurants and bars were recorded. Restaurants were easily identified by their cooked-to-order menus, even when they might not have four walls, hardly a necessity in hot climates. But bars usually serve snack and finger food and were a borderline case in several studies.

3. *City* as the site for the study had been defined as a provincial city of manageable size so that the entire urban area could be mapped. Our definition seemed clear, but the population size of the cities studied varied at the time of research from 38,000 to 250,000. Part of the problem revolved, and continues to revolve, around the lack of definition of "urban." Is it the boundaries of the local municipality as drawn by the government a decade ago? Manikganj in Bangladesh and Ziguinchor in Senegal both enclosed village-like settlements and small gardens that challenged any preconceived idea of urban. In Nigeria, cities had drawn their limits to include agricultural land in anticipation of rapid expansion of residential estates to house their burgeoning populations.[3]

Other city boundaries enclose only a part of several commercial centers within an area that have merged into each other through population increase and residential density. Iloilo "proper" in the Philippines registered a population of 55,000 and was the original focus of that study; but the high commercial density of the area meant that the study area did not really reflect the commercial and squatter areas of the urban region. A second sample census was therefore completed of the entire metropolitan area that then numbered 245,000 inhabitants. Significant insights resulting from this second census was the unexpected increase in the percentage of street food businesses in the neighborhoods.

With these three basic concepts in place, the studies began.

PART I

CITIES AND THEIR
STREET FOODS

The foods we eat, what foods we think it proper to buy or eat on the street, who makes those foods, when we eat those foods—all of these factors vary by culture and climate. To enable the reader to appreciate this variety, and to understand the context in which the sector operates, this section presents sketches of the seven provincial cities studied directly under the EPOC Street Foods Project and describes their distinctive street foods. Recipes of a few favorite street foods in each country are included.

The classification of foods in each city reflects local attitudes to food in general and street foods in particular. One term, "meal constituents," requires explanation: in the case studies it is used to indicate foods that are usually eaten with something else, either on site or at home. Individual servings of these constituents provide variety in the diet. In Ife customers purchase sauces or stews to eat over steamed ground beans or a corn meal loaf, for example. In the Philippines, constitutents are the various dishes offered customers as accompaniment to the rice or noodles they will eat at the enterprise; in Thailand, housewives often purchase similar constituents to take home and serve over rice that they prepare in their electric cookers. In Senegal, most constituents are taken home since eating on the streets is not a cultural tradition.

Each case study portrays the distinctive characteristics of the city that affect street food vendors and their trade. The focus is on the ambience surrounding the activity and on the reality of vendor's experiences rather than the statistical details, which are reviewed for all the studies in Part II. Throughout the book, emphasis is given to the long-term impact, direct or indirect, of the Street Food study on the street food vendors and their relationship to the government. The accumulated power of these findings brings new insights to the nature of microenterprises, the interventions that really help improve income and food safety, and the gender aspects of the street food trade. The concluding chapter illustrates their potential to reframe debates across these many discourses.

Central to each study is the interplay between the municipal government and the research staff. While statistical data provided some insights into the lives and problems of vendors, it quickly became apparent that some sort of vendor organization was essential when the discussion turned to possible interventions or programs designed to improve the income of the vendors and/or the safety of the food they sold. Without a mechanism to reach the vendors, these goals were unreachable; the first recommendation in nearly every country was that the vendors either form a nongovernmental organization or strengthen the one in existence. The ability to form such an organization, and the form it took, depended greatly on the political climate in each country; in several countries contacts with the vendors had come through local administrators or university staff. In all cases of continued relationships, the most important ingredient was the dedication of local individuals who provided both leadership and inspiration over a span of years. Such presence is difficult for outsiders to maintain and was clearly impossible for EPOC.

Note the broad range of efforts made in the seven cities, and the different backgrounds of the individuals who led efforts to work with the street food vendors. Outstanding for its influence on government and its services for vendors is the Street Food Vendors Organization in Minia, Egypt. Issues raised in Minia about self-sufficiency are pertinent in Manikganj, Bangladesh, where a credit scheme started with EPOC support could not be continued by a local NGO for lack of funds for staff. In Nigeria, an organization of street food sellers in Ibadan was formed by the women trained in food handling and nutrition, but to date the organization has not become the conduit of further training; at the study site of Ile-Ife, however, vendor training continues under government auspices. In Bogor, Indonesia, the municipality and university have played more critical roles in upgrading food safety than have NGOs to date. The existing vendor group in Iloilo, the Philippines, sank under the weight of political manipulation; more recently, a sympathetic mayor has brought order and fairness to a street food trade being challenged by foreign fast food chains.

As Thailand joins the ranks of the newly industrialized countries, Chonburi has been drawn even more closely into the orbit of greater Bangkok, affecting both food tastes and administrative authority. Changes in Ziguinchor, Senegal, over the last decade have been toward chaos caused by a persistent civil unrest; but many refugees from Casamance populate the squatter areas of Dakar, where organizations for vendors are being organized.

As the street food trade persists and its contribution to the local economy becomes clearer, most local governments have begun to regulate rather than attempt to abolish street foods. Renewed energy has gone into training vendors in food safety; the Food and Agricultural Organization has supported many such initiatives around the world. The emphasis on clean water found in all the case studies has almost everywhere resulted in new municipal regulations, but also in greater availability of water for vendors.

The ways these twin themes of vendor representation and improved food safety have intertwined in each country is distinct. The uneven power relationships inherent in the poor confronting authority are mitigated both by organizing and by external leadership that is drawn both from universities and from within local government. Difficulties encountered reflect the dilemma of planning: how to incorporate participation and utilize the local knowledge of the affected group while at the same time limiting their choice of sites and altering their food handling practices. The following chapters sketch the political, economic, and cultural setting of each city as backdrop to the detailed study of who makes, sells, and eats food on the streets. This kaleidoscopic presentation is meant to underscore how gender relationships, dietary habits and restrictions, and economic transformation affect the livelihood of these microentreprenuers.

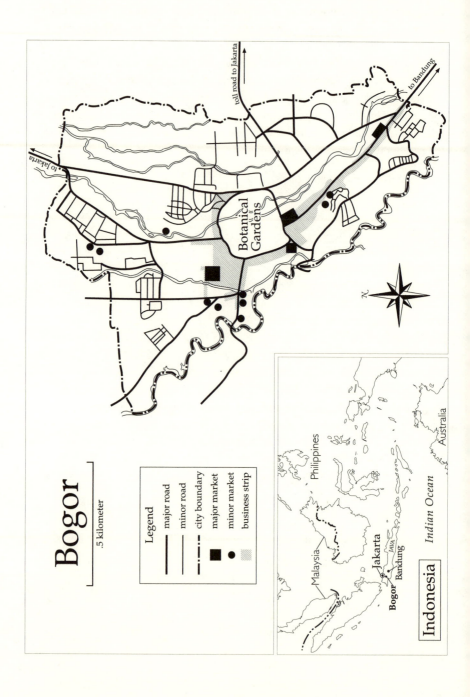

Bogor

.5 kilometer

Legend

— major road
— minor road
—·—·— city boundary
■ major market
● minor market
▨ business strip

toll road to Jakarta

to Jakarta

to Bandung

Botanical Gardens

N

Indonesia

Philippines

Malaysia

Jakarta

JAVA

Bogor

Bandung

Indian Ocean

Australia

CHAPTER ONE

Bogor, Indonesia

Bogor is a street food connoisseur's paradise. Although the typical Indonesian's diet never strays far from rice, the longtime staple, street vendors offer not only a remarkable number of variations on basic meal themes but also many types of "snacks," both savory and sweet. This chapter depicts the diversity of Bogor street cuisine and examines how selling and consumption patterns are shaped by seasonal changes in food supplies and dietary preferences, as well as by rather more persistent gender ideologies. As in some of the other cities, schoolchildren comprise an important market for the street food vendors; for this reason, the EPOC staff helped initiate a program to improve the sanitation and nutritional value of street foods sold around schoolyards.

This chapter also contains findings of a later study on the safety and nutrition of Bogor street foods; combined, the two studies provide valuable information about the overall health content of street foods in and beyond Indonesia. The supportive role of Bogor municipal officers was instrumental in allowing both studies to progress; their attitudes contrasted with others in the central government.

Local Context

Bogor is only 50 kilometers from Jakarta, the steaming, boisterous capital of Indonesia, the world's fourth largest country, with a 1991 population of 190 million scattered over 3,000 islands in the Java Sea. Yet Bogor's 1000-meter elevation is high enough to produce a salubrious climate. For almost 400 years, Bogor served as the hot-season retreat for officials of the Dutch East Indies; the governor general's palace was located near the Botanical Gardens in the center of town. This beautiful garden is the largest in Southeast Asia and spurred the founding of the Institut Pertanian Bogor (IPB), now the leading agricultural and forestry university in the country. Facing the broad avenues that surround the garden are low, open government buildings of the colonial era intermixed with more recent multistory additions. The garden acts as a hub, with spokes leading out past the large old stucco houses set in spacious, well-landscaped enclosures toward the newer housing estates; visible down alleys and across gullies are the densely settled neighborhoods generally accessible only on foot. The streets are clogged with a bewildering choice of public transport: autos and vans and buses compete with bike and motorcycle rickshaws and even an occasional horse-drawn *dokar*. Both transiting passengers and visitors to the Botanical Gardens are treated to a dazzling array of street foods hawked from carts and trays in and around bus stops and the garden entrance.

Bogor has shared in the rapid economic growth taking place in Indonesia since the late 1960s, much of it concentrated in an industrial belt that extends on Java from Jakarta to Bandung. Workers in factories on Bogor's periphery have settled in the city, and a growing number of people employed in Jakarta prefer to live in Bogor. As a result, even in 1983, twenty-five commuter trains ran between Bogor and Jakarta during the work week. An automobile toll road, the only one in the country, links Bogor to the expanding metropolitan region of Jakarta. In the other direction, a major highway continues to several renowned hill stations and to Bandung. Thus Bogor is an important regional transit point for public transport, but the private automobiles of urbanites headed for the cool of the mountains usually rush by without coming into the city.

The prosperity of the city has made it a magnet for rural migrants. Bogor recorded an annual population growth rate of 10% to 12% during the 1970–1980 period, an expansion that engulfed nearby *kampung,* or villages, and transformed their terraced fields into squatter settlements that crowd the valleys between middle-class residential housing on the ridges. This pattern of urban development, with pockets of rural kampung in the city and dense residential areas overflowing municipal boundaries, blurs the distinction between urban and rural (Silas 1989). Indeed, much of Java is so heavily populated, with densities in 1984 of over 750 persons per square kilometer, as to obviate the distinction. Urban migration was abetted both by rapid population growth and by the fact that West Java terrain is more rugged than the rest of the island, lacking the broad areas of volcanic plains that make Javanese agriculture so productive. Nonetheless, many families hold onto their agricultural plots and practice circular migration, a phenomenon documented by Jellinek (1977) in Jakarta and Bijlmer (1986) in Surabaja.

Most Sundanese in West Java are Muslims and practice a fairly traditional form of Islam, in contrast to the more mystical interpretation of this religion that is dominant on the rest of the island. The Sundanese language is also distinct, both from Javanese and from the official Indonesian language, the latter which is itself a derivative of Malay. These differences helped instigate the Darul Islam rebels and other dissident groups in West Java to oppose the leadership of the newly formed Republic of Indonesia in 1949 and to fight a guerilla war for 13 years (1949–1962).[1] Sundanese culture influences male-female roles among Bogor street food vendors, encouraging family enterprises and resulting in fewer women selling alone than is typical of cities in Central Java. Often a husband and wife will sell complementary foods at the same place: the woman makes herbal drinks while the man sells noodle soup. Unlike the rest of the island, women alone are frequently hassled by unemployed single men congregating at bus stops and marketplaces, a behavior alien to the more polite Javanese.[2]

Project Support

Critical to the success of the EPOC project was the interest and support of the Bogor City Planning Office. During the study, Bogor newspapers were filled with stories complaining about the downtown congestion that blocked storefronts and pushed pedestrians into traffic. Blame fell on the many small entrepreneurs offering shoe or bike repair, selling used clothes and books, or hawking food. Despite central government pressure in the early eighties to beautify the city by removing unsightly vendors from congested areas, Bogor generally avoided the "street cleaning" campaigns frequently undertaken in Jakarta and Bandung. In contrast, the city administration expressed sympathy with the plight of the street food vendors and hoped that the results of the EPOC project would help them find a balance among the competing interests. As an alternative policy, the city collects money: in 1983, nearly 60% of the vendors paid a vendor tax and most others paid fees for rental of space in the market or along the sidewalk, for street-cleaning fees, or for a license to operate in the neighborhoods.

The municipal authorities facilitated the Street Foods Project by helping the staff obtain permission for the various surveys and even encouraged a local high school class to carry out their own interviews with street food vendors in front of the municipal offices. In her introduction to the final Bogor report, Chapman wrote, "The most immediate use of the Bogor Street Foods data is by the Bogor planners themselves. I have every confidence that, under the humane direction of their director, a compromise between the need for an efficient city and the need to generate jobs for vendors can be struck" (1984, ii).

The supportive stance of the Bogor officials is particularly striking because, under the centralized governmental system of Indonesia, local governments have limited powers. Further, governmental regulations do not distinguish urban centers from rural areas in this uniformly hierarchical bureaucratic system; as a result, distinctly urban issues are seldom addressed. The resulting government rigidity and top-down decisions are widely perceived to inhibit national development and stifle citizen participation (Walker 1991). To provide an alternative voice for the people outside government structures, in the early 1970s activists began to set up myriad nongovernmental organizations which focused on appropriate technology, women, the environment, education, and alleviation of poverty.[3] EPOC's sponsoring institution in Indonesia, Lembaga Studi Pembagunan (LSP), is an NGO emblematic of this trend. One of its projects involved working with students at universities in Jogjakarta and Bandung to assist vendors and other informal sector entrepreneurs to organize themselves into cooperatives. These student groups were eager to try out any interventions the research might suggest.

In Bogor, the project was affiliated with the nutrition and family resource department of IPB. Faculty participated both as consultants and advisors; 14 of their fifth-year students utilized the project for fieldwork experience, assisting in every phase of the research. Professor F. G. Winarno of the Food Technology Development Centre at IPB had been approached by FAO to conduct a study of food safety in Bogor as a result of EPOC's promotion of street foods; his subsequent project, described later in this chapter, extended the city's active involvement in street foods until 1992.

Street Foods in Bogor

The sheer magnitude of vendors in Bogor is phenomenal: 17,754 enterprises for a population of 250,000, or one vendor for every 14 inhabitants! The figure is based on a total census of the three major and numerous minor markets in the city, two long business strips, the larger schools, and major transport transfer points. To these figures were added a 20% cluster-random sample of residential neighborhoods, which included local markets and primary schools. Such data are critical because they reveal that despite the visibility of vendors downtown, only 15% of all street food vendors—2716 in our census—were found in these congested areas. The overwhelming number of street food sellers in Bogor—15,050 by our count—were in the neighborhoods. They sell from fixed stalls along paths and streets; they use their own kitchen areas to serve food through a window in their home or from benches in front of their houses. More elaborate meals are available from vendors who set up tables under a tent or plastic awning on a vacant lot. Others ply their wares from some type of mobile cart, tricycle, or balance pole (Figure 1.1). Cries of *sate ayam* (chicken kebabs) ring at dusk throughout the alleys, as pervasive as the haunting smell of *kretek*, the clove-laced Indonesian cigarette.

Schools are a center of vendor activity during the day. For example, Chapman wrote of four schools that were within 20 minutes of her house:

> In front and along the side of schools, children were swarming. All the sellers except a boiled peanut seller were men. Either they sold snacks already prepared and packaged into kid-sized (25 rupiah) packets or they were actively frying, dishing up mung bean gruel, etc. The relationship between the kids and the vendors was clearly a warm one, with kids making their own sago sandwiches, pulling and pounding their own doughnuts for deep frying. (Field notes of 26 May 1983).

Traditional views regarding appropriate ways for men and women to carry loads also predict the types of food that mobile vendors sell. Only men, usually from the island of Madura, lope down the street balancing the *pikulan* on one shoulder, from which they sell sate: one tray slung from one end of the balance pole holds food and a small stool where the customer might sit; a tiny charcoal brazier rests on the other

FIGURE 1.1   Two typical street food vendor carts parked in the shade, the smaller one somewhat more mobile, the larger providing benches for customers.

tray. Women sell fruit, cooked snacks, and rice sweets from the traditionally knotted woven scarf tied over their right shoulder in a manner to hold the bundle secure on the back.

Women vendors are more likely than men to sell seven days a week, but their hours were frequently shorter in order to balance their work with household responsibilities. Those with permanent stalls often had relatives take over for a few hours so they could shop for the following day's food both for the enterprise and for the home. Pak and Ibu Sidik ("father" and "mother" Sidik: the usual form of address for adults) typify this practice. Pak sells iced drinks from a mobile cart, parking it near Ibu's fried food stall, which is located at the entrance of their *kampung* and near several schools. Their teenaged children replace Ibu at her stand when they return from school around noon so that she can go home to cook the family meal. Pak might move his cart nearer a transportation center and then return home only in time for dinner.

Women vendors tend to own their own equipment, often cooking in the same pots and pans they use at home; they can sell every day because their location is often near their homes. Men are more likely to work at a franchise location specializing, for example, in cooked chicken, or to sell foods on commission using the carts owned by the bakery or ice cream manufacturer, for which they often pay rent. Thus the number of days men work depends on the supplier and on their ability to work long hours to justify the cost of the cart. Both men and women vendors spend considerable non-selling time each day buying and cooking their ingredients.

The Foods They Sell

Over 200 different kinds of foods are available for immediate consumption on the streets of Bogor—from cassava chips and egg rolls to complete meals of rice with meat, fish, or chicken, served along with a vegetable side dish on a banana leaf. The foods reflect the ethnic diversity of the country and are often sold by vendors dressed in regional garb: they range from spicy beef soup from Kalimantan to fish baked in a banana leaf from Sulawesi. Such a plethora of food choices and the fact that many establishments sold more than one food type made it unreasonable to follow the generic design and utilize food type as one parameter for selecting the smaller vendor sample. Instead, vendors were classed as "permanent" or "not per-manent," the latter being truly mobile or with a structure that could be easily disas-sembled. This division, together with location, was the basis for drawing the 10% study sample.

Street foods also reflect the dietary preferences of Indonesians for meals of steamed rice as often as three times a day. These meals are accompanied by protein, usually cakes of fermented soybean or other legumes, including peanuts and curried vegetables. Meat or fish are luxuries to the majority of Indonesians, who are poor and often malnourished. Eating other street foods in between rice meals is a way of keeping up energy during the day and adding valuable protein, minerals, and vitamins to the diet. In most countries such foods would be called lunch or a light meal; but to Indonesians, only rice counts as a meal: everything else is a snack. A filling chicken porridge would be the equivalent to a rice dish in terms of nutrition, but to an Indo-nesian the porridge is not a meal.

Despite the snacks and rice meals, malnutrition is widespread; blindness, caused by vitamin A deficiency is common, as is anemia among both men and women. National consumption surveys taken in 1980 showed that rural families spend some 74% of household income on food; the figure in urban areas dropped to 60%. In Bogor, located in the most prosperous area of the country, EPOC found that about a quarter of the typical household food budget was spent on street foods.

The 17% of the vendors who sold rice meals included all types of vendors, both ambulant and those with fixed stalls or *warung* (Figure 1.2); also included were the evening-only "restaurants" that set up their tables and chairs under awnings in the downtown parking lots.[4]

FIGURE 1.2 A vendor couple and family in Bogor, including two schoolchildren in uniforms, watch a customer select *tempe* from the many foods being sold at this *warung*.

Ibu Enik, a street food vendor since 1949, raised her eight children with profits from her enterprise and at the time of the study was the primary support for her extended family of eighteen persons, who "all help in making the *warung* successful. A nephew may help lift heavy loads, a niece may help cook, a daughter may help sell food during the day and, of course, the men push the heavy cart from home to selling spot and back. She also points out that they have helped her in the past and she is content because they will support her in her old age" (Chapman 1984, 81).

In the hot dry months, such as July and August when the first census was completed, fruit drinks were sold by 20% of the vendors, or more than were selling rice meals. In the cooler rainy season in March the demand for such drinks was very low, and some drink vendors stopped selling during this period. The varieties of drinks available were enticing and provided an important source of liquid in the tropical climate. Flavored ice drinks made with fruit syrups poured over shaved ice became distinctly Indonesian with the addition of tiny colorful squares of *agar-agar*, a very firm gelatin made from an extract of red algae. Fancy ice drinks might also be decorated with bits of fresh fruit or peanuts, making a sort of liquid sundae. Ginger tea was also served with peanuts, and often with a rice dumpling. Boiled or fresh coconut milk and sugarcane juice were sold in season. Coffee and tea were available year-round.

One of the most popular drinks is *jamu*, a traditional medicinal herbal drink that comes in over thirty varieties, each meant to respond to a particular need or complaint of the customer, from sexual prowess to colds.[5] Typically, women migrants from central Java produce *jamu*, returning to their home villages frequently to obtain the proper ingredients. One *jamu* vendor who was studied walked 10 kilometers (6.2 miles) on her daily route carrying a basket with bottles of eight different drinks weighing about 13 kilograms (29 pounds). Her route took her across a swinging bridge from her low-income neighborhood to a middle-class area, and into "the upperclass neighborhood of Dutch colonial vintage on the cliffs above" (Chapman 1984, 74). Chapman argues that the 15 or more roots, leaves, and seeds that go into the drink provide a vital dietary supplement to the typically high-carbohydrate diet (1984, 73).

A year-round favorite sold by 12% of the vendors is noodle soup: a flavorful chicken stock with wheat or rice noodles, a selection of vegetables, and either meatballs or chicken. The soup is especially in demand during the hot dry season because it both replaces liquid and salt lost by sweating and supplies energy from carbohydrates. This food is entirely sold by men, primarily by Central Javanese migrants.

An ambulant vendor, Pak Kampto begins his 14-hour day around 6:30 A.M. by shopping at a local market. Every day he purchases chicken heads and feet, mustard greens, onions, and seasonings for the broth, and both wheat and rice noodles. Usually he buys beef and sago (a powdered starch made from the pith of a sago palm) to make the distinctive tiny meat balls rather than purchasing them already cooked. Back at home, he cooks the soup and meatballs and prepares various condiments. Local customers come by his house between 11:00 A.M. and 2:00 P.M.; then Pak Kampto loads his cart and tours a middle-class residential area for six hours. Recently he made his own cart for U.S. $55 to replace his first cart, which he bought in 1975 with his earnings as an apprentice to his cousin selling fried noodles in the market. The cart is truly mobile, consisting of a wooden box set on wheels and measuring one by one-third meters, two short legs provide stability when stopping. Such vendors are referred to as *kaki lima*, or five legs, in Indonesian.

Pak Kampto provided us with financial information that illustrated how hard work and careful savings could provide a secure future for his family. After he married a *jamu* vendor, they lived on her income of U.S. $2 per day and invested his profits, about three times as much, in buying a house lot and building a home. Like many of his neighbors, he rents out part of the house to another family, adding to the couple's total annual family income. In 1983, this was about three times that of a beginning—and woefully paid—faculty member at the university, minus fringe benefits of course.

Fruits and a few vegetables are the most usual type of food enterprise in the market areas and are sold by 11% of all vendors in the summer. In the cooler season the number of vendors selling them increased. Many fruits—pineapple or jackfruit, for example—are simply peeled and sliced; yam beet root is cut into sticks and eaten raw; bananas and plantains come in immense variety and are fried or boiled or eaten raw, depending on the type. Distinctly Indonesian is the spicy hot peanut sauce called *gado gado*, which is sold exclusively by women, and which is poured over fresh fruit salad (sold by men) or over blanched vegetable combinations of cabbage, bean sprouts, scallions, potatoes, chamote squash, and carrots. So important is this peppery fiery taste in their diet that Indonesians have separate words: hot, *panas*, and spicy hot, *pedes*. Coconut milk flavored with *pedes* spices is another popular sauce and is served over cooked pumpkins, sweet potatoes, or certain plantains. *Pedes* and sour fruit pickles provide piquancy to the diet while adding important minerals and vitamins; these fruit and vegetable dishes among the top five food types bought by customers in Bogor.

Vendors selling hot fried snacks, which account for over half the enterprise types in both business and residential areas, increased their sales during the cooler season. Squares of *tempe* or *tahu*, soybean curd fermented with or without the beans, are dropped momentarily into boiling fat to serve as a snack; when served with rice, the cakes are more often braised or steamed. While soybean cakes are found across most of the archipelago, the local specialty in West Java is a fermented cake made from peanuts. Other fried snacks, usually cooked at home and kept crisp in large glass jars or plastic wrap, include the familiar chips made from banana or sweet potato. *Krupuk* chips are typically Indonesian; they are porous chips made from rice or cassava flour and frequently flavored with bits of shrimp or peanuts. Also typical are *emping*, crisp thin slices of a local nut. Some foods, such as fried puffed rice balls or fried wheat rolls filled with mung bean, might be either freshly cooked or packaged. The spicy *pedes* peanut sauce alternates with a sweet sauce served with *sate*: small pieces of beef, lamb, chicken, or shrimp threaded on short bamboo sticks and grilled. Both sauces give a uniquely Indonesian taste to this familiar dish.

Sweet or salty snacks accounted for another 11% of vendor sales. Sweets include steamed buns of sweet glutinous rice or wheat dough filled with coconut or mung beans, moist cakes and crisp cookies, tapioca pudding, or pancakes filled with coconut or sweet rice. Steamed or roasted salty rice snacks are also filled or eaten plain. Most such snacks were sold by men pushing carts or carrying baskets throughout the city. Packaged food stalls sell snacks all day long; some vendors had added industrially produced chips to their wares, but the prices put them out of reach for most customers.

Most vendors sell throughout the year; school vacations and major holidays affect their customers and often provide a convenient time for taking four to six weeks off for a visit back to their natal village. Case studies revealed how different vendors adjusted their businesses to Ramadan, the month of fasting from sunrise to sunset that is observed by traditional Muslims but not necessarily followed by other customers, whether Muslim or not. For example, the widow who sold *gado-gado* did not sell at all during Ramadan, but she commented that some other sellers "simply drape an opaque plastic sheeting around their tables to disguise their trade" (Chapman 1984, 77).

Gado-Gado
Cooked Cold Salad with Peanut Sauce

Cooked cold salad

½ cup blanched shredded cabbage

½ cup sliced cooked carrots

½ cup sliced cooked green beans

½ cup sliced boiled potatoes

2 hard-boiled eggs, sliced

1 cucumber, sliced

1 tomato, sliced

½ cup cubed soybean cake

Cool all cooked ingredients to room temperature.

Peanut sauce

6 tablespoons peanut butter

½ cup milk

1 cup water

1 teaspoon chopped garlic

1 teaspoon sugar

1 teaspoon ground red pepper

1 teaspoon lemon juice

1 bay leaf

½ teaspoon salt

Heat oil (in a small sauce pan), add all ingredients except milk and water; cook slowly until the garlic turns yellow. Gradually add the liquids, stirring continuously, until thickened.

Arrange salad on a plate over lettuce leaves. Drizzle sauce on top, or serve separately. Gado-gado should be served at room temperature.

Sate Ayam
Chicken Kebabs with Spicy Hot Peanut Dipping Sauce

Chicken Marinade

2 pounds chicken breasts, skinned and boned, cut in 1½-inch cubes

3 tablespoons fresh lime juice

½ cup soy sauce

½ teaspoon black pepper

2 teaspoons brown sugar

2 tablespoons minced fresh cilantro

2 garlic cloves, minced

2 tablespoons vegetable oil

Spicy hot peanut dipping sauce

4 tablespoons peanut butter

½ cup chicken broth

½ cup milk

1 garlic clove, minced

2 teaspoons soy sauce

2 teaspoons brown sugar

1 teaspoon rice vinegar or lemon juice

1 teaspoon ground red pepper

1 teaspoon sesame oil

Tabasco sauce to taste

Marinate cubed chicken for several hours at room temperature with the rest of the ingredients. Make the peanut sauce by combining all the ingredients and cooking over low heat, stirring constantly until thick. Remove from heat and set aside.

Thread chicken cubes on damp wooden skewers (to prevent burning). Grill, basting with marinade. Dip cooked kebabs into spicy peanut sauce.

Agricultural Linkages

Street foods utilize many secondary agricultural crops in Indonesia, such as corn, cassava, peanuts, and soybeans. Corn is roasted or steamed on the cob or sliced off and mixed with grated coconut as a salad. Cassava flour is used as the base for inexpensive fritters and cookies popular among construction workers, pedicab drivers, and children. Peanuts are sold as snacks or processed into sauces. All three crops are primarily consumed as street foods, in contrast to poorer regions that rely on corn and cassava as staples. Soybeans, however, are processed and eaten as much at home as on the street.

Wheat is increasingly used in snacks despite the fact that the country does not grow it. Its use may be traced to USAID food aid strategies that provided the Indonesian government with highly subsidized U.S. food surpluses. For example, laborers in a "food for work" program in East Java were paid in bulgur wheat. Although these wheat kernels can be cooked like rice, the women and men workers preferred to sell the wheat to bakeries and to buy rice. Further, Indonesian government policies have specifically encouraged diversification of the diet away from its overwhelming dependency of rice, both for nutritional and international trade considerations.

Improving Street Foods for Schoolchildren

Some 30 million Indonesian children eat street foods every school day. In-school feeding does not exist in Indonesia, and the costs of introducing such a program would be prohibitive. Thus, Chapman initiated two strategies to improve street foods for children: one improved the environment around the schools where vendors served the children; the other enhanced the nutritional value of several favorite snacks.

School days begin early in the morning, in order to avoid the afternoon heat. Vendors often provide the children with their first food of the day and offer lunch to them as they leave for home. Most schools have some sort of yard that is surrounded by a fence or wall; because the schools may front on busy dusty streets or alleys, many school principals invite selected vendors inside the yard to serve the children. In exchange for this privilege, why should vendors not be required to improve their food handling practices? Working with an enthusiastic school principal, designs were formulated for a paved area near the front gate that would be shaded by trees or an awning and, more critically, be provided with water. Most urban schools have a water tap behind the school building near the toilets; running a plastic hose away from potential contamination to the food area would be simple. Vendors wishing to sell in this improved environment would be required to take a training course in food handling and nutrition. A demonstration program was then proposed for 20 model schools in Bogor; the principal and the Parents and Teachers Association of each school would be briefed on the goals of the project and given a mini course in food safety themselves so that, once the vendors were trained, parents and teachers could set up a monitoring system. External funds were sought to pay for the costs of erecting the food center and conducting the training; it seemed a logical project for UNICEF, and negotiations for funding continued for two years after EPOC had left Bogor.[6] Ultimately, these ideas were incorporated into other projects. Nonetheless, the model remains a low-cost approach not only to improve the health and nutrition standards among street food vendors but also to teaching children, parents, and teachers about basic sanitary standards for food handling.

Clara Meliyanti Kusharto and Ratna Megawangi, faculty members in the department of nutrition at IPB, succeeded in developing improved protein recipes for four popular street foods: a cassava chip, a fritter, and two types of baked goods made from wheat. In addition, they sought out people willing to produce and market the new product, and they tested their improved versions on potential customers. The most successful was a recipe that added a bean ingredient to a wheat cookie: the children liked the crunch of the legume, and the complimentary proteins made both ingredients more valuable. The other improved products fortified traditional foods with soybean flour; however, the unstable prices of soy flour due to its unpredictable supply resulted in a low profit margin, and the producers ceased to fortify their products at that time.

Broad Policy Changes

During the Bogor study, the authorities in Jakarta declared a *"becak*-free zone" in the downtown areas of the capital and began confiscating any pedicab found on the streets. This zeal against such informal activities extended to roadside vendors, who were forcibly evicted from their downtown locations and offered stalls in new market places that were not only distant from their usual customers but were rented at unrealistically high cost. As a result a large majority refused to move. Street food vendors were required to pay only for a much cheaper authorized parking space, where most could afford the 300-rupiah daily charge. However, because of the excess demand for such spaces, the vendors were often "charged as much as three times the official rate" and so continued to operate nearby "illegally" (Sethuraman 1985, 726).[7] The confiscated *becaks* were thrown into the Java Sea to provide shelter for fish, preventing a recurrence of that form of transport; but of course the vendors were soon back where they had been.

The "street cleaning" efforts drew widespread criticism from local NGOs who rallied around vendor leader Abdullah Suad Lubis.[8] In 1983 he helped found a cooperative for vendors (*Kooperasi Perdagang Kaki Lima Kecamatan Djati Negara*) in his old neighborhood to offer credit to vendors embarking on new income activities.[9] In recognition of his leadership he was awarded an international Ashoka Fellowship, which provides fellows with living expenses for three years to enable them to continue their voluntary activity.

The adverse publicity surrounding the street cleaning eventually affected the central administration. In 1989, the Coordinating Minister for Political Affairs and Security formed a special team to carry out Operation "Tomorrow is Full of Hope" to improve the living standard of street vendors.[10] Over 900 vendors decided to quit hawking and were rewarded with scholarships from the Lions Club of Jakarta to continue schooling or with tuition to attend the Jakarta Vocational Training Center. The head of the ministry had words of advice for the 173 vendors who had completed training and secured formal sector jobs: he told them not to feel disappointed because they earned less than when they were vendors because "in a company your future is secure" (*Jakarta Post* 13 July 1990).

Concern that the Jakarta campaign would spread to Bogor was frequently voiced by the vendors during interviews. However, instead of repressing street food vendors, Bogor began working with vendors to improve the safety of the food served through new regulations on water use and by supporting a major four-year project for development training guidelines for street food vendors.

Chris Bayin, the municipal officer in charge of Pasar Ramayana, one of the largest market areas in the city, was a member of the EPOC advisory committee and took seriously the need to improve water use among the vendors. In an interview in July 1990, he described the recent Law 1/1990 entitled "Cleanliness, beauty, and orderliness in Bogor municipality." Under these regulations, vendors who did cooking on the spot were expected to carry their own water for washing. To help the vendors comply with this requirement, the municipality made water from wells available in several markets where vendors could come to fetch water and where they could wash their utensils under cover. The new regulations also required that all previously cooked food be covered. School children were encouraged to help improve street food safety by buying only from vendors with clean stalls; if vendors did not change food handling practices, the children were urged to bring their own food to school. For added control, vendors at fixed locations were required to have licenses. All of these regulations were part of the attempt by the municipal government to ensure cleanliness of the food.

The IPB Streetfood Project

In April 1988, a four-year project entitled "The Wholesomeness of Common People's Food in Indonesia," or the Streetfood[11] Project for short, was begun in Bogor under the leadership of Professor F. G. Winarno, founder of the Food Technology Development Centre of the Bogor Agricultural University (IPB). Supported by FAO and the government of The Netherlands, and conducted under the joint auspices of one Indonesian and two Dutch research groups,[12] the project focused on testing interventions "to improve the quality and safety of food sold by street vendors"; successful measures would be collected into training manuals for distribution throughout the country by government agencies and NGOs (Winarno 1989, 2).

Although the goals of the project resembled those of the EPOC project, the two differed significantly in design and intention. For example, the IPB project definition of street foods reflected an adversarial approach, emphasizing that "streetfoods are sold in public spaces *which were originally not intended for that purpose*" (Winarno 1989, 5; my italics). In contrast to EPOC's emphasis on all street food vendors, sellers who rented their stalls legally in markets, shopping areas, or parks were excluded. Also included were units that are situated on private ground but are easily accessible to the public.

Clearly, there was no need to repeat the EPOC Bogor study, with its primary attention to the vendors and their income: the IPB study accepted the economic importance of street food vending as a given. Rather, the major emphasis of the IPB project was on a thorough analysis of the safety and nutritive values of street foods, originally with the expectation that the findings would contribute to a new Indonesian food law that would set standards for safety and identify mechanisms for control (Bijlmer, 1992). In addition, several significant theoretical issues were explored that related street foods to city size, the street economy, and to circulatory migration patterns. The IPB project findings in these areas substantially expanded our understanding of the street food trade.

Before focusing on street food vendors, a survey of all economic street activities was carried out in Bogor and four other locations to ascertain the proportion of hawkers selling street foods. The survey was designed to capture different characteristics of the two major types of vendors by method of operation: (1) mobile vendors who actually move about and so are ambulatory and (2) vendors selling at a regular place whether from permanent stalls; from trays, boxes and baskets; or from parked pushcarts or tricycles. Such stationary vendors might be found in the neighborhoods or at "strategic locations" around commercial areas, transport points, hospitals, and the like. From the beginning, the assumption was that food sold by mobile street food vendors would be less safe because "the smaller and simpler the equipment, the larger the chance of contamination" from dust, exhaust fumes, insects, and customer handling (Winarno 1989, 5). Yet even vendors squatting on the ground at crowded intersections were classed as *stationary*, even though they certainly utilize simple equipment and their foods are even more likely to be contaminated by exhaust than is food sold by mobile sellers peddling around the neighborhoods. In fact, this classification emphasized geographic location rather than attributes of the trade in anticipation of organizing vendors for training.

The hawker survey revealed that 78% of all neighborhood stationary vendors sold street food, compared to 44% of all ambulatory vendors and 47% of stationary vendors at strategic locations. Women predominated in the neighborhoods (77%), were a third of permanent vendors at strategic locations, but were only 28% of mobile vendors; overall, women outnumbered men 52% to 48%. This division of vendors into three groups clarified the different needs of each type and informed the subsequent interventions and training modules. The survey also underscored the economic importance of street foods: some 12% of the urban labor force was involved in the trade (Bijlmer, 1992).

Because the project was expected to produce a series of training packages for use throughout the country, the baseline survey was designed to reveal variations in the street food trade from rural villages to urbanized locations; case studies would be done in Bogor and in a neighboring village. The sites selected for study included areas in Jakarta with some 6.5 million inhabitants; Bogor, with 250,000 people; a district capital with a population of 63,500; two market towns with 21,000 and 28,000 people; and ten villages with an average population of 4,600. These sites were scattered throughout the province of West Java and included both highland and lowland areas. The researchers assumed that the addition of toxic chemical coloring agents would increase with city size, but that food handling practices would be less safe in rural areas. Staff also expected pressures from customers and municipal regulations to offset the likelihood of contamination from adverse environmental factors and degraded water supply in urban areas.

In fact, the results of testing 915 food samples showed that contamination was related more to the category of food than to the type or location of vendor. Cold drinks, watery snacks, and meals served cold "proved to be of poor microbial quality in contrast to snacks and meals which were fried or cooked just before consumption" (Bijlmer 1991, 5). Pesticide residues did not prove to be a problem, but the use of chemical additives such as boric acid to improve texture and textile dyes as coloring agents was alarming.

City size was important in predicting the number of persons working in permanent enterprises. Enterprises in the rural commercial areas employed 1.23 persons, versus 1.48 in urban locations; the figures for enterprises in the neighborhoods were even greater, with 1.34 persons per unit in rural areas and 1.73 in urban areas. In Jakarta the study reported nearly three workers per enterprise (Winarno 1989, 11). Data from the survey do not indicate whether these workers were paid, but the Bogor case studies reaffirmed EPOC findings that most help is unpaid family labor.

Another issue expected to vary by city size was the number of circulatory migrants. Because these temporary workers send remittances home and indicated that they would like return as soon as possible themselves, the project staff assumed that they generally worked for large-scale operations such as bakeries rather than in their own enterprise. As such, they would hardly be interested in learning improved methods of food handling. These assumptions were based on Bijlmer's earlier work on ambulatory vendors in Surabaya, Indonesia's second largest city located in East Java. His research focused on the range of *"reception systems* through which rural migrants are received, accommodated and channelled into the highly particularistic and fragmented labour market of the street economy" (1986, 61). He found that half of the migrants in Surabaya stayed temporarily with kin or friends before finding their own accommodations and settling down. The other half lived in some sort of collective accommodations, sharing space and expenses but carrying on independent economic activities. Only a small number operated from the distinctive Indonesian system called *pondok*, in which the owner of a shelter also owns an enterprise. Some *pondok* owners rented carts or *becaks* to their residents, while others provided food or bakery goods on commission to them (Bijlmer 1986).

To test these conclusions in West Java, street food vendors were asked their place of origin, though not how long they had been away from home. Not surprisingly, given the rates of urbanization in Indonesia, migration rates were highest for the largest two cities. In all study sites more migrants worked as ambulatory vendors than stationary ones. Due to lack of data on length of stay in the urban areas, it is unclear whether the migrant eventually returns to the rural areas. Chapman found in the EPOC study that although 55% of the street food vendors were migrants, 58% had been in business more than three years, a fact that suggests a high degree of permanent settlement (1984:37). IPB data on accommodations in a *pondok* show that 55% of urban ambulatory vendors reside there, a finding that underscores the probability of temporary employment. In addition, 37% of the men and women who sell from baskets and crates, but who had been classed as stationary, were living in *pondoks*, data that further emphasize their importance to temporary vendors. By excluding these "stationary" basket and cart sellers, as well as all *jamu* vendors (primarily women), the IPB study found that almost all the remaining ambulatory vendors were men. Identifying this category of male workers, who consider themselves temporary migrants, and who send any surplus home rather than investing it in their own enterprise, corroborated Bijlmer's earlier work and confirmed his conjecture that reaching and influencing these circulatory migrants requires different approaches than those for permanent city residents.

Case Studies

Forty cases studies were carried out in Bogor to ascertain the conditions under which foods were prepared. Descriptions of contaminated kitchen floors and sheds where street food production takes place illustrate unsanitary practices all too vividly, but the interviews confirmed that such food handling practices were the same as those used for home cooking. Of course, a vendor's scale of production allows more points for contamination, and the urban setting, with its lack of water and sanitary facilities, exacerbates these problems. But improving street food safety is obviously difficult if consumers do not demand higher standards.

The case studies were also selected to represent different organizational categories of enterprises: single entrepreneurs, household enterprises, and larger production units. The sample was slanted toward ambulatory vendors, both self-employed and employees, a selection that over-represented male circulatory migrants.[13] Because of the purposive sample, generalizations are not meaningful, but those insights that recur in the studies are valuable in rounding out the picture of the Indonesian street food trade.

Information from the individual cases illustrates the difficulties encountered by *pondok* bosses with their workers, most of whom were distant kin or from their own village. Rental fees for carts often went unpaid for months; men took off for the village without informing the boss if or when they might return; carts were poorly treated. Kin obligations may also interfere with the ability of settled vendors to save. A successful vendor couple in the EPOC study confided that they had moved to Bogor from a smaller town nearer their village precisely to avoid constant demands from their kin; in Bogor they were able to save money toward land and a house (Chapman 1984). Such problems reinforce the tendency of many vendors to replicate their businesses horizontally instead of increasing their size: for instance, building a new cart to rent or opening a second outlet. Only two of the forty vendors in the ITB case study invested directly in their enterprises. Such horizontal replication of the business, together with a "splitting-off" of expertise, results in an amoeba-like pattern of growth.

The IPB case studies found that two-thirds of their sample vendors were able to save money; while the settled vendors saved through traditional rotating savings groups, migrants bought gold and village land. Rotating savings groups are formed by a group of men or women in a similar occupation such as market vendors or housewives. Each contributes a small amount of money to a weekly pool that is then distributed by rotation to one person, by schedule or lot, until each has received the pool. If each of ten members put the equivalent of one dollar into the pool, ten dollars would be available to each member in turn.

These savings groups or organizations for migrants from a particular region were usually the only types of organizations to which the vendors belonged. All vendors in this small sample owned a television set and most owned two radios, perhaps reflecting their extended family living patterns. Even more impressive is that almost all of them subscribed to and read a newspaper! Yet, like most street vendors in the EPOC studies, only producers who hired employees kept any accounting of their enterprise. Bijlmer comments that the difficulties of tracing "net profits does not only frustrate researchers but also hinders a proper monitoring of impacts of supportive measures" (1991, 16). Identifying the primary vendor in a couple-run enterprise is also difficult. In 1980, Ibu Rus set up a small *warung* in the parking lot of a newly constructed bank where her husband worked as a watchman. After two years the *warung* became so prosperous that Pak Muk quit his job to work with his wife and extend the hours of sale. A young male neighbor helps with the *warung*, while Bu's sister and daughter, along with a female neighbor, assist with the cooking. Although Bu Rus works 14 hours a day cooking and selling, she is less often at the *warung* than is her husband, who spends 11 or 12 hours there. Undoubtedly, a survey team would list Pak Muk as the primary owner.

Interventions

The details of these case studies provided the IPB team with information that was invaluable for designing simple interventions. These included adding vinegar to dishwater to inhibit bacterial growth and kill pathogens; replacing hand squeezing with an inexpensive aluminum press to prepare a popular tapioca-based drink; and increasing the shelf life and safety of coconut milk used in many other drinks. Improving the way cooked foods are displayed and sold was also emphasized. Videos, animated films, posters, and role playing were used in meetings with the vendors to educate them about the dangers of unsafe procedures and the ease with which many foods could be made more safe. The project was planning a similar campaign of training for consumers, rightly assuming that consumer pressure was more likely than governmental regulations to improve food practices by the vendors.

The fundamental conclusions of the IPB project paralleled those of EPOC: the goal should be to legalize and organize the trade. The IPB project team noted that local governments continue to focus their wrath on the minority of vendors in congested areas, while they overlook the importance of the trade for the populace and the city; to change this, the team recommended training modules be prepared for government officials so they will understand the important functions played by street food vendors and for consumers regarding food safety. Suggestions to facilitate training by organizing vendors through *pondoks* and associations of migrants from specific regions are innovative. Finally, the team promoted the idea of a provincial NGO to continue the IPB project work in training both vendors and consumers (Bijlmer 1991).

Because of foreign policy disagreements over East Timor between the governments of Indonesia and The Netherlands, all Dutch-supported projects were abruptly terminated by the Indonesian government in April 1992, three months before the completion of the IPB project. Plans to continue the IPB project until March 1993 to test interventions at other sites were suspended pending alternative funding (Bijlmer 1992); Professor Winarno was able to secure funds to continue the training efforts at a more modest level.

Impact of the Two Studies

Bogor is unique in having had a decade-long study done of its street food trade. Both the scholarly and applied information produced by EPOC and ITB has been utilized to educate the national and international community about the importance of street foods as a source of income and food for urban dwellers. This dual nature of street foods was reinforced when the IPB project shifted from its early regulatory and adversarial approach to a supportive stance that emphasized measures to assist and educate the vendors. Because this position was held by many in the Bogor administration, both projects had their full support. In Jakarta, the various federal ministries are divided on the appropriate responses to the street economy, but the compelling research results have encouraged greater efforts to accommodate the needs of the vendors while protecting the interests of consumers and citizens.

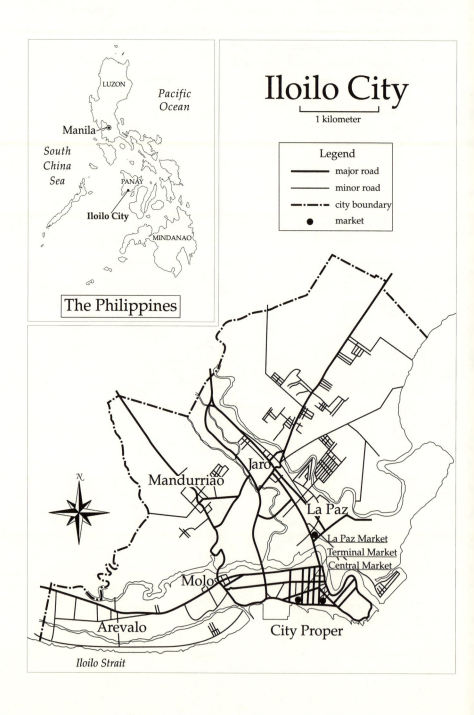

CHAPTER TWO

Iloilo, Philippines

In more ways than one, street foods feed the youth of the rapidly growing city of Iloilo. University students patronize and work for vendors while attending school, and many, weighing the opportunities for profit against the relatively low wages in other sectors, establish their own street food enterprise after graduation. Vendors also feed the schoolchildren, especially since the EPOC staff helped vendors establish direct links to schools, and at the same time improve the sanitation and nutritional value of their products. The Iloilo case study also provides a close look at the important, complex relations of credit, trust, and loyalty along the street food distribution chain: namely, relations between vendors and their lenders and suppliers, as well as between vendors and their customers.

A decade after the study, Iloilo has begun to modernize and street food vendors compete with outlets of fast food chains. Corruption within the vendor association brought its downfall. But in Manila, vendor groups mediate between government and vendors to monitor compliance with new, more sympathetic regulation in a major commercial center. The complex relationship between vendors and school feeding illustrates a middle road between the situation in Thailand or Indonesia.

Local Context

Iloilo is the major port on Panay Island, located 250 miles south and slightly east of Manila, an hour's flight or an overnight sea voyage from the capital. In 1937 the municipality of Iloilo was merged with five adjacent towns to form a self-governing city. The new boundaries also encompassed rice fields, fish ponds, and tidal flats that extend along the Iloilo River and its tributaries. Including rural areas within municipalities helps explain the finding of the Food and Nutrition Institute that 8% of the food consumed in Philippine urban areas in 1978 was home-produced. Although housing estates and new commercial centers have replaced some agriculture, and squatters have claimed less productive land, the city in 1994 still produced about 10% of its own agricultural needs.

While all of the towns retain the typically Spanish central plaza where the government and church are located, the commercial centers are rapidly emulating current international merchandising: Jollibee, the Philippine fast food chain, is located in a new shopping center across the square from a new department store. Local shops have names like Grandma's Fried Chicken or Tony's Fast Foods. While street vendors are not allowed to congregate near the new shopping areas, they cluster on the side streets downtown and in the residential areas; or they sell from stalls provided in the traditional markets, at bus stops, or in entertainment areas along the Iloilo straits, offering a magnificent array of foods, including local specialties—deep fried local plaintains coated with sugar, called "bananacue," or, when stuffed with ground meat, a "banana-burger."

The city's 1980 permanent population of 244,827 has increased by 100,000 in a decade; each year there is an additional vast increase with the influx of students. Over 150,000 students are enrolled in the city's five universities and its many technical, commercial, and vocational schools at secondary and college levels. Not only do the students provide customers for street food vendors, but also many support themselves by working for these entrepreneurs, who are frequently distant kin or from the same village. The need to pay school fees for their children also propels many women back into street food vending after years of home child care. Graduates may find that their new degrees provide employment only in low-paying government jobs, and so return to street selling: 20% of the vendors in the EPOC study had college training.

Agriculture and fishing are the major occupations both on Panay and in the western half of the neighboring island of Negros; this area comprises the Western Visayas Region VI for economic development. Panay exports rice throughout the country; Negros is dominated by sugarcane. Outside the irrigated areas, agricultural productivity is low; efforts continue to introduce new crops and cropping techniques appropriate to rain-fed agriculture. Access to remote areas on both islands has improved with the completion of island-circling coastal roads and coast-to-coast highways, which cut across the mountains and opened new areas to rain-fed farming. Data on the demand for agricultural produce by the street food trade helped identify crops to be promoted. As capital both of Iloilo province and of the Western Visayas Region, Iloilo is an important administrative center, as well an entrepot for regional and export commerce. Small-scale agribusiness investment in food processing and freezing has slowly increased the area's limited industrial sector.

Despite the apparent agricultural abundance, Panay remains one of the poorest islands in the country. During the 1980s, increased landlessness and civil unrest in the mountains encouraged rural-urban migration to Iloilo and out-migration to metro Manila and even overseas; today, remittances are an important source of income in the area. Disparities of income continue, with the richest 10% controlling 36% of the income, while the poorest 30% account for a meager 9.3% A high population growth rate of 2.46% contrasts with 1.9% in neighboring southeast Asian countries (NEDA

1989); during the 1980s, the poverty rate increased from 50% to 65%. Surveys have consistently shown that over 50% of total family expenditures have been devoted to food purchases (NEDA 1983, 116–119). Yet malnutrition persists, with 69% of 7-year-old children classified as underweight.

Squatter houses of wood or split bamboo, with roofs of galvanized iron or nipa palm leaves, are often built on platforms that stretch out over tidal flats, over swamps, and along roads over the drainage ditches; they are connected to each other and to land by complex walkways of wooden slats. In fact, three-quarters of households in the EPOC household survey were squatters and paid no rent. Potable water is sold by vendors and must be carried out to the houses in buckets, a disincentive to cooking at home! Piped water is available only in some sections of town, and then the water pressure is low. Surface well water, used by some households, is frequently polluted. Intestinal diseases are endemic. Yet 28% of homes in the household survey owned a refrigerator, more often for their enterprise than for home use. Indeed, 27% of these households operated a food business from their homes; about half sold street foods and the rest were *sari-sari* (grocery) stores.

In 1994 Iloilo mayor Mansueto A. Malabor identified squatters as the major problem facing the city. He estimates that three-quarters of the squatters occupy private land, and as the economy of the city improves, the owners want them removed. He is also encouraging inhabitants of the pier houses to move because their solid trash is polluting the river and producing unpleasant odors. Land for relocation is expensive, and the sites are some six kilometers from town. Former mayor Luis Herrera, who headed the city for seven years, including during the EPOC study, had purchased land nearer the downtown area for low-income housing, but when the National Housing Authority took over the project, the land was sold instead.[1]

Project Support

An integral part of the EPOC design[2] was the involvement of local scholars and administrators in obtaining as much local support as possible, both for the project and for the long-term welfare of street food vendors. Gerald A. Barth, the EPOC country director, actually set up advisory committees in both Manila and Iloilo. Membership in each committee included Philippine scholars and administrators; the Manila group also featured representatives of USAID. This committee was consulted about city selection and methodological issues, and the final seminar in the capital was held under their auspices. In Iloilo, the street foods project operated under the umbrella of the Regional Development Council; its chair also chaired EPOC's consultative committee. Members included heads of most local development agencies, the mayor and his staff, and professors from several local universities. Most attended the final seminar in Iloilo, along with the leaders of two vendor associations. After an appropriate street foods lunch, the participants broke into working groups to consider ideas to improve street foods themselves and the income of the vendors. Their recommendations, along with the project findings, were further discussed in the Manila seminar.

What Is a Street Food Enterprise?

One question the committee considered was how to determine the boundaries between street food enterprises and formal sector food establishments. In question were *sari-sari* stores and *carendaria* shops, both of which utilize permanent, temporary, and ambulant situations for selling. *Sari-sari* stores are small variety shops selling primarily household necessities and packaged foods and home cleaning products, but many also sell prepared snacks. Further, owners of street food enterprises often aspire to become *sari-sari* store operators and may sell soap along with barbecue. Pragmatically, such stores were included as street foods if significant income came from ready-to-eat foods.

Carendarias resemble the old Horn and Hardart−type cafeteria in that they sell precooked food portions displayed in glass cases; in the Philippines these foods are combined with rice or noodles for a regular meal, or they are added to soup broth for a lighter repast. Because *carendarias* operate out of market stalls or along streets, they were all considered informal sector businesses; they represented 35% of all street food enterprises. In comparison with more than 475 *carendarias* in the city, only 39 restaurants and 51 canteens existed in 1984. These canteens, operating on the premises of various institutions ranging from schools to banks, served the same types of precooked food available at *carendarias*.

The Survey

Because of the large size of Iloilo City, Barth concentrated on the old municipality, along with the contiguous La Paz market. This area, with a 1983 population of 55,400 people, encompassed three major markets, as well as the central business district and the port area. Interspersed among the commercial areas are residential neighborhoods, but there is no open agricultural area in this most urbanized part of Iloilo City. Four women university graduates served as interviewers, primarily using Hiligaynon, the primary language of Iloilo. Because this language does not have a pronoun that distinguishes between gender, both staff and respondents frequently mixed up "she" and "he," a confusion that caused some error in early data collection, but was subsequently corrected.

A census in the commercial areas identified 1,259 street food establishments; slightly less than half of these, or 580, were permanent establishments, while 679 were semi-mobile or ambulant vendors. Vendors in the interior of residential or squatter areas were estimated from a 10% sample count to number another 91, about equally divided between permanent and nonpermanent vendors. The total figures for Iloilo City Proper, then, were 621 permanent and 729 nonpermanent vendors, for a total of 1,350 vendors, or one vendor for each 41 persons in a population of 55,400. Some 25% of the vendors sold in one of the three major markets, and about 7% were located in interior areas; the bulk of the vendors (68%) were located on streets and sidewalks.

To estimate the total number of vendors in all six districts of the expanded city, projections were based on counts made in business areas of the surrounding districts and combined with household samples. The result was 5,100 vendors operating throughout the city of 244,827, or one vendor for each 48 persons. Since three people are needed to operate an average street food enterprise, some 15,300 people are employed in the trade. The total number of households in the city was 42,640, based on a family size of 5.75 persons; using a figure of 35% of the population as economically active, the working population amounted to 85,689 people. Such calculation suggests that as many as 18% of the population earned income through street food vending. Even if most employees were students, the percentage of the permanent labor force engaged in selling prepared food would be nearly 12%.

Iloilo Characteristics

Four distinguishing features of the street food trade in Iloilo emerged from the survey.[3] First, 27% of all enterprises were operated by wife and husband. Second, in contrast to the predominant single-person enterprise elsewhere, an average of three people worked in each enterprise. Third, the distribution and consignment systems were remarkably developed. Fourth, the vendors had a high level of educational attainment.

Couples

All interviews for the survey were conducted with the actual owner of each establishment;[4] according to these data, 79% of the firms had women as owner/operators, compared to 21% for men. When refined to show couples working together, the figures are 62% women alone, 10% men alone, and 27% together. As shown in Table 2-1, enterprises run by couples were the largest and most profitable; a majority were *carendarias* operating out of permanent structures. The average income for women operators was less than half that of couples or of men alone; the least profitable activity was that of women selling peanuts from baskets. However, some men selling alone were engaged in the lowest-paying activity—selling ice cream on commission; their income was closer to that earned by employees of street food vendors.

TABLE 2.1   Vendor enterprises by control and ownership in Iloilo

	No.	%	Avg. daily income (pesos)[a]
Husband and wife operators	37	27	374
Male operator	14	10	363
Female operator	84	62	154

a. At the time, $1 = 10 pesos.

Jointly run enterprises are frequently started by women who continue to run their successful businesses after their husbands join them. Whoever the owner, women both controlled the business income and dominated decision making, a phenomenon observed throughout the Philippines (Hackenberg and Barth 1984).

Paid and Unpaid Assistance

Most enterprises were family businesses, even when they were not controlled jointly by husband and wife. There was an average of 1.8 unpaid workers per enterprise and 1.1 employees. Such unpaid assistance helps account for the higher earnings of enterprises operated by men, since case studies showed that wives, whether working or not, normally helped their husbands in the business, sometimes even taking over from them.

Nene, a 45-year-old widow, specializes in a local noodle soup called *batchoy*, which she sells from the same stall, near the entrance of one of Iloilo's major markets, that her husband had run for fifteen years. Nene, a college graduate, continues to work as a bookkeeper, but now also supervises the food stall and stops in on her way to work. She has hired a neighbor, who has six children and whose husband drives a taxi, to open the shop at 5:30 A.M., prepare the soup, and sell during the day. After her office work is finished, Nene returns to the stall, where she is joined by her two sons, who are college students. They sell soup and drinks until about 9:00 P.M., when they go home for the evening meal. Nene was going to quit her bookkeeping job because the food enterprise is much more profitable, but her employer asked her to stay on and is very flexible about her hours. Having a well-located stall is an important asset for Nene. But the income of the stall has gone down because of the cost of hiring help. Yet the importance of multiple sources of income keeps Nene working at two full-time jobs.

Multiple strategies for income earning is common among the vendors in Iloilo even though street vending was the primary source of income in 80% of the families. Forty-six percent of the vendors had a spouse with a job; 19% of the vendors themselves had another occupation. In addition, 31% had other sources of income, including remittances, contributions from children, pensions, or rental from land, room, or house.

Loreta has been selling food since she was a child. At 53, with eight children, she was running a *carendaria* in the port area where her husband worked as a stevedore. After having her cart confiscated by the police, she erected a stall and home against the warehouse where her brother works. Loreta starts selling coffee and rolls at 3:30 A.M., but her largest income is from the meals she cooks in the morning and sells, mostly to regular customers, at lunchtime. She stays open until about 7 P.M., serving beer and soft drinks once the food is finished. The food also feeds the seven members of her family who live at the stall. They include Loreta, her husband, her brother, two children, and two grandchildren; the adult members all help her with the work. Her married children also often eat with her or take food home for their families. Despite feeding so many people for free, Loreta earns more than twice as much as her steve-dore husband.

Paid employees were hired primarily by half of the enterprises with permanent structures and only by 6% of the semi-mobile or ambulant enterprises. Pay was low, about the same as for a domestic worker; employees were also provided with meals, and most (70%) with a place to sleep. One-fifth of these employees were related to the owner. Most were in their early twenties and slightly better educated than the owner, both factors suggesting that they were college students. Mayor Malabor him-self actually worked in a *sari-sari* store when he was a student in Iloilo.

Consignments and Deliveries

Many vendors make more food than they can sell directly to customers, so they also sell to other retailers or wholesalers, either for cash or on consignment. The tropical heat and lack of refrigeration precludes storing most foods for later sale. For example, Meding's liver and pork barbecues supply five wholesale buyers who sell throughout the city, paying her only after they have made their own sales. In the late afternoon, with help from her daughter who has returned from school, she sells in the neigh-borhood. In addition to her own barbecues, she sells baked goods and native sweets delivered to her on consignment from a supplier in the Central Market. Her husband helps out whenever he is not driving a jeep and making deliveries for another whole-saler; once again, his income is about half of his wife's daily profits.

More than one-half of the vendors in the survey had some items delivered to their enterprises. Beer and soft drinks are sold only for cash, but beverage companies fre-quently supply a refrigerator to the vendors and may give them counters that adver-tise their products. Some 36% of the vendors bought items on consignment as well. Goods sold were usually paid for at the end of the day; 10% of the firms, primarily the ice cream vendors, operated exclusively on this system.

Vendors must constantly weigh convenience against cost. With time in short supply, having food and beverages delivered becomes cost-effective. Vendors using chicken for barbecue or meals save time by purchasing ready-to-cook chickens rather than live ones at lower prices. Often, when a couple is operating the enterprise, the husband might go to the country and buy chickens at a much reduced price, adding to the profitability of their enterprise. Several prosperous enterprises bought jeeps so that husbands or sons could transport raw and cooked food items around town.

For 43 years Corey has been preparing native sweets made of glutinous rice sweet-ened with coconut milk and or brown sugar and steamed inside palm or banana leaves. She sells in the market in the morning and makes the sweets each afternoon; one son helps her carry the sweets to the public jeep for the early morning ride to town. Besides those she sells herself, Corey supplies sweets to six other women; three of these also sell in the market, two are ambulant vendors, and one sells from her home. As a widow with nine children, two still of school age and living at home, Corey seeks additional sources of income. When needed she serves as a midwife, which earns her an income equivalent to four days' work. One year she set up a *sari-sari* store in her neighborhood, but a daughter's hospital bills used up her operating capital. A waitress daughter who lives with her contributes to the household budget.

Education

The vendors interviewed had an average schooling of just under eight years; no vendors were illiterate, and one-fifth of the vendors had attended college. Preliminary data suggested that there was a significant link between college attendance and higher earnings; however, later analysis indicated that the important variable was years of vending experience rather than education per se.

Letty is a college graduate who worked for a year as a secretary before quitting to try her hand at supplying food to street vendors. Starting with banana bread, she soon added cakes and muffins; her customers have expanded from vendors to several university canteens. Her sister sells any leftover items as well as others that she bakes at a Saturday market. A third sister started as Letty's assistant but now is both a retailer and wholesaler of banana cakes. The three sisters live in a middle-class section of town with their parents, who operate a *sari-sari* store from the front of the house. Each sister has her own kitchen shed behind the house and each cooks with a modern gas oven. Each of these various entrepreneurial activities brings in considerably more than the typical white-collar job available in Iloilo; collectively, the family is well off.

The Foods They Sell

Most street food vendors in Iloilo sold a variety of foods, from self-produced items to industrially packaged snacks and beverages, thus acting as producers, traders, and food servers. Barth found that only 25% of the vendors only sold the food, with no preparation involved. Over half (56%) cooked the food at place of sale, while 16% cooked food at home. Most vendors (92%) bought some items from wholesalers. Fifty-eight percent purchased goods directly from the producer, while 13% also utilized a middleman.

Throughout the Philippines the custom of *merienda*, or snacking throughout the day, is well entrenched. As a result, street vendors offer light foods all day long. Local and Western-style eggs, sandwiches, buns, fruits, and fried snacks are sold by 22% of the vendors. These include deep-fried *bananacue* or banana-burgers, deep-fried chips made from bananas and sweet potatoes, popped rice and corn, fried cashews and peanuts, batter-fried shrimp, and fried *lumpia*, the local version of egg rolls. Sliced green mango is served with fried local shrimp paste. Eggs are a popular boiled snack, including duck eggs, fresh or fertilized (*balut*), quail eggs, and chicken eggs.

Typically Philippine are the "native cakes," steamed sweets using a base of glutinous, sticky rice or sometimes cassava; these snacks are sold by 5% of the vendors. *Puto maya*, a muffin-sized sweet, uses ground rice mixed with coconut milk and ginger; *puto bumbong* uses a variety of naturally purple rice cooked in hollow bamboo; other *puto* are flavored with brown sugar or anise.

Industrially manufactured food items, usually shipped from Manila, rival locally produced candy, snacks, and beverages. In 1983, these manufactured items were the primary food sold by 19% of the vendors; however, 78% of Iloilo street food sellers sold some items made in Manila. Beer was then manufactured near both Manila and Cebu, and shipped to Iloilo; along with soft drinks, it constituted a major item for many vendors. Even instant coffee had largely replaced locally brewed coffee. Locally made beverages were sold by a mere 3% of the vendors. Nonalcoholic drinks that remained popular were fruit drinks and a local specialty called *tahu*, made with ginger and hot water; also available was an alcoholic drink, *tuba*, made from the fermented sap from the coconut palm tree. At the time, ices and ice cream, sold by 6% of the vendors on commission only, were still locally made.

Half the vendors sold more substantial foods: meal constituents, soups, barbecue, sandwiches, meat, and eggs. Because by local custom a meal must include rice, or at least noodles, 35% of all street food establishments were *carendarias* offering dishes locally known as *viands*. Specifically served over rice, these dishes or meal constituents are usually offered cold by street food vendors; they include shrimp, chicken, pork, with or without vegetables and are served dry or with a minimum of sauce. *Viands* are displayed in enclosed food cases so that customers can easily make their selection, and they are generally eaten at tables provided by the vendors. Most *carendarias* operate out of permanent structures in market or vending areas built by the city. Others are self-built stalls with galvanized tin roofs that shelter a counter and stools. Often the counters are supplied by beverage companies such as Coca Cola or San Miguel beer in exchange for free advertising. The space between the wall and the counter is used for cooking and serving food; refrigerators, liquid petroleum gas tanks, charcoal grills, and cases of soft drinks line the perimeter. Posters decorate the walls and a radio plays incessantly. Bedrolls may be spotted under the shelves at one end; an amazing 44% of all vendors surveyed lived in their stalls.

Many *viands* are made from fresh or dried fish, shrimp, crab, squid, or snails. Chicken and pork in all its forms are the base of many dishes: pig's ear is a local favorite. Because beef is imported it is less used. Vegetables, seaweed, mung beans and their sprouts, jackfruit, bamboo shoots, and coconut are used to produce hundreds of viands. Most vendors vary their dishes in response to seasonal food supply and in order to keep regular customers.

Customers

Even though the customer survey[5] was conducted during college vacation, 16% of the street food customers were students. This figure surely doubles during term. The 4% of all customers who never cooked at home included many students. Unlike most other surveyed countries, customers were equally split between women and men, although certain enterprises, mainly those selling beer, catered to a largely male clientele. A quarter of the customers, many of them students, were from outside the city. By occupation, nearly half were blue-collar workers or market traders; one-fifth were white-collar workers, and another fifth were students. Two-thirds were buying snacks,

Shrimp Lumpia
Variation on Chinese Spring Rolls

Filling (for four lumpia)

3 ounces shrimp, shelled, deveined, and
finely chopped

¼ cup julienned bamboo shoots

2 tablespoons finely minced scallions

1 small carrot, peeled and coarsely grated

1 teaspoon soy sauce

1 garlic clove, finely minced

salt and pepper

Wrapper

2 eggs

¼ cup cornstarch

3 tablespoons all-purpose flour

¼ teaspoon salt

¼ cup water

vegetable oil

Soy dipping sauce

½ cup water

1 tablespoon sugar

2 tablespoons soy sauce

2 teaspoons cornstarch

1 clove garlic, minced

1 teaspoon fresh gingerroot, minced

hot pepper sauce to taste

Make filling by combining all ingredients; set aside.

Make wrappers (or used packaged ones). Beat eggs with a whisk until frothy. Blend in cornstarch, flour, and salt. Whisk in water in a slow stream. Beat until ingredients are thoroughly combined. Brush an 8-inch heavy skillet with oil and ladle 3–4 tablespoons of batter into the pan, tilting so that the batter covers the bottom. Cook over medium high heat until the wrapper is opaque and slightly blistered, about 1 minute. Turn with a spatula and cook the other side for about 15 seconds. Slide onto waxed paper. Repeat, separating wrappers with more waxed paper. Makes four wrappers.

Divide filling into four portions. Place each portion about one-fourth of the way up the wrapper. Fold the short end of the wrapper over the filling. Fold the left and right sides of the wrapper toward the center. Roll up from the bottom to form a rectangle.

Heat 1 inch of oil in a heavy skillet to 350 degrees F. Fry lumpia, seam side down, until golden, about 1 minute. Turn and fry on the other side for another minute. Remove with a slotted spoon and dry on paper towels. Serve with soy dipping sauce at room temperature.

Make the dipping sauce by combining all ingredients in a saucepan and cooking over low heat until the sugar dissolves. Bring to a boil and cook until the sauce thickens. Pour into a serving bowl and allow to cool.

Camote Chips
Sweet Potato Chips

Select 2 pounds of sweet potatoes for their cylindrical shape. Peel and slice thinly. Soak in ice water for 15 minutes, then drain very thoroughly and blot dry.

Heat oil in a deep-fryer to 375 degrees F. Fry about one-third of the potatoes at a time until tender and brown along the edges, 4 to 5 minutes for each batch. Remove and drain. Serve at once.

Sweet potato chips are a common street food around the world. In the Philippines and Indonesia, the chips are sprinkled with sugar before serving; in Nigeria, salt is preferred; in the Caribbean, spices are often added.

---

meaning that they did not consume any rice. Most of the food was eaten on the spot, but a fifth said that they were taking it home for their families. The relatively high percentage of low-income customers reflects the time constraints of women and men working at multiple jobs. Street foods are not only more convenient but also cost less than transportation home and back for lunch.[6]

As elsewhere, street food sellers maintain their regular customers with special services rather than with lower prices, since by custom the cost of a portion tends to be the same throughout the city. Called *suki*, these relationships result in the customer being served larger portions, getting better quality, or receiving faster service. Often the total purchase price of the food was rounded off to the customer's advantage; this action was considered a courtesy and not thought of as bargaining. Regular customers, who totaled 37% in the study, were often allowed to buy on credit until their next payday. *Suki* relationships exist throughout the marketing system between vendors who sell on consignment and those who sell to wholesalers.

The dietary importance of street foods is underscored by the customers' estimate that 35% of their food intake was from prepared food; the amount spent equaled 28% of their monthly food budget. Nearly two-thirds (58%) of the food purchased is *merienda*, the rest is for meals—12% for breakfast, 24% for lunch, and 6% for dinner. A household survey[7] found that 30% of food costs were spent on street foods, including 13% street foods eaten where purchased, 10% street foods brought home, and 7% food eaten at formal institutions. Seventy percent of the food expenditure was on foods for home preparation. Of the food brought home, 61% were snacks, and the rest supplemented meals—24% for lunch, 4% for breakfast, and 11% for supper. Food brought home was usually purchased in the neighborhood, but 13% of the respondents actually had this food delivered. Households with incomes in the lowest quartile brought the most food home. The lowest three quartiles all spent two-thirds or more of their total family income on food; the average amount spent on food by the highest income group was five times that of the lowest group, but this amount represented only 40% of family income. Both figures are affected by the fact

FIGURE 2.1   Roast corn is sold to customers in cars or truck and to schoolchildren as they walk home along a residential street in Iloilo.

that three-quarters of households in the survey did not pay any rent; presumably, these are the households spending 65 to 75% of their income on food.

Working and Surviving

Most street food vendors report that they work seven days a week all year round.[8] The fact that nearly half of the vendors (44%) live in their stalls clearly contributes to their continuous schedule. The only strictly seasonal vendors are the sellers of grilled corn on the cob, who appear during the summer months: 110 more vendors were counted in August than in either February or April, selling only corn for about two months (Figure 2.1). A second increase in the number of vendors was noted in November as the holiday season approached. Not only did more vendors appear in the central markets, but also there was a 10% increase in vendors in the neighborhoods as many *sari-sari* stores increased their proportion of prepared food sales, an activity that takes more effort and time, but which provides rapid turnover of capital. Variation also occurred in income: 84% of the vendors said their sales were lower during the dry season that begins in March and coincides with school vacation. Most of the fruits and the vegetable snacks listed in February had completely disappeared before the April survey, but they reappeared in May, beginning with the arrival of small green mangoes.

Survival of Street Food Enterprises

Despite incomes well above the minimum wage, street vendors in Iloilo lead a precarious existence due particularly to illness-incurred debt and periods of police harassment. This instability was documented by the EPOC study: 9% of the enterprises that were included in the survey could not be located six months later.

A majority of vendors used their own savings to start their business; about one-sixth used supplier credit, for which they paid no interest. Another 15% borrowed funds from a moneylender at rates from 5% to 40% *per month*. When hospital bills or school fees forced vendors to borrow their own operating capital, many more sought out the moneylenders. Over 37% of all vendors had outstanding loans at these usurious interest rates. Banks would only grant loans to registered stall holders: only three vendors in the survey had ever had a bank loan. Government credit programs that were supposed to reach the poor were not observed in Iloilo in 1983. For example, the Ministry of Social Service and Development could give "social credit" loans; in Manila about half the recipients were female vendors.[9] In contrast, in 1994 this same department, now decentralized to city control, offered interest-free loans of 1,000 to 5,000 pesos to vendors needing funds to expand an existing business. Three-quarters of the loans went to women. Repayments were postponed in the case of family emergencies.[10] Throughout the country, nongovernmental organizations (NGOs) are organizing cooperatives in order to provide small scale credit for the poor, utilizing group accountability instead of material collateral.

While the issue of legitimacy and legality bothered all vendors, those selling in the markets seemed more secure than those on the street; vendors operating out of their homes away from the downtown area were seldom bothered. Regulations did not recognize these differences. Legally, all enterprises were supposed to obtain licenses to operate a business and to sell certain items, as well as permits from the Bureau of Internal Revenue and the local sanitary and health department. This latter license required vendors to attend a week-long training program and to pay 20 pesos to obtain a license; among all the vendors in the survey, only Letty had attended. Not surprisingly, only 10% of the nonpermanent vendors had any license. Indeed, at the EPOC seminar, some administrators voiced their reluctance to grant such permits because it might legitimize "illegal" vending. In contrast, two-thirds of those enterprises operating out of permanent structures held licenses.

Vendors in the markets pay rent for their stalls. While in theory these stalls are obtained through lottery, in actuality perhaps 70% of the stallkeepers were not officially listed in their own name, but had either inherited or purchased the right to rent the stall. Marketplace vendors without a stall bought daily cash tickets that legitimized their operation.

During the 1980s when the study was conducted, the city administration under Mayor Luis Herrera took a remarkably benign attitude toward the vendors selling on streets and sidewalks; in contrast, in Manila, police raids were an almost daily occurrence. The vendors in Iloilo were left alone as long as they obeyed certain rules: keeping the area clean, covering all cooked food, cooking only in designated areas, occupying only half the sidewalk, and obtaining the agreement of the store owner. In 1983, nearly a quarter of street food vendors belonged to one of two vendors' associations active in the downtown area, one in the market and the other for street vendors of all commodities. This street vendors' group represented 400 vendors at the time and hired its own guards to enforce the mayor's rules, watch for pickpockets, and preserve the selling places of members. At the final EPOC seminar, representatives from this organization asked for a change in the law to recognize sidewalk selling as legal.

During the study, no vendor indicated that he or she had had to pay fees either to a *tong* or to the police. The situation changed rapidly during the subsequent decade. The mayor who succeeded Herrera drove out many newly installed vendors from the Central Market, whose capacity Herrera had increased from 500 to 900 stalls, unless they agreed to make a "donation" of 30,000 pesos. Corruption also grew within the vendor associations. Those vendors not paying protection money were beaten up, while vendors who ingratiated themselves with the association and administration were allowed to set up their stalls or carts anywhere they wished, even on the city's historic plazas. When Mayor Malabor was elected in 1993, he fulfilled his appellation of "Mr. Clean" by cleaning up the plazas and abolishing the corrupt vendor associations. He reinstated the conciliatory approach of Herrera and made a small credit program available to vendors. After being confronted with the explosive issue of relocation, he dealt with the vendors on a case-by-case basis. Iloilo is modernizing; when a new shopping area broke ground, vendors in the area were offered stalls nearby in the less congested Solis Street where they pay no rent as long as they observe sanitary rules.[11] Competition from the new megamalls is not too severe. In 1994, a cold bottle of Coca-Cola cost 5 pesos at a *carendaria*; at Jollibees (the Philippine version of McDonald's) the same amount cost 9.45 pesos plus 4% tax. Clearly, while Jollibee caters to a middle-income group, many middle-class customers are happy to save money by eating on the street.

Street Food Policies in Manila

Rapid population growth, economic development, and political machinations have all contributed to the increasing disparity of incomes in the Philippines. The more open political climate since the overthrow of President Ferdinand Marcos has brought into power many politicians devoted to alleviating poverty. The national NGOs who opposed Marcos were offered representation in many local level decision-making bodies where they champion the interests of the poor; these groups also help organize and offer services to community-based Peoples' Organizations. The impact of these changes on the street food vendors in Manila is palpable.

Police harassment and brutality against street vendors of all types was legendary under the Marcos administration. Not only were carts confiscated or destroyed, but also vendors, like any petty criminal, could be jailed indefinitely without charge. The upscale city of Makati, part of Metro Manila, was a frequent site of confrontations between vendors and police . Today, all vendors who registered their stall locations in Makati before October 1992 with the Association of Vendors have the right to continue selling in this area of modern office buildings and expensive shopping malls as long as they follow basic health and cleanliness standards. Vendors are also urged to adopt standardized carts to lend the sidewalk a trim appearance.

The compromise that persuaded vendors to agree to these and other regulations was formulated by Makati Councillor Nenita "Nini" Ramos Licaros, elected in 1992 to her first government position. In an interview she recalled the intense ingrained opposition to her stance from political bosses with police connections. They sprayed her car with paint remover, sent a funeral wreath emblazoned "Rest in Peace," and finally had a mock coffin delivered to her on the eve of her birthday! Her family connections to the president of the Philippines certainly helped protect her from more serious retribution. To gain allies, she has solicited free carts from a bottling company and encouraged NGOs to offer credit to the vendor organization. She even contacted a women's livelihood organization to make and sell aprons and head-coverings to the vendors, who are required to use them in accordance with new regulations. And she arranged for clean water to be delivered to the street food stalls.

Once the Makati Council passed the regulations, all existing vendors were enumerated; the list was then computerized and distributed to the newly formed Makati Vendor's Association, which monitors the compliance of its members. At first only residents of Makati were going to be registered, but bidding on the rights for stalls was pervasive, so a decision was made to recognize all vendors who were selling on the streets in October 1992. Although the agreement curtailed additional registration, much pressure is being applied to open up the rolls again; even some police have applied, Licaros noted with a smile. Current registration is about 500, of which 350 are stalls. Officially, street foods are still illegal, Licaros said. In Makati, vendors break rules by locating on the sidewalk and by providing stools (Figure 2.2): the council wants customers to buy the food and go. Licaros observed that it is politically necessary to allow some seating at the ends of the cart, but not in front where they further disrupt the traffic. However, vendors have been suspended for fifteen days for infractions of health rules (Licaros interview, 10 June 1994). Nini Licaros, like Mayor Malabor of Iloilo, used political power to overturn corruption within the police and among the vendors in order to establish a fair balance between the rights and needs of both vendors and citizens.

FIGURE 2.2 New carts licensed by the city council in Makati, an upscale commercial section of Manila. The stool legs are perilously close to the curb.

A second type of initiative for helping vendors in Manila came from within the administration. Patrocinio De Guzman, deputy director of the Food and Nutrition Research Institute (FNRI), was a member of the Manila advisory committee for the EPOC Street Food Project in the Philippines and attended the seminar in Manila in January 1984, when Gerald Barth presented the final project report on Iloilo. Since 1985 the FNRI has been studying nutritional issues related to street foods; in 1988 the FNRI worked with UNICEF to outline methods of improving the nutritional status of schoolchildren. These two issues intersect in the Philippines because many children prefer to eat street foods in place of, or in addition to, food available in school canteens. With funding from FAO, De Guzman began a project in 1992 that was designed to improve "the food management practices and nutrition awareness" of providers of food for schoolchildren: street food vendors and school canteen operators.[12]

School canteens throughout the Philippines are operated by teachers who are relieved of some classroom time to supply the meals. This policy was first initiated in 1906 and has changed considerably over the years. In 1966 the Bureau of Public Schools amended the guidelines at a time when funding for schools was low (De Guzman et al. 1974). The revised system not only supplied meals for the children, often utilizing food distributed through foreign aid programs, but also provided a source of income from the meals to be used for home economics instruction, medicines for the school clinic, or school building maintenance. In rural schools, children and teachers often grew their own vegetables with seeds supplied through foreign assistance. Although the policy is still in place, many teachers are buying foods from street vendors because they lack the time and skill to provide meals. Recognizing this trend, from 1975 until 1982 the Health Department in Iloilo held one-day training sessions for vendors.[13] The unique features of De Guzman's project are the training of teachers and municipal health officers to train the vendors and the emphasis on school canteens and street foods as complementary sources for feeding urban schoolchildren.

At San Juan elementary school in Manila, one of two pilot schools in the project,[14] the canteen was managed by two teachers whose regular subjects were home economics and livelihood training. Students from grades 4 through 6, boys as well as girls, help with the cooking that takes place in the school. Meals are served three times during the day, with *merienda* breaks in the morning and afternoon for the younger students who attend school in two shifts. In addition, the older students and the teachers, who are in school all day, are provided with a noontime meal. Of the 2,450 students and 75 teachers (71 female and 4 male), about 1,000 eat in the morning and at noon, about 800 in the afternoon.[15] Food costs per meal are 15 pesos for students and 20 pesos for teachers, either for rice and sauces or for sandwiches and juice. These figures show that many schoolchildren and teachers patronized street food vendors who, until the project began, crowded the narrow street that is the only access to the schoolgrounds.

Today, vendors at San Juan occupy a covered, cemented area on the edge of the campus that has its own water supply, and they are gradually buying their newly designed carts. All these vendors attended four Saturday training classes taught by the teachers and municipal health officials trained under the project. Safe food-handling practices were emphasized, and new recipes that made favorite foods more nutritious were offered. For example, the nutritional level of the widely consumed fish balls can be greatly enhanced by the addition of squash and fish protein concentrate. Selling fish balls, fried to order and dipped into one of several sauces, is quite profitable for vendors, but homemade balls are often contaminated and low on fish content, while the ones available frozen at supermarkets are expensive. FNRI is promoting the enhanced balls to individual vendors and is trying to convince a large-scale food manufacturer to produce them.

These two initiatives in Manila both seek to regularize, if not legitimize, street food vending and to improve the safety and contents of the food they sell. Their approaches reflect the locations in which the vendors sell. In high-profit, congested commercial areas, where a balance is necessary between the competing rights of vendors and the public, a political solution would appear necessary and is clearly preferable to earlier policies of harassment and destruction. Iloilo's policy of providing alternative downtown sites is prohibitive in Makati because of its expensive land prices. Municipal vendor markets with stalls rented at affordable prices along the Singapore model is the long-term goal of De Guzman. In outlying areas such markets might be erected on a small scale; perhaps the school vendor program will lead the way.[16]

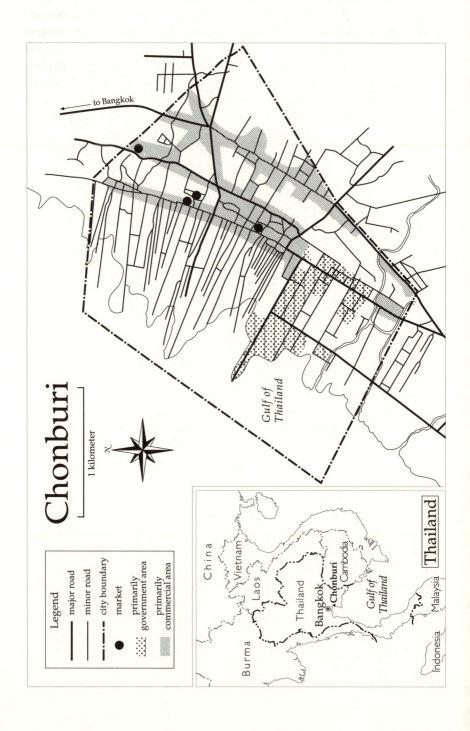

Chonburi

1 kilometer

N

to Bangkok

Gulf of
Thailand

Legend
— major road
— minor road
—··— city boundary
● market
⬚ primarily
government area
▨ primarily
commercial area

Thailand

China

Vietnam

Laos

Burma

Thailand

Bangkok

Chonburi

Cambodia

Gulf of
Thailand

Malaysia

Indonesia

CHAPTER THREE

Chonburi, Thailand

Chonburi is one of many cities in Asia undergoing rapid industrialization and economic growth. The conversion of former agricultural hinterlands into vast industrial zones has not just transformed the city's economy and demographics; it has made it difficult even to define what is "urban." But the proliferation of agro-processing industries and fast-food restaurants has not hurt business for the city's vibrant street food sector. Economic change has reinforced the traditional expectations that Thai women will contribute significantly to family income. As a result, the street food trade is dominated by women.

Long an important part of the urban Thai diet, meals and snacks purchased on the streets of Chonburi and Bangkok are now especially convenient for the many busy working women who buy takeout provisions for their families' suppers. Their widespread appeal and low cost has also won street food vendors contracts with schools and hotels, as well as selling space inside modern shopping malls. In this context, it is perhaps not surprising that many vendors earn as much as or more than their customers, and running a street food enterprise remains a respectable occupation even for well-educated men and women.

Local Context

Chonburi, located along the rapidly industrializing eastern seaboard of the Gulf of Siam, is the capital of a province neighboring the burgeoning Bangkok metropolitan area. One of 76 provinces in Thailand's hierarchical and centralized bureaucratic system, Chonburi has eight districts reporting to it. Historically, Chonburi's coastal location made it an important fishing port and an early industrial processing center for the rice, sugar, and tapioca that is cultivated nearby. Many original migrants to the area came from China, resulting in a population that is currently about half Sino-Thai. Labor for the rapid industrial expansion after World War II came from throughout the country, overflowing the 4.5-square-kilometer municipality that is located between the seashore and the main coastal highway. Nearly one square kilometer consists of wooden and a few cement piers that stretch from solid land into the protected waters of the bay and are lined with houses built on stilts. Old Chinese temples are found near the entrances of many walkways. Toward the end of piers, the sea is more apparent, and inhabitants often keep a small boat to use between their home and shore or fishing boat.

Excluding this foreshore, Chonburi consists of only 3.4 square kilometers. Four large covered markets, three of them private, are located within this small area; vendors in two of the markets come primarily from outside the official city limits, and over half of the street food customers live beyond the municipal boundaries. Residential areas ring the governmental town center and the commercial area that includes small-scale food processing factories, as well as shop houses offering food and services.

At the time of the study, Chonburi, with a population of 47,000, was the fifth largest municipality in Thailand; its density was more than 10,000 persons per square kilometer. Despite this high density, the city's architecture is dominated by Chinese shop houses; in 1985, only a few modern hotels or banks and the wats were more than three stories tall. Bangkok's primacy in Thailand is so overwhelming that in 1984 the next eleven largest municipalities represented only 7.3% of the country's urban system. The capital is 87 kilometers away, but the bus ride through the congested, increasingly industrialized areas between Chonburi and Bangkok takes three hours. This proximity to the many universities in Bangkok explains the absence of a local center for higher education.

The absence of development nongovernmental organizations, as opposed to philanthropic Buddhist organizations, reflects the inhospitable climate created by military governments in Thailand until the latter part of the 1980s. Student groups promoting radical reform were suppressed after the 1976 coup; nonprofit groups strayed little from the traditional charitable models, supporting temples and joining with international groups to work with refugees fleeing neighboring countries (Pongsapich and Kataleeradabhan 1994). Even today, most change-oriented organizations do not register because of governmental restrictions and regulations. Most such organizations are located in Bangkok (Pongsapich 1993).

Chonburi's population increased rapidly during the 1950s, but then grew much more slowly, particularly in comparison with many other provincial towns outside the Central Region or with the suburban areas between Chonburi and Bangkok. Many of these areas are *sukhapiban*, or sanitary districts, created after World War II to encourage industrial development and housing estates by providing formerly rural areas with urban infrastructure. Taxes levied on industries located there are lower than those in municipalities, and the revenues collected go into the provincial budget: both these factors provide strong vested interests opposing the expansion of municipal boundaries to enclose their urbanized periphery. In Chonburi, the availability of urban services outside the dense inner area actually led to a decline in population from its maximum in 1982 of 50,345 to 46,862 in 1983. While the municipality was experiencing a decline of 6.9%, the surrounding Muang District was increasing at a rate of 12.5%; its 1982 population was 125,843 compared to 141,553 the following year. Some food processing plants have moved to the district from Chonburi; new economic activities such as mechanical repairs and construction are also expanding in this peri-urban area.

These changes in and around Chonburi reflect the rapid industrialization policies of the Thai government, which reported an average annual 7% growth rate for the period between 1960 and 1980. Since then, though there have been significant fluctuations, the rates are still strong and reached an amazing 13.2% in 1988. National data show a steady reduction of people living below the poverty line; in 1988 the proportion had fallen from a third to a quarter nationally, but regional disparities remained with 43% in the Northeast compared to 5% in municipal areas (Pongsapich 1994).

Women's Economic Importance

To support greater household income, more women are working for cash in both rural and urban areas. Rural Thai women engage in export-oriented homebased work to increase family income; only 5% indicated that their income was for personal use only (Pongsapich et al. 1989). These activities add to women's workload, with no commensurate additional work by their husbands (Pongsapich 1994). Because women's wages are seen only as supplmentary, their pay in sawmills or tapioca production comes to 60% to 85% less than men. Such discrimination makes the selling of street foods attractive to Thai women since they control their own income. Typically, women support education for their daughters and sons, and they often provide money to their husbands for leisure activities such as drinking and gambling, pursuits which are considered culturally appropriate for Thai men. The assumption is that if the wife did not provide this money, potential rivals might do so. "Although a married woman gave her earning of her own free will, her absolute contribution remained a form of culturally condoned blackmail" (Blanc-Szanton 1990, 93).

In contrast, women's labor in Sino-Thai households selling street foods is unpaid family labor; girls are seldom allowed higher education unless the family is well off. The Chonburi household data clearly demonstrated these differences: Sino-Thai households tended to be larger and to operate their businesses as household enterprises, with all family members contributing their work. While adult members in Thai families may all work, they typically work separately and in smaller businesses. The single large business tends to be more profitable: our data showed that the average Thai family earned 5,700 baht per month compared to an average of 6,500 baht for Sino-Thai families.

The Street Project with CUSRI

Chonburi was selected specifically to provide data on a provincial town that could then be used in further research on urban food and poverty, subjects of growing interest to our partners in the Thai study, the Chulalongkorn University Social Research Institute (CUSRI). As the first social science research unit in the country, CUSRI recognized the importance of both urban and rural studies and began to study the effects of internal migration and modernization throughout Thailand. Amara Pongsapich, vice-director of CUSRI at the time of the study, assumed overall supervision of the project and brought her considerable experience in gender-sensitive research to the study design. Napat Sirisambhand became the full-time project coordinator for CUSRI's survey team as data were collected and analyzed during 1984. Cristina Blanc Szanton, who had written her doctoral thesis comparing the roles of young women of Thai and Chinese business families (1982), became EPOC's consultant to the study and visited Thailand frequently, working closely with Sirisambhand in all phases of the project.

The critical role that street foods played in Thai society, particularly in Bangkok, was readily apparent when the study was first discussed. Acutely aware of the rapidly changing urban scene in Bangkok, CUSRI and EPOC initially proposed a comparative study street of food vendors in a village, a town, and Bangkok in order to trace the impact of urbanization and modernization. A preliminary reconnaissance by CUSRI staff in as many as ten provincial towns, where they were conducting other research, demonstrated clear differences in the street food trade by city size. As in Indonesia, smaller towns had fewer vendors than medium-sized towns. In these small towns, most vendors were women who sold local food specialities and Thai sweets from stalls clustered around municipal markets. Carts and poles were used by both women and men to move about medium-sized towns; in Bangkok, male vendors used tricycles and motorcycles, usually the property of food manufacturers, to roam widely through residential areas, often selling foods on commission. The variety of regional foods increased by city size, as did the frequency of police harassment (Khan 1994). After a particularly severe sweep of Bangkok streets, street food stall owners marched on the king's residence, swimming all the way to the gardens across the moat, respectfully demanding, and receiving, leniency.

Funding for a comparative study was not forthcoming, however, so a medium-sized town was selected. Chonburi proved to have several advantages. Previous studies of local industry and commerce provided valuable longitudinal data allowing for a clearer understanding of the momentous socio-economic changes that took place during the 1980s. In addition, Chonburi was composed largely of migrants from both China and Thailand. These vendors offered a wide variety of regional street foods: Thai curries of fermented fish sauce from the south, green papaya salad and sticky rice from the northeast, or special sausages eaten for the evening meal in the north, or late-night Chinese snacks. Central Thai staples such as noodles and rice with curries or red pork, roast duck, or chicken were of course also sold.

Study Design

The visibility of street foods begged the question of the dietary importance of ready-to-eat foods. So CUSRI decided to supplement the EPOC methodology with a household survey using random sampling of 4% of the 6,600 households in town, reflecting three distinct types of land use: general residential, commercial, and government offices. The census, conducted in January and February 1984, counted a total of 948 vendors, selling year-round on the streets. An additional 412 vendors were counted during the hot season in April and May, making a seasonal increase of 44%; the vendors primarily sold seasonal fruits, cold drinks, and ice cream. The census was also administered in two peri-urban areas where most of the manufacturing expansion of the town was located. The municipality was trying to incorporate these areas for the extra tax revenue; another 90 vendors were located here. In May, 23% (219) of the vendors were interviewed for the economic survey. Also in May, 414 customers were interviewed; the household survey followed in September. With experienced survey staff on call, CUSRI was able to complete these surveys with great speed. Similarly, experience and data from the Chonburi study were immediately utilized in other projects.

Street food vending was by far the major source of prepared food outside the home; a census of other food establishments yielded only nine formal restaurants and three ice cream parlors. One-fifth of the vendors sold foods that are usually or frequently taken home to eat, often with rice cooked in the family's electric rice cooker. And vending was an important source of income in the city: even in the cool season, street vendors accounted for 14% of all households.

The importance of street foods to the Thais is reflected in the words they use for different types of vendors. Pole vendors are *haap rae*; pushcart vendors are *lot kaen*; those who sell from tables are *phaeng looy*; and the shop houses, often with carts in front of them, are called *hong thaew* (Szanton and Sirisambhand 1986). In Bangkok, new terms have yet to be adopted to distinguish between traditional shop houses and Western-style fast food franchises (Yasmeen 1992).

Vendors

Nearly four-fifths of the 948 vendors in Chonbury were women (78%) and were equally divided between Thai and Sino-Thai ethnicity; women sold all types of street foods. The ethnic balance did not hold for men: only one-fifth of the male vendors, or 4% of all vendors, were Thai. Men sold foods in all broad categories except two Thai specialties: steamed crab or shrimp dumplings and a steamed sweet made of rice and coconut. The ratio of women and men in most categories was fairly consistent except for sweets and desserts, items largely sold by young unmarried Thai women.

Most vendors were between 26 and 50 years old, but there was a difference in average age: while most female vendors were mature women, a majority of the younger women sellers were Thai. Women usually stopped selling after age 55, once they had paid for their children's education; but over a quarter of male vendors were both elderly and Chinese. These men who continued selling Chinese specialities into their old age represented the less successful immigrants; they were usually selling alone with no family support.

Women's income from street foods was critical: 23% were the primary supporters of their families. Unexpected was the high proportion (36%) of women not currently married: 22% were unmarried, 9% widowed, and 5% separated. Unmarried women, aware of the demands marriage placed on their earnings, "openly preferred to remain single and visiting expensive nightclubs for fun in the evenings" (Blanc-Szanton 1990, 93). About two-thirds of both women and men vendors were married; nearly two-thirds of the male vendor's wives (60%) earned an income. The pressure on women's time to provide both income and food for their families adds to the demand for street foods.

Both women and men vendors were reluctant to answer questions about the source of their capital to start the business. Most said they used their own funds or borrowed from people they knew, without interest. Some funds probably came from the revolving savings group, call *len share*, that are common in the markets.

Given the small size of Chonburi, it was not surprising to find two-thirds of the vendors clustered in or around the four marketplaces (35%) or along nearby commercial streets (29%) (Figure 3.1). Another 17% sold downtown only in the evenings; no more than 19% of the vendors were found in residential areas. Since most of the housing estates were located outside municipal boundaries, the actual spread of street food vendors into neighborhoods was not recorded. Vendors paid daily or monthly fees for selling both inside the covered marketplaces and on the pavement nearby; special agreements were made by vendors selling in front of larger enterprises.

Street vending provided a minimal income to some 60% of the vendors and a substantial income to the more successful of these entrepreneurs. The estimated monthly net income of the lower income group was 2,430 baht; this amount was considered barely sufficient for a family of five to survive, but it was more than the salaries paid to policemen and soldiers, wage laborers, or elementary school teachers, and about that of petty bureaucrats. The top 12% of vendors made an income comparable to top professionals or foreign company employees but of course relied on considerable unpaid family labor. The middle income group (28%) averaged 5,500 baht per month, an income in the range of that earned by doctors, lawyers, contractors, and truck drivers for large businesses, jobs not available to women. Not surprisingly, the educational level of the vendors was high, with 4% of the women and 11% of the men having some college education. Only 8.5% of the vendors were illiterate.

Nearly one-half the vendors (42% of the women and 48% of the men) ran family enterprises with one or two relatives assisting. Given the high level of profits, it is not surprising that 16% of the women actually paid children or relatives to assist them. Those selling snacks prepared on the spot had help in preparation and serving, while some complicated sweets required help to make at home. Children would mind the enterprise after school, sitting in the back doing homework until needed. Long hours selling in addition to preparation meant long hours for both women and men. Length of time spent reflected the type of food prepared and sold rather than a gender difference. Over half the women vendors and 61% of the men vendors worked at their trade between 5 and 8 hours; a striking 35% of women and 24% of men spent between 9 and 12 hours on their enterprises. Only 5% of the women and 7% of the men worked less than 4 hours a day.

FIGURE 3.1   Street food vendors vie for road space with automobiles; others sell from sheltered open shops where the cooking area is decorated with flowers.

The Foods They Sell

Over 200 varieties of street foods were recorded in Chonburi. Most common street foods were of Thai origin, especially the meats and curries eaten with rice at home, and the vegetable and fish soups. Light meals and snacks draw on Sino-Thai traditions while sweets are primarily based on historic Portuguese recipes.

One-third of all vendors were engaged in selling light meals; three-quarters of these vendors, or nearly one-quarter of all vendors, sold some type of noodle dish. These noodles may be thin white rice noodles or Chinese wheat noodles: they are sauteed or deep fried and served in chicken broth, often with bits of chicken, pork, fish, vegetables, or peanuts. The alternative light meal has a rice base that may also be served in soup or along with Thai curries, sate, chicken, or red pork. All these foods have ties to other countries: noodles and red pork to China, sate to Indonesia, and curries to India. Most of the foods sold have taken on a distinctly Thai flavor, often through the addition of coconut milk or hot chilies. Most are also sold by both women and men; in contrast, Chinese men are the predominant sellers of red pork or steamed buns (*dim sum*), while the few male Indian vendors usually sell *roti* (Indian flatbread) or Indian curries.

Sweets, desserts, and fruits were the second most popular type of food (sold by 27% of the vendors) in January and February when the census was taken. A third of the women in this category sold typical Thai gelatins or custards, foods undergoing rapid commercialization in Bangkok, where they are produced by male-owned shops and distributed from motorized carts by male sellers on commission. Both glutinous rice prepared with bananas or coconut milk and sweet hot snacks prepared on the

Khao Pad Karee Gai
Fried Rice with Chicken and Curry Powder

2½ cups cooked rice

2 tablespoons oil

2 garlic cloves, finely chopped

2 teaspoons medium-hot curry powder

1 tablespoon fish sauce

¼ teaspoon sugar

3 ounces boneless chicken breast, finely sliced

1 scallion, cut into 1-inch lengths

½ small onion, finely slivered

white pepper to taste

Heat oil in a wok until a light haze appears. Add garlic and fry until golden brown. Add curry powder and cook for a few seconds. Add chicken and cook until meat is opaque, 1–2 minutes. Stir in fish sauce and sugar. Add rice gradually, mixing well after each addition. When the rice is thoroughly reheated, pour into a serving bowl and garnish with scallion, onion, and pepper.

Gaeng Judes Wunn Senn
Vermicelli Soup with Meatballs

2 ounces dry rice vermicelli

4–5 pieces of dried Chinese mushrooms

2 tablespoons oil

2 garlic cloves, minced

4 ounces finely ground pork

2 cups chicken broth

1 teaspoon preserved radish

1 tablespoon fish sauce

1 tablespooon soy sauce

1 small onion, finely chopped

¼ teaspoon sugar

¼ teaspoon ground white pepper

1 scallion, slivered lengthwise

Soak the vermicelli for ten minutes in cold water; drain. Soak mushrooms in water to soften, then drain and coarsely chop them. In a small pan, fry garlic in oil to a golden brown and set aside. Shape pork into 10–12 small balls.

In a medium saucepan, heat the chicken broth with the preserved radish. When liquid is simmering, add pork balls and cook for a few minutes. Add drained noodles and stir thoroughly. Add fish sauce, soy sauce, mushrooms, sugar, onion, and white pepper; mix well. By now the meat should be cooked through.

To serve, pour a little of the fried garlic and oil into each bowl, add soup, and garnish with the scallion.

spot with rice flour and coconut milk are traditional Thai treats. Ice cream and iced liquids were lumped into a single category because only these foods were sold cold, and therefore from special carts. During the fruit season from March until July, many vendors switch from selling sweet or salty snacks to selling cooked or fresh fruits: mangoes, durian, rambutan, jackfruit, mandarins, and ripe papaya. The most popular fruit dessert is durian or mango served with sweet glutinous rice cooked in coconut milk. Because fruits prepared in this manner were considered a dessert, all fruits and vegetables were listed under this general category, including papaya salad and broiled corn or yams. Some foods sold varied by time of day. Certain liquids or light foods, such as ginger and soybean drinks and rolls—all of Chinese origin—were sold around 5 A.M. as a quick morning breakfast. Rice porridge and noodles were generally served after 6 P.M. as a "warm snack" to cinema goers and again later in the evening to "night workers" earning their living on fishing boats or as truck drivers. Such groupings illustrate the difficulties of translating food concepts across cultures.

Buns, white and flat breads, and various other locally produced bakery products were sold by about 5% of the vendors, while packaged sweets and cookies were sold by 8%. In Bangkok, mobile commission sellers are increasingly handling the distribution of these packaged goods.

High-protein foods such as dried beef or pork are often eaten with local beer or whiskey, or they are brought home to add variety to a rice-based meal. More substantial carry-home foods such as cooked poultry or meats, curries, meat or fish patties, fried bean curd, sausages, and meatballs are widely available. A local specialty, *krapah pla*, or fish soup, is also taken home. Northeastern migrants have created a demand for their distinctive half-cooked beef and broiled chicken, as well as for the spicy green papaya salad and sticky/glutinous rice that usually accompany them. The Thai report groups these foods in three categories: "meal constituents" (4.3%), "salty snacks" (along with steamed buns, 10.32%), and "Northeastern food" (4.5%); taken together, a fifth of the vendors sold these take-out foods (Figure 3.2).

The numbers of vendors selling drinks, 8%, seems low in comparison with many other countries, even if iced drinks are included. Both the popularity of soups and the high percentage of food taken home may both help explain the relatively low sales of liquids in this tropical country. Coffee with cream and sugar, served either cold or hot, is the favorite single beverage; coffee and herbal teas are sold by nearly half (47%) of vendors selling drinks. Fruit and soya milk–based coolers—often dressed with sweet beans, nuts, candied fruit, bean curd, or cereals—are a favorite snack served over ice in a plastic bag. Beer, whiskey, and soft drinks often accompany the evening snack but are sold by a mere 3% of all vendors.

Distinctly Thai Aspects

Several characteristics of street foods in Chonburi set this town apart from other studies. Unusual is the "night market"; 17% of the vendors only sold foods at night. Special foods available at this time include porridge served with pickled vegetables or

FIGURE 3.2   Male vendors in Chonburi predominate in selling salty snacks to accompany beer; here they are preparing food in the government area.

marinated soya bean curd. Originally, these were cheap foods served to Chinese immigrants who worked nights at the shipyards and docks some 60 years ago. Today the night market sells both Thai and Chinese food to members of these ethnic groups.

Also unusual is the ease with which women eat on the street. This "public eating" is more dominant in Thailand than in other Southeast Asian countries and contrasts with prevailing concepts of modesty in many other countries (Yasmeen 1996).

This freedom of women in public space is further illustrated by the fact that women, especially housewives, are the major purchasers of street foods. Women working outside the home or full time in the family enterprise, often in the shop located below their living quarters, reported spending half their food budget on street foods as compared to non-working women who nonetheless spent 40% of their food budget this way. One of the busiest times of day for street food vendors is in the late afternoon, after most businesses have closed, when working women stop on their way home to buy meal constituents or salty snacks to add to the evening meal. Vendors jokingly call these women *mae ban tung plastic*, or "plastic bag housewives."

Of the 62% of customers who are women, nearly half are unmarried and often supporting their parents at home. Over half (54%) of the customers live outside the city boundaries: 20% just outside, another 19% in the surrounding district, and only 15% outside the urban area. Most customers work in the city. In contrast, factory workers in the free trade zone surrounding Chonburi, mostly young women from the Northeast region, seldom buy street foods in the city; rather, factory owners encourage local women to provide both rooms and meals for their workers. Migrants who work on cassava and sugarcane fields in the hinterland also seldom come to town to eat as they can receive food on credit from their employers.

Also unusual among the countries studied, schoolchildren in Thailand are *not* major consumers of street foods. Even though there are 17 schools and two vocational colleges in the municipality enrolling over 10,000 students in Chonburi, together they account for only 15% of the customers. In Thailand, most schools contract street food vendors to supply food within the schoolyards; children are prohibited from patronizing vendors outside the school premises until after classes have been dismissed. Of course, many children have money to spend on snacks and sweets after school, but they do not rely on street foods for their breakfast or lunch. Vendors cluster around the schools in the evening, enticing especially the younger children with colorfully packaged cookies or candy manufactured in Bangkok. Still, these purchases do not amount to an important income for vendors, compared to other groups of customers.

This practice of contracting street food vendors to prepare food for students on school and university campuses, often in kitchens provided by the institution, extends throughout the country except in tiny schools in remote areas. This arrangement apparently originated as a convenient way to provide school lunches, rather than from concerns over food safety.

Street Food Dependency

Buying prepared food outside the home is common in Thailand. The National Statistical Office household survey of 1990 confirms the popularity of eating out, in restaurants and from street foods,[1] everywhere in Thailand: 24% of the total household food budget was spent on prepared food; 15.2% was eaten out, and another 8.8% was carried home. Figures for Greater Bangkok emphasize the increase with city size: almost half of household food expenditure was on prepared food, consisting of 32.9% eaten out and 14.8% taken home; Chonburi data show 47% of the food budget spent on street foods; lower-income families spend a higher percentage of their income on street foods, but higher-income families spend a greater amount. This eating out is not consistent across families; many people live in rooms that constitute 23% of the available housing stock in Bangkok. While some roomers might plug in an electric rice cooker, which they have learned to use for many other types of meal preparation, 17.6% of households surveyed said they never cooked (as quoted in Yasmeen 1992).

A study of household energy use in Bangkok, Chiang Mai, and Ayutthaya that did not consider roomers as separate families found that 3.8% of households had no cookstoves in their homes and that 20% of households ate most or all of their meals outside or brought the cooked food home. Data were also collected in this study on street food–producing families who live above their shops, which are open to the street once a metal shutter is rolled up. These food shops are heavy users of charcoal: preparing grilled foods over coals gives an essential taste to certain Thai foods. Overall, households that prepare and sell street foods consume twice as much energy as ordinary households do: 25% more electricity, twice the amount of fuelwood (i.e., all types of biomass), twice the amount of gas, and four times the amount of charcoal (Tyler 1990).

In Chonburi, the household survey found that almost 70% were dependent on street foods in their diet: 13% said they did not cook at all, compared to the higher figure of 17.6% in Bangkok. In Chonburi, another 56% reported that they only cooked at home for certain meals. Many of those that did not cook were small households or single households of government employees who had been transferred to Chonburi without their wives. Midday meals were seldom prepared at home, with 72% of households eating street foods and another 7% supplementing home-prepared food with street food. Evening meals are the most often eaten at home, but over half the households supplement some home-prepared food by purchasing dishes that are complicated (such as curries), or time consuming (such as soup), or uneconomical to prepare in small quantities (such as chili paste).

Food Safety

The speed of Thailand's economic growth has stimulated urbanization throughout the country and enlarged the demand for street foods. Health officials are increasingly worried about the safety of street foods, particularly outside Bangkok where vendors are not required to register for a health certificate or as an enterprise. A recent study in a district town in Saraburi province thoroughly tested the safety of foods sold by vendors and found many unsanitary practices. Vendors used their hands to transfer noodles from a serving bowl to the customer's plate. As elsewhere, fresh fruits and vegetables and iced drinks showed higher bacteria counts than cooked foods, even those carried home in plastic. Enterprises serving food to seated customers had high counts of contamination, from both utensils and air pollution. Ice for drinks was scraped from blocks placed in chests that were also used to keep other foods cold. Legislation requiring all vendors in medium- and large-sized towns to register and undergo training is being considered.

Effects of Rapid Political and Economic Change

In Bangkok with its horrendous traffic congestion, vendors are being restricted to sites that do not intrude into motor or pedestrian traffic. Signs prohibit vending around the many upscale malls; instead, some market complexes such as Mabukrone provide street food vendors with space indoors in an atrium setting. As with the upgrading that took place in Singapore, few of the new indoor street food sellers are successful vendors who were able to afford the more expensive surroundings; rather, the new entrepreneurs represent a middle-class investment (Yasmeem 1996). More than one hotel offers street foods along with cocktail service, so popular are Thai street foods.

The combination of the gradual democratizing of the Thai governmental system with several mayors in Bangkok concerned with the welfare of the poor resulted in less harassment of vendors in most parts of the city. In Chonburi, where harassment had never been as severe, police seldom restricted the spread of Northeastern vendors onto the street pavement in front of the municipal hall in the evenings. Tables would be set up along the side of a garden where many families would picnic on the grass. Thanks to the street lights throughout the gardens and the petrol lanterns and cooking fires of the vendors, the area had the appearance of a fair. Music was often played for everyone's enjoyment.

These changes in governmental structure have resulted in Chonburi in weak enforcement of safety standards. While the food sanitation division took orders from the central ministry, the local health officer lacked both time and resources to monitor street vendors or to investigate the frequent reports that lead paint was being used to add color to shrimp!

The elected mayor in Chonburi was preoccupied with infrastructure projects that would strengthen road and water communications with Bangkok and enhance his political future. The competition set up among business, bureaucracy, and elected officials discouraged research and encouraged corruption. As a result, Chonburi was the only EPOC city that did not hold a briefing seminar in the town itself; in contrast, the Bangkok seminar in 1985 aroused great interest in the university and development community. As anticipated, only a few representatives of development NGOs attended.

Street food vendors in Thailand prosper throughout the country without market associations and without intermediary NGOs. Production of some foods has been taken over by industry, but the daily food on the street is apparently so central to Thai life that even in congested Bangkok the government has not dared to restrict it entirely. In the small side streets, or clustered around bus stops, vendors sell foods from early morning until late at night, seemingly little affected by the proliferation of American fast food restaurants or upscale shopping malls with their versions of street foods. As the urban areas expand, mobile vendors reach out into the new residential areas and squatter settlements, and noodle shop-houses appear. Despite the incredible social and economic changes in the country, Thai street food vendors continue to play a dominant role in feeding the urban populations.

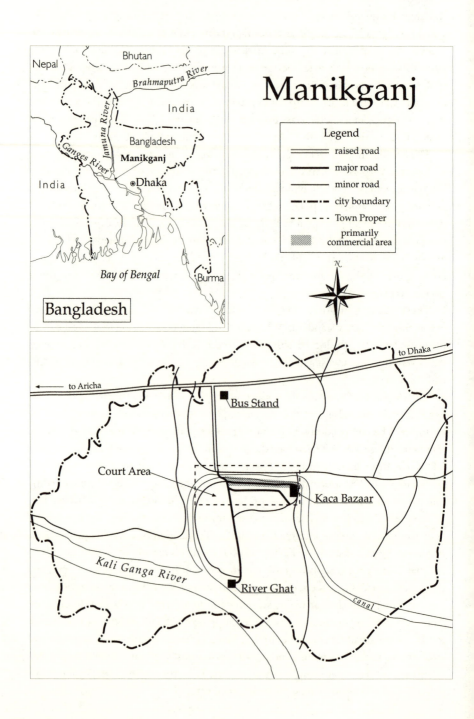

Manikganj

Legend

═══ raised road
━━━ major road
─── minor road
─·─·─ city boundary
- - - - Town Proper
▨ primarily commercial area

Bangladesh

Nepal

Bhutan

Brahmaputra River

India

Bangladesh

Manikganj

⊛Dhaka

Jamuna River

Ganges River

India

Bay of Bengal

Burma

N

to Dhaka

← to Aricha

■ **Bus Stand**

Court Area

Kaca Bazaar

Kali Ganga River

■ **River Ghat**

canal

CHAPTER FOUR

Manikganj, Bangladesh

Many of the characteristics of the street food trade in Manikganj reflect the poverty of the local population, as well as the cultural influence of Islam, most notably in the almost total absence of women vendors. The family nature of the trade is illustrated by the importance of spouses and female relatives in the production of the street foods for sale. Compared to most other cities except for Ziguinchor, demand for street foods is relatively limited, as is the variety of products offered.

As in many of the world's poorest countries, street food vending serves for many households as one part of a varied and shifting survival strategy. Thus enterprises come and go as vendors pursue other income sources or, under less fortunate circumstances, fall into bankruptcy. Also, as is typical of microenterprises in the least developed countries, capital scarcity is a constant problem, and so it was one of the first the EPOC staff tried to address. Although development organizations abound in Bangladesh, street food vendors have received little attention or assistance in the past, largely because most such agencies have in the past focused on the rural poor. EPOC's emphasis on the needs of the urban and peri-urban poor has encouraged more urban programs; EPOC's partner in the credit project has concentrated more recently on assisting women and men who produce street foods.

Local Context

Manikganj, is a small administrative center about 40 miles northeast of Dhaka, located on the major road that links the capital to the western part of the country by ferry across the Brahmaputra River before it joins the Ganges; *ganj* means "market." The confluence of these two great rivers created Bangladesh, their discharge precipitating the vast and mobile delta, with its hundreds of connecting rivers, meandering streams, and fragile sandbars that encroach on the Bay of Bengal. The area around Manikganj is typical of delta country; annual floods inundate the rice fields with silt as well as water and help maintain the fecundity of the land, but they also wreak havoc on transportation and communications systems as rivers shift and roads are wiped out.

With great effort since its independence from Pakistan in 1971, Bangladesh has become self-sufficient in rice, despite a population growth between 2.5% and 3% per year, which, according to projections, will result in a density of 2,500 persons per square mile by the year 2000. The country remains one of the world's poorest, with an annual per capita income in 1990 U.S. dollars of $210 (World Bank 1992). Using the purchasing power parity index (WRI 1994) this comes out at U.S. $1,160. Land ownership is skewed; 65% of rural households lack sufficient land to provide basic subsistence. As a result, Muslim families have adopted the practice of dowry, signifying that women are no longer considered a labor asset for the farm but rather have become a burden (Chr. Michelsen Institute 1986, 82–3).

Manikganj is district headquarters within the central administrative service; its officers oversee three subordinate units of local government. The district of Manikganj is one of the poorest in Bangladesh; floods limit rice production to once a year in more than half the region. The town was incorporated as a municipality in 1972 and since then has gradually expanded its boundaries to increase its revenue base. In doing so it has encompassed a rural landscape of hamlets and rice fields connected by raised earthen paths that accommodate bicycle rickshaws but no motorized vehicles. Even so, 45% of the street food vendors live outside the boundaries. The town center is dominated by administrative and court buildings, but also contains a hospital, four high schools, two colleges, a sports stadium, and two cinemas. Its food processing industries include ice cream, ice and candy factories, bakeries, and a cold drink bottling plant. A twice weekly periodic market (or *hat*) and three daily markets attest to the town's continued centrality as a traditional trading center. Travelers, students, and people coming for courts or markets are all important customers for the street food trade.[1]

Bangladesh as a traditional Islamic country seems an unlikely place to study women as street food vendors. Women are noticeably absent in public places throughout the country, even though the prime minister and the leader of the opposition party are both women. Although very few women wear a veil, the long end of the *sari* makes it easy to cover head and face when necessary. The isolation of women is seen as the primary cause of continued high fertility rates, despite myriad efforts by government and NGOs to introduce family planning.[2] More education, more jobs, and more mobility for women are considered essential if the country is to modernize. Finding out women's role in the pervasive street food trade helps show one type of work, albeit invisible, in which women are already engaged.

With a population in 1983 of only 38,000, Manikganj was the smallest city studied, but, like most of urban Bangladesh, its population is increasing by over 6% per year.[3] Migrants did not cluster in squatter areas; rather, they were dispersed throughout the municipality, building bamboo and thatch huts among the more substantial tin-roofed wood or brick houses. The average family size was 7.62 in the region at the time of the study. Hindus made up nearly 20% of the regional population, compared to the 12% national average.

Street Foods and Survival

Two characteristics of the street food trade in Manikganj are unusual: the absence of women sellers, and the persistence of periodic markets. Still, Manikganj provides additional evidence that the production and sale of street foods is often a family survival strategy, albeit not necessarily the only one.

Periodic *hats* are held in different towns on different days, once or more each week; hat days in Manikganj are Sunday and Wednesday. Both buyers and sellers may follow the markets in search of local products, including homemade snack food traded by middlemen in bulk. The influx of people provides additional customers for street food vendors. Previously, *hats* were held on open ground with vendors sitting unprotected from sun or rain. After independence, the Bangladesh government gave grants to local governments to erect all-weather market structures with tin roofs. Manikganj constructed two such buildings, at the main market and in the commercial section. Stalls in these structures are rented to vendors of all types. Vendors who do not rent stalls set up around the main market, erecting bamboo stalls, attaching plastic or jute shades to the walls, or squatting on the ground. Some pile up bricks for the customers to sit on and are referred to (by English-speaking Bengalis) as "Italian restaurants" because the word for "brick" in Bengali is *it*. Only vendors in the main market where the *hat* is also held, and who comprise nearly two-fifths of those in Manikganj, must pay a daily fee to a local collector, theoretically adjusted by sales and product; however, an extra gratuity may help reserve a vendor's regular spot.

Of all the countries studied, only in Bangladesh is street vending not an occupation for woman; however the trade is a critical family strategy for economic survival in this extremely poor country. The census of vendors in Manikganj produced a total of 550; of these, only six were women. Interestingly, each of the regular women vendors had a different focus: full meals, tea, fruit, grocery shop, and dry snacks respectively. This indicates that it is the activity of selling itself that is the obstacle to women's participation, not the type of food sold. One woman only sold sporadically, when bananas from her own tree were ripe.

Salima runs a tea stall near the bus stop. Although tea is widely sold as a street food, almost half (46%) of the customers interviewed said they never touch it. In the shop, Salima keeps four kettles of water hot on a wood-burning stove made of uncemented bricks. A woman water-carrier fetches the water from a nearby teacher's training school that also supplies many of Salima's customers. The tea is steeped in one kettle and then strained into one of only six teacups that Salima owns. She always rinses out the cup with boiling water before pouring the tea, boiled milk—purchased daily from a vendor who brings it to the shop—and sugar, which she stirs with one of her two teaspoons. Salima serves no sweets, but her customers often chew *pan*, and they frequently offer her a piece.

All six women (of which four were Muslims and two Hindus) were without family able to support them. Four were widows, including the Hindu woman who ran a small grocery store (*mudidokan*). One husband was a drunk. The other, incapacitated by

FIGURE 4.1   In Manikganj, women are not vendors, but they fetch water, prepare food, and clean up both at home and in the town. This women has cooked rice and *bhaji*.

asthma, was a caring house-husband. Such destitution removed religious barriers to modesty and allowed women to be seen in public. In addition to the women selling alone, 10% of the vendors hired and paid female assistants to work at the selling location (Figure 4.1). Another quarter of the vendors received assistance at home from one or more female family members, while 2% utilized unpaid family members, usually little girls, at the site. This means that 36% of the male vendors had female help. Adding the 1% of female vendors brings women's involvement in the trade to 37%. Not surprisingly, as they were selling alone without home assistance in a milieu not receptive to women vendors, the six women earned incomes lower than most men in each category of food. This was primarily due to a low volume of sales; their rate of return at 29% was not so far below the total male average of 32%.

Alternatives to street vending for women with little education are extremely limited in rural Bangladesh. Until recently, women in land-poor families pounded rice for wealthier neighbors and received payment in kind.[4] During the last 10 years, the rapid diffusion of rubber roller rice mills has replaced this activity. A few women produced basic snacks for traders. Increasingly, NGOs are forming women's groups to increase production of snacks and ground spices and to assist in marketing these goods in major urban centers. Poverty, new technologies, and male migration have increased the acceptability of female agricultural labor. However, pay for agricultural laborers remains low; men are paid about half the daily earnings of street vendors, and women are paid even less. Food distribution agencies have instituted food for work programs, usually repairing roads by breaking up fired bricks to form a solid base. Over the last decade, the establishment of garment factories in and around Dhaka has opened up new work opportunities for young rural women; families without resources to pay for dowries often encourage their daughters to migrate, even though such work breaks purdah restrictions.[5]

The pervasive insecurity of life in Bangladesh is reflected in the unusually high turnover of vendors in Manikganj. While nearly a quarter of the vendors had been in business before Liberation in 1971, the total number of vendors in Manikganj changed abruptly from one season to another and declined by 40% during the year of the study. This fluctuation was not caused by migrants moving in and out; indeed, two-thirds of the vendors living in Manikganj had been born there, and half of the rest had resided in the town for more than a decade. Rather, the move in and out of vending is part of the economics of survival. Most vendors had multiple strategies for making some income; a quarter said they stop selling completely one or more times a year to take up other jobs. On slow days, vendors might drive a rickshaw or work in the brickyard. But on average, street food vendors earned about the same income as a skilled carpenter, and three times the prevailing agricultural wage. Ninety-four percent of the vendors owned neither land nor the shop from which they sold. Owning land is a goal of most rural families.

One village family produced and packaged a particularly tasty *canacur*, a spicy crunchy fried snack mixture of fried vermicelli-like bits of dough, made from wheat or pulses, that are added to heated and pounded rice (*chira*) and peanuts. Narul, the elder brother, developed the business to support his extended family, which consisted of two younger brothers, three wives, and nine children. Most nights Narul slept in his rented shop near the bus stop; twice a week he purchased ingredients at the *hat*, walking the three miles to his village to make a fresh supply of *canacur*. Before his return, his wife Roshan would already have removed the ashes from the below-ground cookstove located in the courtyard under a straw-roofed shed.[6] One of the sisters-in-law fetched clean water from a neighbor's tubewell. The women mixed food coloring and spices into the batter of pulse flour, and the vendor then pushed the batter through a strainer into the hot oil to form vermicelli. Meanwhile, Roshan made a dough of wheat flour and cut it into squares for frying. Peanuts were sorted and fried; then all these ingredients, mixed with the *chira* and chili powder, were packaged in plastic bags, each bearing the family label.

Narul sold the *canacur* to other vendors, while the younger brothers hawked it themselves, primarily at the bus stop. The enterprise supported the entire joint family and allowed Narul to save money. Eventually he was able to purchase enough farm land for his nuclear family and withdrew from the joint enterprise; the business then passed to the middle brother, who is now supervising the *canacur* production using the same recipe and the same label.

Street Foods in a Poor Country

A count of street food vendors in Manikganj in early 1983 found 550 sellers throughout the municipality, nearly three-quarters at one of the three daily market areas. The market near the bus stop developed as a sort of suburban center and might be considered a commercial area rather than a traditional market. Another 12% sold along the main road in the commercial area, where the only push carts were found, while 8% could be found near the courts. Only 43 vendors, or 8%, were found scattered among 13 outlying villages. This pattern of immobile vendors clustering primarily near markets conforms to observations made by street food researchers in other countries when they considered possible study sites: as town size increased, the number of mobile vendors increased and places of sales diversified.[7] Thus the Manikganj study provides a view of urban change, as the street food trade expanded to the northern edge of town to include a major transportation node.

The position of Manikganj at the early stages of urbanization may help account for a another difference from the other cities studied: foods sold by vendors were also available on the same fast-food basis within four-walled structures. In other countries, a sizeable gap existed between the type and cost of food sold on the street and that sold in formal restaurants. Here the differences were small: street food sold from three walled shop houses was served at tables on the premises, and the owners of the establishments paid rent. Owens estimates that the 550 vendors tabulated represented only about 80% of the sellers of fast foods in the town.

Also excluded from the study, after some lively debate, were the pan sellers. Pan is betel nut and leaf topped with spices and lime and served on ceremonial occasions, but it is often also taken with, or as a substitute for, tobacco. All preparations of *pan* are chewed, and the residue is often swallowed after all extractable juices have been either absorbed or spit out. Like cigarettes and *biris* (indigenous cigarettes), *pan* also often replaces a snack; in colloquial Bengali the term for eating and smoking is the same. At the bus stand so many vendors sold only *pan*, cigarettes and *biris* that if they had been included in the count they would have constituted 22% of the street food sellers selling there! Hashish and opium, sold by a single licensed dealer, were also excluded, as were covertly sold Western alcoholic beverages.[8]

Location

Vendors located in permanent structures were a slight minority (47%); some rented space in government structures in the main market or commercial area, while some rented from private owners. Half the vendors built their owns stalls or squatted on the ground. The sellers near the courthouse rented government land across from it, where they had built semi-permanent structures of bamboo and wood; tea and snacks were offered freely to the district officers. Similar stalls, albeit illegal and non−rent paying, were set up along the highway. Like all roads in Bangladesh, the highway was built some five feet above the surrounding fields. Earth to raise the foundation was dug up along the route, creating ponds that are often filled with fish and ducks. Vendors often build platforms out over the water so that their shops can front on the highway. In all the selling areas, a few vendors jointly arranged to occupy a veranda of an office building or house.

The five vendors with wheeled pushcarts were all found in the commercial area selling *chatpotti*, a favorite evening snack. Some *chatpotti* vendors clustered by the cinema, or near several ayurvedic and allopathic medicine shops that have become gathering places, to gossip and to drink one particular ayurvedic medicine that has an alcoholic base. *Chatpotti* goes well with the drink, which we categorized as medicine, not street food!

Mahbub, a 17-year-old *chatpotti* vendor, is assisted by his 10-year-old nephew, who is learning the trade and who helps by fetching water and washing the dishes. His mother Nazra prepares the various ingredients, then puts them in jars or on plates on the pushcart: they include boiled potatoes, some in pieces, some mashed with *dal* (cooked pulses) and spices; hard-boiled eggs; raw chopped onions; and chopped coriander. Water and tamarind are mixed and put in a kettle. Nazra also fries tiny circles of bread called *fuchka* that may be used like toast or crackers, topped with the mixture or eaten on the side. Besides these foods, the pushcart holds two kerosene stoves to keep the *dal* and potato mixture hot, a kettle for drinking water, jars of spices, tin plates and glasses, spoons for those eating from a plate, serving utensils, and a bowl for washing dishes. To assemble the *chatpotti* for the customers, boiled potatoes and onions are moistened with tamarind juice, then spices and coriander are added to order. Sliced egg and the warm *dal* mixture are spooned over it all.

The semi-permanent street food vendors near the main market sell every day, but are joined by transient vendors on *hat* days. As noted, all daily vendors in this area must pay a market fee through a local collector to the government. No fees are collected at the other markets, even from those selling from verandas or stalls, since they pay rent to the property owners, who in turn pay property tax. No vendor or health licenses are required for nonpermanent vendors; however, a trade license is required for those in permanent structures. This is assessed by the Food Department of the central government, but paid to the municipality. Two-thirds of the permanent vendors in fact had licenses. Overall, harassment of vendors by the local government is not a problem; indeed, the officials displayed considerable empathy.

In contrast, shacks built by vendors near the bus stop have been cleared off the shoulders of the road several times by representatives of the central government that owns the highway (Figure 4.2).[9] Consequently, many vendors simply squat under the trees, waiting for the buses to stop so they can hawk their wares though the open windows of the intercity buses or the vans, called "coasters" locally, that ply between Manikganj and Dhaka whenever they are filled.

Not surprisingly, two associations had been formed in this area for vendors of all types of items, not only street foods: one with a membership of 53 for hawkers with no selling location and another with 100 members for those with stalls. Both groups collect dues and provide loans to members; both lobby influential people in an effort

FIGURE 4.2   Street food vendors near the bus stop sell fried snacks and full meals to passengers and to villagers who walk to work or town on the broad shoulders of the raised highway.

to legalize vending at bus stops. The hawker group had ambitious plans to buy and run a local bus as a money-making endeavor for its members. Permanent vendors in the markets also belonged to their own organizations, which focus on settling quarrels between sellers, providing night guards to prevent theft, deciding on holidays, and collecting funds for government celebrations or charitable causes.

Vendors

A third of the vendors had never attended school, another third had less than six years of schooling, and only one vendor had more than ten years' schooling. Nonetheless, the 22 case studies revealed that even the more successful illiterate vendors kept accurate mental records of their business expenses. Accurate information on age is difficult to obtain in Bangladesh, since written birth records are virtually nonexistent. The team estimated that 33% of the vendors were between 26 and 35 years old; they found only 5% who appeared to be under 16; and 12% seemed to be more than 55 years old.

The percentage of Hindu vendors in the sample was 24%, greater than their 20% share of the regional population. They tended to sell traditional sweets and dairy products or to run the small grocery stores (*mudidokan*) and tea shops. Owens found that the Hindu vendors generally enjoyed a higher sales volume and greater profits than their Muslim counterparts, perhaps largely because they were able to start their businesses with greater capitalization despite having been in business a shorter time.

In 90% of the cases, start-up capital came from savings or family. Considering that moneylenders may charge interest as high as 25% per month, vendors knew such loans were dangerous to their survival. Another 5% of the vendors started their businesses by taking goods on credit. Of the remaining 5%, half borrowed from moneylenders to supplement other funds, while the other half took low-interest loans from the vendors' associations. Commercial credit is generally not accessible to small borrowers. The immensely successful loan programs started by the Grameen Bank and BRAC (Bangladesh Rural Advancement Committee) were at the time only available to rural men and women (Chen 1989; Sharif 1983; Tinker 1989; Yunus 1983).

Working capital is of much greater concern to small entrepreneurs; fear of money-lenders and lack of low-interest loans certainly contributed to the fluctuation in the number of vendors in Manikganj. Still, 76% of the vendors acquired some or all of their stock on credit, while three-quarters of them insisted that such goods did not cost more than if they had paid cash for them. Almost all settle their accounts weekly. Taxes and fees for most vendors are either nonexistent or amount to less than 1% of sales. Nonpermanent vendors paid no rent or license fees, although those selling near the main market paid a daily fee. Including this fee, 54% of vendors pay for the space where they sell.

Most vendors walked to and from work; only those who purchase supplies at regional *hat* incur substantial travel expenses. Cooking fuel costs were negligible because women and children scavenge twigs, cow dung, and agricultural refuse for use both at work and home; electricity for lights at place of sale were a more signif-icant cost. About one-third of all vendors hired employees (20% hire men, 10% women), and paid them about a quarter of their profits. Two-thirds of the vendors or their families consumed some of their own street food every day, while another 30% did so every week. The loss to profits of this consumption was figured at 7%, assuming stable demand. For some, customer default on credit sales was a major problem; one restaurant near the courts went out of business for this reason, and another vendor moved his location to avoid demanding, highly-placed customers. Beggars were ubiquitous, and the larger establishments kept small change available for them.

Vendor families are large. At the time of the study, they averaged 7.42 persons, containing an average of 1.94 earning members in addition to unpaid family labor. Income from street foods provided more than half the family income in 67% of the homes and was the sole income for 47%. Income was extremely variable, with the most successful making over 300 times as much per week as the least successful. By excluding the two enterprises with the highest income, this falls to 165 times as much; average weekly income is then 470 taka, or some US $20 at the 1983 exchange rate. Yet even this income was equal to that earned by a skilled carpenter and three times the going rate for agricultural labor.

The Foods They Sell

Altogether, 128 different ready-to-eat street foods were identified for sale in Manikganj during the year. For the purposes of the study the foods were grouped into eight categories, revealing both food preferences and attitudes toward meals. Wetness was a concept applied both to the rice meals (7% of the vendors) and to sweets with syrup (2.5%). Dry foods (7%) were considered meal substitutes only because they lacked rice, while dry snacks (56%) included sweet biscuits, hard candies, *gur* (date sugar), and munchies such as the distinctively Bangladeshi *canacur* and *muri* (puffed rice). Wet meals were only served in a "hotel," the English word being used in Bengali to signify "restaurant" (overnight accommodations are available only at a "residential hotel"). Dry meals were served in a "restaurant," a term used to signal that egg dishes, seasoned bread, or *bhaji* (fried spiced vegetables) rather than full meals are served. Tea, however, was served in a tea shop (4%). The popular dry snacks, offered by 56% of all vendors, were sold by mobile hawkers and from market stalls, as well as by *mudidokans*.[10] Fruit juices were sold by 20% of the vendors in the census; this number fluctuated with the seasons, as did the sale of ice cream and other dairy products (3.5%). Those foods that did not fit these categories, and hence were classified as "other," were sold by fewer than 1% of the vendors.

Because of limited demand for street foods, not quite half (49%) of the vendors offered three or fewer items for sale; indeed, 29% sold only one item, with dry snacks, fruit, or juice accounting for 87% of these single-item sales. Of the 128 foods, 45 tended to be sold mainly by their producers, but the only items always made by the seller were those made to order at the place of sale such as tea, *bhaji*, and *ruti* (toasted flatbread). Certain items, made both by Dhaka industries and local shops, were never sold by those producing them; among these were ice cream and ices, bottled soft drinks, hard candies, and all fruits except bananas.[11] Many items, especially *canacur* and *muri* were sold by both producers and retailers, but another popular dry snack, *chira* (flattened baked rice), was sold only by nonproducers. Thirty percent of the vendors sold only what they produced, 57% were only retailers, and 13% sold both self-produced and purchased food items.

Among the 43% of vendors who produced at least some of the food they sold, most had the help of women at home. All vendors of *acar* (varieties of chutnies or pickles) and of *canacur* were assisted in production by women. Women were also essential in the production of date sugar (87%) and of *muri* (76%). Half of the vendors selling the sweet or salty milk curd drink *matha*, as well as those selling the many versions of *dal*, had help in processing; about a quarter of the *bhaji* sellers also had women's help. All these foods are normally consumed in the home, so most women would know how to prepare them. This helped subsistence-farming families in nearby villages to engage in sporadic production of these foods when agricultural labor demands were low or financial needs great. In fact, women with outstanding products often expanded their production to sell to middlemen or wholesalers outside their family. Increasing women's ability to package and market these homemade products has become the focus of several NGOs in the region.

Family cooperation helped two brothers, Mujib and Ahmed, to expand their enterprise selling *bhaji* with *ruti* near the teacher training institute. When they started they squatted on the ground; within a few months they had erected a two-sided bamboo and jute stall with a tin roof. Customers sit on benches at a long wooden table; another bench demarcates the shop from the next one. *Bhaji* is prepared daily by their mother, who washes potatoes with water from a neighbor's tubewell, fries them with onions and spices in soybean oil, then simmers the vegetables in water to form a thick sauce. The *bhaji* is then placed in a covered aluminum bowl and taken by one of the brothers to his stall. The men make the *ruti* themselves, washing their hands carefully before mixing the flour. Dough balls are weighed before being dry-cooked on a freshly washed iron skillet. Water is brought from the institute by a woman water-carrier who is paid 2 taka per day. Food is served and plates are washed by a young boy who receives food and 3 taka per day, while a third employee sweeps the stall and fetches fuel from the sawmill for 0.30 taka a day.

Seasonality

Seasonality is revealed not only in the types of food available in the hot. cold, and rainy seasons, but also in the cultural attitudes about what is appropriate to eat at what time.[12] For example, *canacur* can easily be made the whole year round, but because it is considered a "hot" food, that is, one that heats the body when eaten, some vendors sell it only in the winter. Eggs and meat are also considered hot foods, while fish and papaya are regarded as "cold" foods and are thus more widely sold in the hot season. Despite these influences, 57% of the vendors always sell the same product, while another 20% sell the same type of food year-round. Only a quarter regularly switched foods by season, for example, from ice cream in the summer, to *canacur* in the winter, to fruit during the rains.

The major change in year-long food patterns comes during the fasting month of Ramadan, when observing Muslims consume neither food nor drink from sunrise to sunset. Special types of foods called *iftari* are prepared to break the fast. These are types of foods, rather than particular dishes. Nine new vendors tried to earn money on these foods, but only two lasted for a week and only one was still selling at the end of the month. This man had sold *iftari* foods for the last seven years, taking time off from selling wood; he also made and sold *acar* on a casual basis, and so had adapted his business skills to foods. During Ramadan, many regular vendors either added *iftari* foods or stopped selling their regular items to sell *iftari*.

Customers

Because of purdah (seclusion of women from public observation), most women do not visit the markets; only ten people in the customer sample of 436 were female

Samosas
Fried Potato Dumplings

Pastry (for 30 samosas)

3 cups all purpose flour

½ teaspoon salt

3 tablespoons clarified butter

¾ cup ice water

Filling

1 medium-sized onion, finely chopped

1 10-oz. package frozen peas, thawed and drained

1 tablespoon fresh ginger, grated

1 fresh hot green chile pepper, finely chopped

3 tablespoons cilantro, finely chopped

3 tablespoons water

1½ pounds new potatoes, boiled in

jackets, peeled, and diced into ¼-inch pieces

1½ teaspoons salt

1 teaspoon ground coriander

1 teaspoon curry powder

1 teaspoon ground cumin

¼ teaspoon cayenne pepper

2 tablespoons lemon juice

vegetable oil for deep frying

Make the pastry. Sift flour with salt into a deep bowl. Add clarified butter and mix with fingertips until the mixture resembles coarse meal. Add water all at once and knead vigorously. Form the dough into a ball; knead on lightly floured surface, folding in and pressing down, for about 10 minutes, until smooth. Form the dough into a ball again, brush lightly with oil, and place in a bowl. Cover with a damp towel to keep it moist, and let it rest for at least 30 minutes and up to 5 hours.

Prepare filling. Stir-fry onions in 2 tablespoons of oil until lightly brown. Add peas, ginger, chile, cilantro, and water. Cover and simmer until peas are cooked. Add diced potatoes, salt, spices, and lemon juice. Mix lightly, then turn off heat and allow to cool.

Roll out dough and thinly as possible, and cut into fifteen 6-inch circles using a large cookie cutter or a bowl. Cut each circle in half. Moisten the edges of a semi-circle with water, then shape into a cone. Place 1 tablespoon of filling into the cone. Moisten the top of the cone with water and fold over to form a triangle. Repeat.

Fry the samosas in deep oil heated to 375 degrees for 2–3 minutes, turning once, until golden brown. Drain on paper towels and serve hot. They may be kept hot in a 200-degree F oven.

Bhaji
Hot Spiced Vegetables

4 cups green beans or other vegetable
(zucchini, okra, cauliflower, etc.)
2 tablespoons clarified butter or
vegetable oil
1 teaspoon black mustard seeds
1 teaspoon salt

1 teaspoon turmeric powder
2 tablespoons chopped onion
2–4 tablespoons water
6 tablespoons dried unsweetened
coconut (optional)

Trim green beans or vegetables and slice into small pieces. Heat butter or oil in a heavy pan and add mustard seeds. Cover and allow to brown but not burn. Stir in turmeric, salt, and onion. Add vegetables and only enough water to prevent burning: zucchini or okra require less water, cauliflower requires more. Reduce heat and cook until tender. If desired, stir in a coconut a few minutes before the vegetables finish cooking. Adding 1 tablespoon of curry powder instead of the coconut makes the dish more spicy, less sweet.

(2%): they included four children, three wage laborers, one housewife, a school-teacher, and a beggar. However, approximately 45% of the customers interviewed were taking food to be eaten elsewhere, often home to their families. Case study vendors brought home street foods other than those they were selling. Mostly these were treats for the children such as fruit, dry snacks, or ice cream. Four groups of customers each represented about one-fifth of the total: businessmen, including some vendor-owners (23%), farmers (22%), laborers (20%), and white-collar workers (19%). Children under 14 represented 9%, while college students were only 3% of the total. Half came from outside the municipality, as would be expected with bus stops, court, and markets being the primary locations for sale. Generally the income of the customers was lower than that of the vendors, a fact that reflects the general poverty of rural Bangladesh.

In contrast to most countries studied, the frequency of purchasing street foods was quite low, reflecting both poverty and cultural preferences. Except for those purchasing *ruti*, *bhaji*, and tea, few customers bought street foods daily, though most bought them at least once a week. Most families prepare meals at home; findings indicate that some meals are prepared at home and eaten at work, but that no "real" meals are purchased out for eating at home. Only 22% of the street foods surveyed were seen as constituting a full meal for the customers; the rest were snacks. However, the data do support the general findings of the EPOC studies concerning expenditure: the higher the income level of the customer, the more money is spent on street foods, while this amount represents a proportionately lower percentage of total income.

Food-handling and water-use practices were remarkably safe, a fact that might seem inconsistent with the level of development. However, clean water was available in all selling and producing areas, both in town and in the villages.[13] I noted the care with which a female attendant in a tea shop near the courts rinsed out each cup with boiling water before adding more boiling water to a tea infusion kept in a tightly closed bottle. The middle-class interviewers were asked to rate all vendors, including those whose homes they visited, as "very clean," "clean," "OK for most items," "dirty/would hesitate to eat," or "very dirty/would never eat." They rated 21% as "very clean," 61% as "clean," and 15.7% as "OK." At the *bhaji/ruti* stall of Mujib and Ahmed, for example, staff observed that the *bhaji* was not covered on site and that dishwater was used for two servings before being replaced; yet they rated them "clean." No vendors were placed in the last category, but four establishments were considered "dirty": two "hotels" and two stalls at the bus stop, which sold, respectively, dry snacks and fruit. Samples tested in Dhaka were all found fit for human consumption and showed either no or low counts of bacteria. *Matha* and *bhaji*, both wet foods, revealed the highest counts, a finding that supported the local folk wisdom, which says that dry street foods are safer than wet ones.

Working and Surviving

The extreme fluctuation in the numbers of vendors throughout the year—only 57% of the total number counted in the winter at the bus stand were still selling a year later—was caused by variations in both supply and demand. Date *gur*, for example, cannot be stored in the hot season, so half of the *gur* sellers switched to other snacks while the other half worked elsewhere until winter arrived. Several vendors sold fruit they grew themselves, then stopped vending until the next season. Most vendors of meals or owners of *mudidokan*, in contrast, made few changes to the foods they sold during the year. Social attitudes toward the appropriate foods to eat in each season, as discussed earlier in this chapter, also affected demand.

The changing agricultural seasons not only affected what foods were available but also the extent of alternative employment opportunities. The floods that prevented much of the region from planting year-round forced agricultural laborers in and out of the trade. Twenty-two percent of the vendors selling at the bus stop at the edge of town in the winter had stopped selling by the spring; about a third of them shifted to agricultural work and a fifth to nonagricultural jobs. Half of them could not be traced.

The fasting month of Ramadan had the greatest impact on street vendors. In 1983 it fell in the summer, and 45% of the vendors stopped selling. Social pressure on Muslims against eating during the day, even though travelers are technically absolved from fasting, meant almost no dry snack and fruit sales at the bus stop. Restaurants and tea shops had curtains to provide anonymity for those wishing to eat, or, indeed, for non-Muslims.

At the autumn count 86 vendors reappeared, but 16 had stopped selling; by the fall rainy season 78 had left and 19 resurfaced. A second winter/spring count would have indicated whether this pattern was largely seasonal or whether the decline might have been permanent. Two factors clearly influenced the total numbers. First, Owens estimates that 9% of the vendors left because of business failure; this correlates closely with data collected showing that 11% of the vendors had been in business less than a year. Besides the 24% who started their enterprise before Liberation, a third had been vending for one to five years, and another third for six to twelve years. These data, combined with the preceding discussion, show both stability, particularly among vendors with stalls or those making sweets, and high turnover among the more casual snack and fruit sellers who predominate at the bus stop and markets.

Changes in the system of local government also affected street vendors. Manikganj had been a district headquarters when the study began; its courts serviced seven smaller units as well as the district. Decentralization of the court functions to the lower units reduced the number of litigants coming to the town; the anticipated higher status of division for Manikganj, which could be expected to add administrative functions, had not yet occurred. It was expected that new customers would be found eventually among additional administrative workers, increased numbers of college students, and new visitors to the court, compensating for this decrease in patronage.

Vendors responded by supplementing their income in many ways. While vending was the sole income for 53% of the vendors, 29% had a second income; additionally, over half of these vendors grew food for home consumption or sale. For 18% of the vendors, street food was a supplementary activity. Large families provided another survival strategy; over half the vendor families had other earning members, while unpaid family labor allowed higher incomes to vendors than would have been possible had they done the same work alone or utilized paid labor.

Interventions

There are hundreds of foreign and indigenous nongovernmental organizations operating in Bangladesh, most of them focusing their programs on assisting the rural poor. Many ran programs in the Manikganj area, and because each had its particular requirements for eligibility and program, street food vendors, being a heterogeneous category, failed to fit into any one NGO activity. A "fair" was considered where these NGOs would present themselves to the vendors so the vendors would be able to identify the most likely NGO to approach for assistance. Ultimately a handbill was prepared that described the activities of each NGO, and EPOC staff held small meetings around the town to distribute the handbill and describe the available programs.

Because vendors had expressed the need for low-interest loans, and because such loans were available in some rural districts but not in urban areas,[14] EPOC secured additional funding of U.S. $5,000 to set up a revolving loan program for vendors. The Manikganj Association for Social Service (MASS) which had been operating in the town under the leadership of Mujiber Rahman, a college professor, would run the program. Applicants were screened by a motivator working with a board member of

MASS. The scheme replicated that used by BRAC, which works in villages but has its headquarters near the bus stand. Both the motivator and the board member attended their two-week training program. One part of the grant (U.S. $1,500) was set aside to pay these men for one year, while the remaining portion was deposited in a local bank to collect interest at 14%; this amount served as guarantee, against which loans ranging between 500 and 1,000 taka could be made for up to two years at 16%. Women vendors and enterprises that utilize women's labor were given preference for the loans. The 2% spread was intended to defray possible losses.

Since the program substituted group responsibility for collateral, vendors formed themselves into groups of five in order to start saving and become eligible. Twenty groups were formed in the first year and loans were granted, primarily to retailers rather than producers. Fifty-seven vendors borrowed U.S. $2,000; only one vendor was in arrears (after a divorce). The program, however, did not earn sufficient interest to pay staff, so when the initial funding ran out, the remaining balance was turned over to BRAC as previously agreed. BRAC then offered loans to vendors resident in the villages. Few town vendors seem to have received loans after the switch.

Data from the Street Food study were presented to local NGOs at two briefings in Manikganj and Dhaka. Among the possible interventions that were discussed, two ideas seemed most promising. The first concerned the construction of an open street food market near the bus stop that would protect sellers and customers from the elements and provide clean water, electricity, and shared seating. This was enthusiastically supported by the vendors' association, which agreed to collect rents if an NGO could provide capital to build and secure permission from the unsympathetic central government. To date, nothing has changed.

The second idea would improve the capability of women producers to assist in packaging and marketing. Since BRAC was already working with nearby rural women in the production of ground spices, it also hoped for some marketing connection with the vendors for products its members were making, such as bamboo dish covers to protect food from flies and dust. Unfortunately such activities had a low profit margin compared to the production of food. BRAC planned to investigate bottling *matha* and adding soybeans to dry snacks to enhance their nutritional content. MASS turned to working with producers once the loan program funds were turned over to BRAC.

EPOC staff tried to promote a *mohila mela*, or women's market, that would be held on Friday at the local school. Only women and children would be encouraged to attend; women's food production and handicrafts would be displayed so that the NGOs' female staff could contract for various goods. The *mela* would have provided an opportunity for inoculating children and for disseminating health and family planning information; most importantly, it would have given women a day out.

Plus ça Change, Plus la Même Chose

Positive changes abound in Bangladesh: self-sufficiency in rice, cement pillars for rural homes to survive floods, employment for women of varying education levels.

Among these are literate women in garment factories, secondary school graduates at the Grameen Bank, and university graduates in government jobs, reflecting 10% quotas requiring their employment. Rising Islamic fundamentalism counters these trends for women, while the increasing population pushes per capita income lower every year. Indigenous NGOs grow in power and sophistication; foreign NGOs increasingly act as resources and funding for them. Programs still concentrate on rural areas; women as street food producers are receiving both technical and marketing assistance and focusing on the urban market.

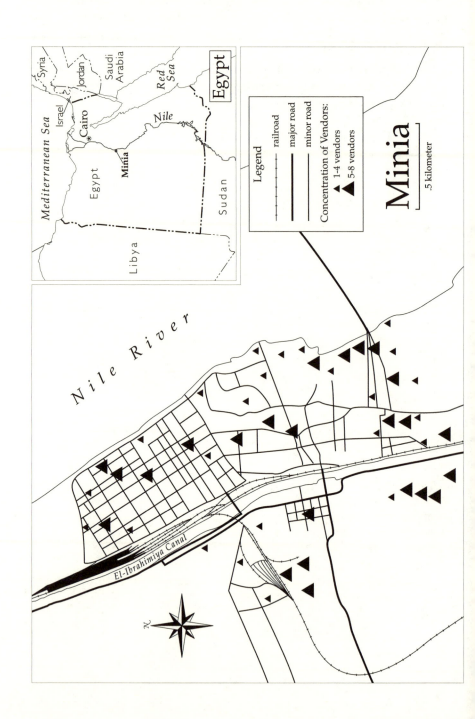

Egypt

Mediterranean Sea

Syria
Israel
Jordan
Saudi Arabia

Cairo
Nile
Minia

Egypt

Libya

Red Sea

Sudan

Legend

railroad
major road
minor road

Concentration of Vendors:
▲ 1-4 vendors
▲ 5-8 vendors

Minia

.5 kilometer

Nile River

El-Ibrahimiya Canal

N

CHAPTER FIVE

Minia, Egypt

The Minia study was one of those in which the EPOC study itself helped spark the formation of a local group devoted to assistance, advocacy, and intervention on behalf of the street food vendors. Thus a substantial part of this chapter focuses on the creation, organization, strengths, and weaknesses of the Street Food Vendors Organization (SFVO), which differs from the vendors' groups discussed in other chapters in that nonvending community members play an important role in its administration and policy making. Before the study, Minia government officials tried to enforce regulations so strict that many vendors were forced to violate them simply to make a living. Today many of those same officials have become supportive members of the SFVO.

Like most countries in the Third World, Egypt has had to liberalize its economy in recent years and reduce the role of the central state. This case study documents how the resulting market instability has affected Minia street food vendors' ability to find affordable basic supplies; it also shows how the SFVO has tried to address the supply problem, which is no doubt a common one in the many other countries undergoing liberalization. Finally, the Minia case further illustrates how much street food enterprises are really family projects, with women and men often exchanging vendor roles as family opportunities and fortunes change.

Local Context

The city of Minia, a relatively small town of 179,060 along the Nile River in Upper Egypt, is the capital of Minia Governorate, one of the poorest regions in the country. It is easily reached in six hours by express train south from Cairo. Government offices and the modern commercial center stretch along one side of the major north-south boulevard, separated from the river on the other side by a series of well-tended public parks and private clubs. Several old mosques with distinctive slender minarets mark the older commercial part of town to the south, where decaying villas give way to rows of shops interspersed with schools and hospitals. Surrounding these areas, and spilling across the canal to the west, are the apartments, housing projects, and squatter areas where the bulk of the population lives. Distances are not great, so the town does not support a motorized taxi service; horse carriages are the alternative to buses or walking.

Escarpments that mark the Nile valley in Upper Egypt are visible in the distance. The high cliffs confine agriculture to the valley floor; but wherever irrigation can reach, green fields and palms belie the arid climate. The desert, unseen from the valley floor, creeps to the edge of the escarpments. Thus agricultural areas of Egypt are seldom far from the Nile: the narrow ribbon of cultivation varies between 1 and 12 miles wide except near the Fayoum depression, where an indentation in the cliffs allows irrigation to penetrate further into the desert. This geography helps explain why most of Egypt's estimated 1995 population of 59 million live in 4% of the country's land area, along the Nile; half are urbanized, with some 12 million living in greater Cairo. Villagers from the area around Minia regularly come to the city to shop. About 8% of the vendors who joined the Street Food Vendors Organization live in villages as far as six kilometers away.

As the Nile approaches the Mediterranean Sea and creates a delta of interlaced channels, irrigation and agriculture penetrate further into the desert. In the days before the high dam was built across the Nile at Aswan, yearly floods brought nutrients and mud to the valley fields. The dam has reduced the flooding, but also the fertility of the soil. Peasants must now buy fertilizer for their fields and concrete for their houses instead of using mud from the Nile. These additional monetary needs push many into various forms of microenterprise, including street food vending, in their villages or in urban areas.

In the past few decades many rural families have left the land. High-paying jobs in the Saudi Arabian peninsula have provided an alternative source of income for both women and men. The better educated work as nurses and teachers in the newly rich oil countries, while unskilled laborers build roads and buildings. In any village, a typical modest adobe home will contain a television set and a refrigerator; two-story houses reflect even more remittances from family members abroad. Recent slumps in some of the Gulf states' economies, however, have reduced the availability of such employment for the educated, farmers, and street food vendors.

Since 1952 Egypt has been controlled by the military. Early presidents introduced land reform, subsidized basic foodstuffs, and expanded health services in an effort to mediate the extremes of poverty and affluence. But persistently inadequate health services and recent reductions in food subsidies have directly affected the street vendors. Their children, many of them put through school by the vendors' earnings, are even more concerned by the 1990 termination of a government policy that had promised public sector jobs to *all* graduates of high school or university, women and men alike. This policy used to account for the high education levels and low pay of the white-collar class in Minia; it also explains the presence of so many women in the bureaucracy. Since it was lifted in an attempt to cut costs and inefficiencies in the state bureaucracy, many women have kept their secure if low-paying jobs, while their husbands have joined private firms or gone abroad. Still, only a third of all women in Egypt are literate, as compared to two-thirds of the men. Class and income inequalities persist; at least a third of the population of the country remains below the poverty line (Grant et al, 1989). Landlessness and unemployment are particularly acute around Minia and have fostered migration to urban areas and abroad.

In Minia, many women who started street food enterprises with their husbands have continued to run them alone as men sought better paying alternatives abroad. Henana, for example, only began selling street foods after her husband went off to Iraq and did not send money home to support her or her seven children; he has returned and helps her now. Among the evening street vendors in Minia are many schoolteachers, who supplement their meager earnings by selling sweets. Twenty-eight-year-old teacher Rafat learned to make pastry from his father, who lives with him and his wife in their tiny two-room house. He buys the dough and his wife fills and bakes the pastries during the day; then he sells them at the evening market from a small, covered cart. Both Henana and Rafat's wife are listed as the primary vendor in the records of the street vendors' organization.

Over one-fifth of the population of Minia is Christian: traditionally most were members of the ancient Coptic Church, but many have become Protestants. The street vendors' organization does not keep data on members' religion, but the staff indicated that most of the vendors are Muslims. Perhaps poor Christians have had more alternatives available to them through the Coptic Evangelical Organization for Social Services (CEOSS), a local NGO that receives development funds both through USAID and from the World Council of Churches. For over a decade CEOSS has worked in over 40 villages to improve farming techniques and set up microenterprises that range from sewing to carpentry. Of course their programs are open to members of all religions. But as Islamic fundamentalism had increased in cities further south, the issue of community cooperation/conflict was a subtext, unspoken but recognized.[1] When the vendor's organization arranged for its members to use the CEOSS clinic for their health examinations, it was welcomed by members as an improvement over the government clinics. Discussions with the members indicated that they would prefer their own clinic but that their organization could not afford it; the sponsorship of the clinic was never mentioned. Nor was there any evidence of cultural limitations on the movement or activity of women of any religion in Minia.

Street Foods in Minia

The demand for street foods in Minia was much lower than in any other city EPOC studied; in 1985 a total of 784 street food establishments existed, or one for every 228 people. Even so, with each individual vendor serving an average of 60 customers per day, about 47,000 people would eat street foods every day, a number equivalent to a quarter of the city's total population. These vendors offered over 70 types of food

FIGURE 5.1   A vendor couple selling roast sweet potatoes by weight from a colorful traditional push cart in a new commercial area of town.

and beverages, a significant variety, but low in comparison with street foods enumerated elsewhere.

Foods sold on the street usually require considerable preparation time. Often the entire family is involved in preparing and selling the foods. While only 11% of the 1,348 vendors in the 1985 census were women, women were present in 17% of the enterprises; a visual survey done later in 1985 estimated the number of women vendors at 25% (Figure 5.1). Moreover, 14% of wives and an impressive 17% of husbands assisted during the preparation, selling, or cleaning up. In addition, other family members assisted in buying and preparing ingredients. Nevertheless, the economic contribution of family members is not considered a cost since none of the women and only a few of the men, usually sons, were paid. A 1992 survey of members of the vendors association found that women members, who might not be visible on the

FIGURE 5.2 Frying *tamia* near a hospital in Minia, this vendor
uses a gas cylinder to heat the oil; bread is kept in the glass-
enclosed cupboard.

street, constituted about a third of the vendors of the major street foods—sweets, sandwiches, and *foul*—and over a quarter of all other categories.

Case studies show that vendors borrowed electric grinders to crush beans for *tamia*, stored perishable ingredients in neighbors' refrigerators, and had help from parents, in-laws, children, siblings, cousins, and spouses in the many tasks involved in producing street foods. Family members stood in line early in the morning for bread, bought flour and sugar in the market, mixed ingredients, fetched sugarcane in their trucks, and loaned carts and utensils.

Slightly over half the vendors sell in residential areas. The largest number of street food vendors cluster in the low-income southern section of town, selling meals and snacks to schoolchildren, hospital visitors, and fellow workers throughout the day (Figure 5.2). Intercity bus stops are particularly popular for vending in the western

Foul
Stewed Beans

1 medium onion, chopped
3 garlic cloves, crushed
6 tablespoons olive oil
¼ teaspoon cayenne pepper
¼ teaspoon black pepper
½ teaspoon salt

2 pounds fava or broad beans
¾ cup water
1 teaspoon coriander
½ teaspoon allspice
3 tablespoons lemon juice

Fry onions and garlic in oil until golden. Add pepper, salt, and beans and fry for three minutes before adding the water and spices. (Egyptians generally use more oil and more hot spices in their foul.) Cover and cook on low heat for 25 minutes; add lemon juice and simmer another 10 minutes.

Serve in small pita bread and garnish with chopped tomatoes, onions, and cilantro. A hot sauce is often poured over the foul for additional spicing.

Tamia
Deep Fried Chickpea Patties in Pita Bread

Filling

1 cup fine bulgur wheat
1 large onion, chopped
2 garlic cloves, chopped
2 tablespoons chopped fresh parsley
1 teaspoon ground coriander
1 teaspoon salt
2 teaspoons ground cumin

1½ cups cooked, mashed garbanzo
    beans (chickpeas)
1 egg, slightly beaten
3–4 tablespoons flour
1 tablespoon lemon juice
1 teaspoon dried red hot peppers,
    ground or finely chopped (optional)

Tahini sauce

1 cup tahini (sesame seed butter)
3 garlic cloves, crushed
1 teaspoon salt

½ cup chopped fresh parsley
¼ cup finely chopped fresh mint
¾ cup fresh lemon juice

Prepare tahini sauce by blending all ingredients until smooth and the consistency of mayonnaise.

Prepare filling. Cover bulgur with boiling water and set aside for 30 minutes. Drain. Fry onions and garlic lightly in a tablespoon of oil. Stir in parsley, lemon juice, spices, and red peppers; then add mashed garbanzo beans, egg, and flour. Add enough bulgur to that the mixture forms a ball without sticking to your hands. Add a little flour if mixture is too thin. Make the balls about the size of a quarter and flatten them slightly.

Preheat oil in deep fryer to 365 degrees F and fry the balls until golden. Drain and serve hot in small pita bread, several balls to each pocket. Garnish with tahini sauce and sliced onion, tomato, cucumber, and radish.

extension. Vendors around the government buildings specialize in sandwiches for early morning through noon. Other vendors sell pastries and sweets at the lively, crowded evening market. These vendors are often unlicensed because, they say, inspectors don't work at night.

The Foods They Sell

By far the most popular foods, accounting for one-third of all sales, were the Egyptian classics *foul* and *tamia*, both using dried beans as the major ingredient. The deep-fried *tamia* also uses large quantities of oil. Both foods are eaten at all times of the day but less in the evening, alone or in sandwiches made with Egyptian flatbread, accompanied by eggplant or pickles. Other sandwich fillings include meat—especially liver paste—eggs, or fried vegetables. Nearly one-quarter of the vendors sold mixed sandwiches; these, together with *foul* and *tamia*, were by far the most popular street food items, sold by over half the Minia vendors.

In 1985, 18% vendors offered substantial meals such as kebabs (grilled chicken and fish) or *kushary*, an Egyptian favorite combining rice, macaroni, and black lentils with fried onions and hot tomato sauce. One-quarter of the vendors sold snacks, predominantly prepackaged industrially processed chips, cookies, and candy, but also sometimes yogurt, cheese, nuts, and grilled corn. Sweets and pastries accounted for 8% of food sold. Among members today over a quarter sell sweets, probably because of the high return for these items.

Bottled soft drinks accounted for 75% of the beverages available in 1985, and health restrictions on homemade beverages have accelerated the shift to commercial soft drinks. Tea is widely sold, often at stalls where customers can also smoke water pipes. A few vendors sell sugarcane juice, cocoa, and seasonal fruit juices.

Two-thirds of the vendors sell the same food year-round, except during the fasting month of Ramadan, when daytime vending ceases. While a majority sell seven days a week, men are more likely to take time off. Sandwich sellers who cater to government workers often sell snacks at mosques on Friday, the government holiday. In the summer, some *kushary* and sweets vendors switch to selling ice cream along the corniche.

Regulations

Many street foods are sold illegally according to national regulations dating from 1967 and 1968.[2] Cooked meats, fish, vegetables, macaroni, and salads are prohibited. Thus most sandwiches, including those based on *foul* and *tamia*, are also forbidden. Enforcement appears to be particularly stringent against *kushary* sellers, perhaps on the theory that this dish, along with sweets, is considered a luxury food bought by the middle class, and so should be held to higher health standards than might be expected for basic foods such as *tamia* and *foul*. It is also illegal to squeeze sugarcane or fresh juices on the street, or to sell fresh juices, milk, or homemade ice cream.

The condition of the carts and cooking utensils, as well as the type of food, is under the purview of local health authorities. Fresh pastries must be kept in glass cases; dry sweets must be properly packaged and, like ice cream, must come from licensed producers. Inspectors rarely visit homes to observe the conditions of production, but they have been known to confiscate ice cream vendors' carts if they cannot prove their ice cream comes from a licensed source. Since few carts are truly mobile, regulations govern location as well. Obtaining permission to place a cart on a corner regularly is much easier than obtaining rights to a permanent kiosk, despite the fact that many "mobile" carts have secured access to water and electric connections.

To obtain a food seller's permit, all vendors must submit and regularly update a health certificate stating that they are free from communicable or parasitic diseases and serious skin infections. They must also submit proof that they have not been charged for criminal activity; released prisoners must wait five years before receiving this certificate.

Given this myriad of regulations, many open to a variety of interpretations, it is no wonder that vendors have traditionally seen inspectors and police as their harrassors and enemies. Since over half the foods sold are illegal under one regulation or another, vendors are forced to break the law to make a living. In particular, many vendors obtain licenses for selling legal foods such as tea or sweets or *tamia*, then sell other foods. The readiness of vendors to ignore health regulations is not a trivial problem, given that research staff in 1985 found one-quarter of their establishments were unclean.

Today, local policies have changed dramatically. Instead of harassing the vendors, fining them, or confiscating their carts, the officials in Minia now advise and train vendors through the Street Food Vendors Organization. This change in attitude came about in part due to the EPOC study. The research findings convinced local officials that the street foods trade assures economic survival for many families, and it also provides convenient and affordable food for visitors and workers. The active, visible support the governors of Minia province have since provided for the ongoing street foods project cannot be underestimated.

General Salim Ibrahim, governor when the project began, assigned the secretary of the governate to function as head of the steering committee and appointed officials from the health, planning, and environment departments as members. The governor attended the final project seminar in December 1985, and participated in the discussion of ways to design a more flexible regulation system, one that would balance realistic food safety concerns with the vendors' economic needs. He then supported the recommendation that the vendors form an organization to act as an interface with the government. Subsequent governors have continued to work with the new organization, attending the official opening of the SFVO office, assigning officials to the board, and advising the leaders on government regulations and restrictions.

Changing the Policy Climate

Two strong women have been instrumental in changing the lives of street vendors in Minia: Sarah Loza, who conducted the Street Food Project in Minia, and Haga Fatma, a local activist. Both are professional women who are also dedicated to helping Egypt's poor. While their backgrounds and approaches are very different, their distinctive skills combine to make a model of the Street Food Vendors Organization.

Sarah Loza, a Canadian-trained sociologist, is a founder and president of SPAAC (Social Planning, Analysis, and Administration Consultants), a consulting group located in Cairo that conducts studies for national and international agencies. By involving the provincial governor and key municipal leaders on a steering committee for the Street Foods Project, she was able to engage the leadership of the city in the plight of the vendors. From the beginning of the project, Loza began looking for practical interventions to help the vendors. During the study, the staff initiated training programs on food handling and polled vendors on their opinions about forming their own organization. On the basis of these polls and the steering committee's final recommendatations, Loza and her staff served as consultants through the long process of setting up a new organization.

The first question addressed was what type of organization was appropriate for organizing the vendors: a cooperative, a trade union, or a nongovernmental organization (NGO)? The basic differences revolve around membership: cooperative and trade union members include only people involved in a specific economic activity or officers employed by them. In contrast, NGOs are controlled by individuals concerned about a specific problem but whose work is unrelated to the goals of the organization.[3]

The vendors' poll revealed a variety of attitudes toward organizing. Opinions ranged from enthusiasm about the protection and security an organization might offer to skepticism over the ability of vendors to work together, given the "severe competition" among them (SPAAC 1985, 53). Most vendors felt that they had too little time and influence to set up their own organization. Women, who already sold for fewer hours than men because of family responsibilities, had even less time than men. The vendors' lack of time for or interest in the organizing effort made the trade union or cooperative approaches less feasible. Since the steering committee members were more available for this initial stage, for them the obvious choice was to register as an NGO with the Ministry of Social Affairs (MOSA). Most of the 14,000 registered NGOs in Egypt are charitable organizations, primarily connected to mosques or churches. In the 1960s, MOSA created a subclassification for community development associations (CDAs); some 3,200 groups have registered under this category, mostly in villages. CDAs include village leaders as well as the poor and are eligible for loan programs.

Assigning an urban informal sector activity to this category was an innovative concept. A board of directors would consist of members of the steering committee and vendors. The balance between these two groups would change gradually through the yearly electoral process and could eventually become a board of vendors only. In the interim the "influentials" could continue to act as advocates for the vendors to government and funders.[4] Ex-officio members represent the university, youth, the Ministry of Supply, and the Governor's office.[5] In December 1986, the Organization for Development and Support of Street Food Vendors in the City of Minia, generally called the Street Food Vendors Organization (SFVO), was established. Establishing bylaws suitable both to the organization's unique design and to the official MOSA guidelines for NGOs required many drafts; it took nearly two years before the government accepted them.

Chair of the board of directors since its inception, Haga Fatma Abdel Hamid Osman is a government officer in the real estate tax section who served on the steering committee as a representative of volunteers in social service organizations.[6] Coming from a traditional Muslim family, she was not allowed to go to Cairo to attend the university. Instead, she completed two years of a government secretarial training program after high school and has been in government service since then, serving as an elected member of the local officers union. When her husband, a member of the education department, took up a well-paying position teaching English in Saudi Arabia, she left her political activity to join him for five years, from 1975 to 1980. While there she started a kindergarten, then managed a larger school. Both before going to Saudi Arabia and after her return, Haga Fatma was active in charitable groups such as the Young Muslim Women's Association and the Red Crescent. Her experiences in such diverse organizations have made her a forceful advocate of SFVO, both in Minia and in Cairo. Haga Fatma is an active chair of the board who uses her office daily; her desk is surrounded by a comfortable living room set of furniture and a TV.

The Street Food Vendors Organization

The office of the SFVO is on the first floor of an apartment building across the street from an old mosque that faces on the river. It is a pleasant 15-minute walk along the Nile corniche from the modern commercial part of town, and close to the major vending areas. The staff consists of three men—a coordinator, a loan officer, and a warehouse manager—and a woman who serves as the financial and administrative officer. Records are currently maintained by writing, but a new computer will improve record-keeping as the staff becomes more proficient in its use. The SFVO has also been assisted by two young women interns who are completing their required public service.

The staff keeps evening hours from 5:00 to 8:00 P.M., in addition to morning hours from 9:00 A.M. to 2:00 P.M., for the convenience of the vendors. The offices have clearly become a center for the vendors, who drop in with increasing frequency. Men and women, often dressed up for their visits, come by to discuss loans or to ask advice throughout the day, but especially in the afternoons.

Members

From the initial 28 members who joined in 1986 and the 47 members officially registered when the SFVO began operation in January 1988, the membership increased steadily to 315 by August 1990, and to 529 by the end of 1992. Unexpectedly, nearly one-third of the members are women, numbering 169, a considerably higher percentage than reflected in the 1985 census. Even that figure apparently underrepresented women's involvement by neglecting their assistance to male vendors in the home.

Interviews with vendors underscore the cooperation and flexibility required to run a street foods enterprise. Member lists include some 50 couples who work together, usually but not always at the same stall.

Dalal took over the sandwich enterprise after her husband was injured; he now sells tea and offers a water pipe just up the street from her stall. Raget and her daughter used to assist Raget's husband Yehia in selling sandwiches from an improvised shop, crowded in among the many other enterprises in a vacant lot on the corner of a major intersection in the western commercial area. Recently she became the major food vendor after her husband began to sell the antiques he buys in Cairo from the same stall; Raget's daughter sells soap from a separate table set next to them, but continues to help her mother when she herself is not busy.

Board

Two critical members of the original steering committee, in addition to Haga Fatma, continue to serve on the Board: medical doctor Kamel Michail, then governorate deputy of health affairs and now retired, and Nabil Zeidan, director of the development directorate, an appointed member. In addition to these three and the four vendors, in January 1993 the board included another woman from the NGO community, two additional health officials, an elected member who works at the State Ministry of Social Affairs, and an ex-officio representative of the Ministry of Supply.

The board meets at least once a month and keeps formal minutes. The four special committees for health, provisions, social affairs, and credit are less formal and include members not on the board. One board practice exemplifies the organization's mixed approach, between that of an NGO and a self-interested group. Following the practice in Egypt where poorly paid government officials need incentives to attend meetings, 10 Egyption pounds (LE) per month is available for "travel expenses" for all board members, including the vendors. Only Haga Fatma refuses the money; she feels it violates her volunteer status.

Accomplishments

Most activities of the SFVO fall into two distinct categories, again reflecting the dual nature of the board: the "influentials" pursue advocacy and intervention; the vendors suggest assistance programs. The SFVO's major services now include a loan program and bulk buying outlet, a crisis fund established by the members themselves, and a health clinic. SPAAC recommendations to expand markets—by building and renting out kiosks or setting up canteens at schools and holiday fairs—have yet to be implemented, perhaps because they came from outside the organization. SFVO does arrange periodic social activities for the vendors and their families, but these are primarily the result of staff initiative, and they reflect more charitable than economic concerns.

Advocacy

Efforts on behalf of street food vendors are directed at both government and donors. By funding projects for the vendors, the donors make clear to the government their priorities as advocates for the poor. Support for SFVO gives the project itself greater visibility through donor reports. The political role of international NGOs has not been well documented, but the funding and program support flowing from the major development organizations are of great importance in the lower-income countries such as Egypt. Not surprisingly, both Sarah Loza and Haga Fatma have strived to maintain good relations with the government in Minia and Cairo and to initiate contacts with international funders.

From the initiation of the Street Food Project in Minia, Sarah Loza courted the provincial and city officials. As EPOC found elsewhere, once administrators understand the economic benefits flowing from an active street food trade, they focus on improving health safety and controlling congestion rather than using the blunt instruments of harassment and destruction. The governor and his staff welcomed the formation of the SFVO as a conduit of information and cooperation.

While the creation of SFVO conferred legitimacy to the sector, vendors are still expected to comply with the national regulations, which are still the law of the land. Both the police and health inspectors carry out enforcement. One health inspector now on the board emphasized that his attitudes have turned around 180 degrees since joining the SFVO. Along with the two other health officials on the board he participated in training sessions for the vendors and continues to argue for the flexible application of rules. The municipal police force[7] charged with enforcing regulations concerning vendors has been less forthcoming. No officer has been willing to serve on either the steering committee or the board; representatives have attended board meetings and arranged meetings in each municipal subdivision between the local officials and vendors selling in that area so that standards could be agreed upon that would minimize future harassment. Laws restricting the sale of specific types of food continue to be fairly rigidly enforced, but the recognition the SFVO has received from the governor helps protect the vendors from undue pressure. Overall, the self-esteem of vendors has been greatly enhanced both by organizational contacts and from the attention the vendors receive from visitors and press.

The SFVO has also lobbied for local government help to assure the vendors' access to affordable street food ingredients. When the organization first formed, insufficient quotas for flour, oil, and sugar forced vendors to limit their production or else buy these ingredients at the much higher "tourist" price. For example, the monthly quota for oil allocated to each vendor lasted no more than two days; then the vendors had to buy at the much higher unsubsidized prices. As a result of an appeal by the SFVO, the undersecretary of the State Ministry of Provision increased monthly allocations of oil from 20 to 30 kilograms for vendors in Minia at a time when quotas were dropping elsewhere in the country.

Bread for sandwiches was also difficult to procure, even if vendors arrived at the bakery at 5:00 A.M.; there was always a line, and often the number of loaves sold to any one person would be limited. As a result of the advocacy efforts, vendors were assigned to specific bakeries and were thus assured of a stable supply of bread.

Local shortages of beans and oil persist during the current transition to a market economy, as farmers often send their produce to markets in bigger cities. Minia's major cooking oil producer has also felt the pinch, resulting in an appeal for help to the governor, who can no longer control local businessmen but may possibly influence them.

Two international NGOs working in Upper Egypt have already contributed funds to the SFVO through a cofinancing scheme initiated by the Ford Foundation, the funder of the original study. Ford decided to seek cofunders as a phaseout strategy, as Ford is not an implementing agency and because it wished to involve other groups in this innovative project.[8] Ford staff suggested several possible donors to Haga Fatma, who then met with current donors, the Catholic Relief Services (CRS) and the Canada Fund for Local Initiatives, in Cairo. CRS is already applying the model of the SFVO in other towns in Upper Egypt. Haga Fatma would like to see a network of organizations linking similar groups throughout the country. Loza received a grant from Ford to replicate the SFVO in two slum areas of Cairo. The interest of these significant international donor organizations in assisting street food vendors adds credence when these active women solicit government assistance.

Rotating Credit Fund

The most popular service offered by the SFVO is their loan program. Set up as a revolving credit fund in June 1988 with capital from the Catholic Relief Services (CRS), 40 loans were made in the first two months, often to buy supplies.[9] As of 31 December 1992, slightly more than half of the 529 members had received a total of 725 loans; of these loans, 499 went to men and 228 to women. These figures indicate that some members were utilizing the fund for two or three loans each, while other members did not receive loans at all. Interest on the loans is 2% per month. Costs for bank and administration charges and a possible penalty fee are taken out of the cash provided when the loan is taken out. If the vendor repays on time, the penalty fee is returned. Loans are granted for cash or for supplies direct from the warehouse, and for 4, 8, or 12 months; the maximum loan has now been raised from LE 800 to 1,000 (equivalent at rates in December 1992 to U.S. $303.)

SFVO staff visit loan applicants both at their place of sale and at home, since much of the food is processed there. Cleanliness of operation, as well as character reference, is important in assessing whether to grant the loan. An average of 30 requests are filed each month and only about two are refused. Staff-approved applications go to the board for final agreement. Repayment must be done at the Cairo Bank, a requirement meant to familiarize the vendors with the formal banking operation. Because the bank is a 30-minute walk from the office, many vendors come to the office to repay. As a courtesy, Khalid deposits for those who are sick, disabled, or insistent. Between a quarter and a half of all vendors now pay at the office.

The default rate has been consistently low, but recent cases indicate that several of the more sophisticated members are questioning the interest rate or refusing to repay their second or third loan. They have learned enough about the SFVO to know that the revolving fund was given free to the organization, and they wonder why they also cannot have money without cost or as a gift.

Achmed has a tea and water pipe stand along the main street in central city. After repaying his first two loans he defaulted on the third loan of LE 600. The organization investigated and found he spent the money sending several of his children to language school, so they took him to court where he was given a three-month jail sentence. After his second hearing at the court he decided to repay rather than go to prison. When Said el Areese, a *kushary* vendor, was sentenced to six months in jail and then picked up by the police, his wife begged several board members to forgive the debt. They were not sympathetic. Said had used his loan of LE 800 to buy a house, then told the loan officer that the money had been stolen. After discussing the problem with a vendor leader from his area the loan was rescheduled and Said repaid LE 250 in small installments before he stopped entirely. In a chaotic session, the board and staff worked out an agreement with Said's wife that they would drop charges if she sold off some possession, like her TV set, in order to repay the loan immediately. Ragat's husband nearly defaulted on his first loan because he drank the profits from their enterprise. So she herself took out the second loan, also for LE 800, but she stopped repaying after she learned the origin of the loan fund. After SFVO took her to court, she agreed to repay within two months.

SFVO is reluctant to go to court, not only because the staff try to be responsive to crises in a vendor's life, but also because a lawyer costs LE 50. Staff knew that the reasons Omer hadn't paid on his loan for the last four months was because he was still paying medical bills for a leg injury. The injury was so severe that he had to sell his *kushary* cart. But with LE 25 from the *Sandoug* (see page 109) and a loan of LE 320 he bought a new cart once he was able to work again. While I was in the office, he came in, dressed in jacket and tie, to reschedule his payments.

The credit needs of vendors are clearly not limited to their productive activities, so many use the loans for other purposes. Vendors do not have the collateral to obtain a bank loan and, unlike most other countries, there are no moneylenders in Egypt today.[10] The staff is considering offering social loans at a higher interest rate as an additional service.[11] The Islamic restrictions on the taking of *fida* (interest) appears to be of little concern; technically the cost of a loan is called an administrative fee.

Warehouse

In response to the erratic supply conditions of Egypt's liberalizing economy, the SFVO set up a warehouse in March 1993 to sell items used by its members. Even the store manager had difficulty keeping oil and beans in stock; both items had been exhausted for three weeks at the time of my visit in January 1993. Most other ingredients for street foods were available, including beverages such as tea and cocoa, and both hand and dishwashing soap. The store operates on a 6% profit margin, a level that covers the costs of running the warehouse. Savings from bulk purchases reduce prices for the vendors, who often use loans in cash or kind to cover their purchases. The staff is now trying to develop a credit card system that would save the vendors the effort of applying for a loan and repaying at the bank.

Carts

City authorities' concerns about Minia's tourist appeal have a great influence on their attitudes toward street food vendors. Vendors in areas frequented by visitors are more carefully scrutinized than those in the working-class areas of the town. Officials do acknowledge that vendors give life and character to the streets, but want them also to look clean and attractive and to serve safe food. A SFVO committee decided to hold a contest among students in the university art department to design a cart that would be both appealing and functional. Many suggestions were rejected by the vendors as impractical: wood trim that would need painting yearly and made carts too heavy; the addition of two tanks for water, one for clean and the other for waste water, made even aluminum carts difficult to manage.

The Canada Fund for Local Initiatives agreed to assist in funding ten model carts that cost LE 1,745 each, and which could be purchased on installment over three years after paying 10% down. Each cart includes a water tank on top with a hose that runs into a basin in the cart. Despite the cost there is a waiting list for the carts and additional ones may be built. In addition, a retrofitting project for older carts is being planned for sale to the less well-off vendors.

In January 1993, ten of these new carts were being tested throughout the city, and modifications were still being made. Because of the regulations the carts must be mobile, but most of the model carts seem to be permanently anchored in desirable areas. Their gleaming white exteriors advertise cleanliness. But the new carts, like the older types, are not designed for processing or cooking foods. Vendors who deep-fry *tamia* or *zalabia* (deep-fried sweet dough) keep the hot oil kettle to one side. A single cart design is clearly not adaptive to the many types of street food vendors.

Kiosks

An even more ambitious idea for solving health issues while addressing tourist appeal was to build kiosks in areas frequented by tourists. These kiosks would be permanent but lightly built structures that would be large enough to allow food processing to take place inside. Clustered in groups of five, they would be supplied with water, electricity, and sewerage. Such amenities would enable the vendors to legally sell foods that they now sell in spite of government regulations. Further, a fixed address automatically makes the entrepreneur eligible for social and health insurance.

In 1988, the SFVO received tentative approval to set up ten kiosk clusters in scattered sites around the city. Each cluster would be 10 meters long and 2.5 meters deep; thus each of the five vendors would be provided with a space slightly larger than 6 ½ by 8 feet square. The SFVO plans to build the kiosks and rent them to vendors, especially the unemployed educated children of current members.[12] A pilot cluster to be built near the new railroad station was being considered for funding by CRS. Vendors currently selling in the area would be given priority for renting these kiosks.

Health Issues

Many of the government regulations about street foods are meant to ensure safe and nutritious food for the customer. One of the first activities of the SFVO was to begin training programs for vendors to improve their food handling and sanitation practices and to warn the vendors about the hazards of using additives such as red dye in their products. The health officials on the board assisted in developing a training course for the vendors. The first session, where the governor of Minia greeted the participants, was held during Ramadan in early 1988. In the field, health officials gave advice to vendors and tested foods for safety rather than automatically shutting down vendors selling "prohibited" foods such as *kushary*, fruit juices, and pastries. Certificates are awarded to vendors who attend health training seminars; these are scheduled for two hours in the early morning over a five-day period. In 1989, a videotape to be used to educate members about sanitation and safe food practices was prepared. Many of the vendors who were interviewed found this training very helpful. One vendor, Sharbat, whose name appropriately means syrup, makes cookies from dark honey at home; her son, one of seven children—all in school—takes them to the bakery. She particularly appreciated the cleanliness lessons and later enrolled in a SFVO-sponsored literacy class to keep up with her children.

Most vendors were more concerned about the required health certificate than about receiving training in food safety. Hosni sells *bellila* (wheat porridge) in the early mornings at the railroad station; his wife prepares the food at home each day. She would like to increase their income of LE 3 per day by selling *zalabia* from his cart.

Hosni is already licensed, but he complained about the time spent obtaining the physical checkups and does not want to subject his wife to such an ordeal. In response to such complaints, the SFVO has arranged for its members to receive all health services at reduced prices at a clinic run by CEOSS.

Crisis Fund

In Egypt, health insurance coverage is tied to social insurance schemes that cover workers with a fixed place of employment; vendors without permanent place of work are not eligible.[13] The only pension or social insurance scheme available to vendors was set up to cover war widows and provides only tiny benefits. However, if vendors could qualify as self-employed businesses, then their contribution in Egyptian pounds would result in a significant pension. Those part-time vendors who are employed by the government, a figure reported at 40% in the original study, received coverage through their place of work; spouses of such employees are also covered. Full-time vendors with no working spouse lack coverage. The SFVO has been lobbying to change the law; Haga Fatma is now taking the issue to the media in hopes of providing broad coverage to informal sector workers of all types.

Meanwhile, on their own initiative, members of the SFVO set up their own crisis fund, the *Sandoug el Zamalah*, drawing on traditional concepts of group responsibility. Six vendors, representing the different areas of the city but including all the elected vendor board members, sit on the governing board of the *Sandoug* along with the officers of the SFVO. Started in April 1988 with 16 members, the fund had 367 members in January 1993, nearly 70% of all SFVO members. Each member is supposed to pay LE 1 per month into the fund; the Governor gave the *Sandoug* a grant of LE 500 when it started. To date the fund has paid out LE 1,552 to members for death of a spouse, a destroyed cart, or illness; of this amount, 23 men received a total of LE 765, and 20 women received LE 787. Due to its growth and the difficulty of collecting payments from all *Sandoug* members, the fund was reconstituted in January 1993. Some LE 3,000 was put into a savings account to draw interest; the remaining LE 400 is in a current account for swift distribution. Outstanding loans are now canceled on death. The *Sandoug* has become so successful that most SFVO members now expect gifts in time of crisis, whether or not they are paid up members of the *Sandoug*. Vendors and board members are now debating whether the *Sandoug* should continue with separate membership or whether paying into this fund should be required of all SFVO members.

Social Events

Soon after the SFVO was established, the board voted to hold two events to build trust between the vendors and the staff and board. The first was a visit by 45 vendors and their families to Fayoum by chartered bus; the SFVO paid half the cost. The second was larger and less costly: a festive occasion in a public park in Minia where vendors prepared and consumed their own specialties. Annual events include receptions at the office to mark the end of Ramadan and the Prophet's birthday. A party is also held once a year for young children of vendors. A woman's club for vendor's wives was proposed by a public service intern in order to access funds from the Ministry of Social Affairs for women's activities. The idea was to encourage women to come out of their homes by offering classes they might find useful, such as sewing, or for income, such as making new sweets for sale, or preparing vegetables for sale in the warehouse. Attendance was low, which is not surprising considering the extent of women's involvement in their husbands' trade. Special literacy classes for women drew 22 participants.

Such activities fit the older view of charitable organizations and seem to have had their origin from nonvendors. While no one questions the utility of such events, it is not clear why the SFVO organization should be running literacy classes or holding parties. Staff is already very busy with affairs of the organization. In middle-class organizations, members or their wives form committees for this purpose. Given the long hours most vendors and their families work, it is unrealistic to expect volunteer time for noneconomic matters.

A Model for Street Vendors

Details of the activities and accomplishments of the Street Food Vendors Organization in Minia provide a model for improving the lives of vendors and increasing the safety of the foods they sell. In Egypt the mixed-membership NGO model is already being replicated in other cities and adapted for other types of informal sector entrepreneurs. Haga Fatma is lobbying for a national organization that will represent the concerns of these microentrepreneurs to the government, much as the SFVO does in Minia. Sarah Loza is trying to replicate the study and model in the much more sophisticated climate of Cairo.

No design is without weaknesses. Of course there are problems and disagreements among members and staff of the SFVO and between the organization and its funders. Most are generic problems, characteristic of groups trying something new in countries where NGOs are kept under tight control. More fundamentally, they relate to the processes of social change and the roles of the educated elite in assisting the poorer segments of society, particularly through the mechanisms of development NGOs.

The SFVO with its new organizational approaches to instigating social change symbolizes innovation in process, but inevitably creates tensions among members, board, and staff. Can the organization develop leadership among the vendors or staff as long as the chair plays such a dominant role, not only on the board but also in the day-to-day administration?[14] Can or should the board become one of vendors only? Although several are learning how to play the intervention role with the government, without power or contacts will the vendors continue to need the support of the influentials? Staff/chair conflict is frequent among NGOs everywhere when the identity of the chair is tied to the organization; many felt that only if Haga Fatma moved up to the head of a national organization could the staff assume its expected professional role.

Issues between the donors and the SFVO are rooted in the contradictions between the long-term commitments needed for social change and the short funding cycles of donors that compel them to push for speedy and often unrealistic results. Donors, who are understandably reluctant to continue funding the same people over many years because such guaranteed funding might create dependency, instruct their recipients to seek institutional self-sufficiency. The balance between precipitous withdrawal and continued dependency is a difficult one. Can and should an organization dedicated to helping the poor be expected to become self-funding? When subsidies are liberally handed out to industries, for example, why should the least able be expected to pay their own way? Yet many of the vendors were making an income equal to the influentials in Minia. If the social safety net were extended to them, then could they not afford to support their own organization? What of the really poor vendors? Should the SFVO be expanded to all microentrepreneurs in order to provide a larger membership base?

Regarding the SFVO, services such as the loan fund or the warehouse should largely pay for themselves, but staff and organizational costs may need long-term subsidies. Alternative sources of subsidy should be sought, perhaps by seeking government subvention for services rendered or by involving local businessmen as "big brothers." Utilizing vendors, staff, and board members as consultants for expansion of the SFVO to other cities would enhance both the Minia organization and the speed of replication. A federation of organized informal sector workers might be a long-term goal to enhance their ability to advocate changes in laws regulating social insurance and NGOs. But activities peripheral to the goals and objectives of the street food vendors—literacy classes, health clinics, child care, and income-generating training—should not be attempted. Other NGOs or the government already offer these services.

The Street Food Vendors Organization of Minia clearly presents a commendable model for organizing microentrepreneurs in developing countries. The institutional innovation of a mixed board, and the tensions this creates, deserve continued observation. The street food vendors themselves have clearly benefited from organizing: self-esteem has been increased; harassment from the police has largely disappeared, and health inspectors work with vendors to help them provide safe and nutritious food. While obtaining ingredients in a timely manner is still a problem, caused now by free market forces instead of resulting from government allocation, the credit program and the warehouse have reduced costs by allowing bulk buying. New carts provide a water tank so that vendors can clean plates and utensils more easily. Fewer hassles and less cost are involved in obtaining the required annual health checkups at the NGO clinics, where members can also go for regular medical treatment.

These accomplishments have rightly attracted worldwide attention. The extent to which this model of a mixed-board NGO is applicable in other countries will be discussed in the chapter on impact. The debates on self-sufficiency and leadership raised by the experiment will be further expanded in the final chapter, which reviews the implications of the entire Street Foods Project.

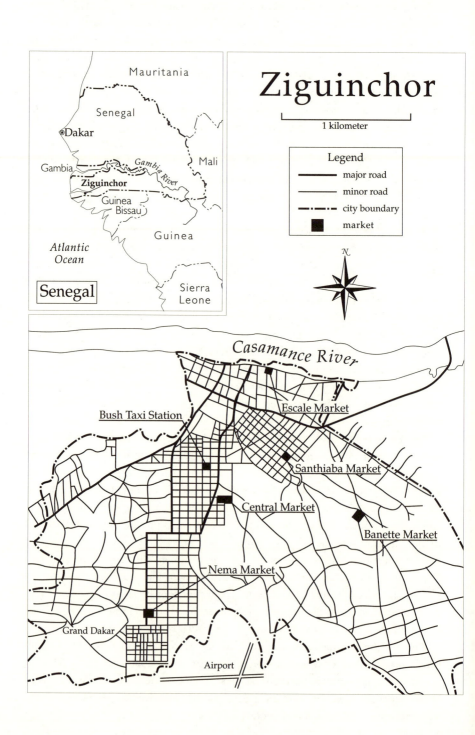

Ziguinchor

1 kilometer

Legend
- —— major road
- — minor road
- —·—·— city boundary
- ■ market

N

Senegal

Mauritania

Senegal

⊕Dakar

Gambia

Gambia River

Mali

Ziguinchor

Guinea Bissau

Atlantic Ocean

Guinea

Sierra Leone

Casamance River

Bush Taxi Station

Escale Market

Santhiaba Market

Central Market

Banette Market

Nema Market

Grand Dakar

Airport

CHAPTER SIX

Ziguinchor, Senegal

Much recent economic development, controlled by a centralized administration, has largely bypassed Ziguinchor, which is isolated from Dakar by the tiny state of Gambia. The resultant feeling of neglect and a prolonged drought that severely affected the rice production in this semitropical region has led to sporadic civil unrest. The EPOC study was carried out in a quiescent period, as the urbanized sections of the town were expanding into the still-cultivated fields enclosed within the municipal boundaries. The seasonality of agriculture was matched in the street food sector, as many women who perform most of the agricultural labor sold peanuts and other crops on the street. As in Nigeria, separate budgets mean that women must contribute food or money to the household. Household surveys reveal the differential spending patterns of women and men in their predominantly polygynous living arrangements. Ethnic differences in women's work and in products sold on the street document the importance of culture in everyday life. As we are unable to revisit Ziguinchor, the focus on current trends examines street foods in Dakar, where many people from Ziguinchor have migrated; their remittances are essential to maintaining families at home.

Local Context

Ziguinchor, the capital of the southern province of Casamance, is the fifth-largest city in Senegal.[1] As the administrative capital in a centralized governmental system, Ziguinchor is the regional headquarters of most government agencies and home to the province's only surgical hospital and secondary school. All post-secondary education in Senegal is found in Dakar, which in all respects illustrates the concept of the primate city: its population of 1,382,000 in 1985 was nearly nine times that of Thies, the next largest city.

The tropical rain forest climate of Casamance is distinct from the Sahelian climate characteristic of the rest of Senegal. Its land is fertile and—except in drought—well-watered, making the region normally self-sufficient in rice. The tropical beaches have become popular winter vacation destinations for many Europeans. The province is geographically isolated from the rest of the country by Gambia, the tiny former English colony and trading port that straddles the Gambia River. A map of Senegal resembles a face: Dakar is located on the tip of the nose, Casamance is the chin, and Gambia is the mouth. Land transport between Ziguinchor and Dakar is unpredictable due to delays at the ferry crossing of the Gambia River that often result in spoilage of perishable crops. Boat traffic between the two cities takes two days, inhibiting intra-city street food trade. In contrast, Ziguinchor is only 15 kilometers from the border of Guinea-Bissau to the south; Portugal controlled both areas for 250 years before being selling the land to the French in 1857.

These physical and historical distinctions are compounded by tribal, linguistic, and religious differences with the Muslim Wolof, who compose the largest ethnic group in Senegal. The Diola, who compose the largest ethnic group in Casamance, do not speak Wolof; many continue to practice their traditional animist beliefs. Christians are found among several ethnic groups as well. Radio broadcasts are primarily in French and Wolof; television was not available in 1983. This sense of neglect is reflected in the deteriorating infrastructure of the province. Casamance leaders claim that the French promised the region autonomy within Senegal before independence in 1960, but the independent government of Senegal has maintained the French centralized governmental system.

The economy of the province began to erode after the newly independent government nationalized the peanut trade in 1960, causing most of the largest French commercial establishments to move to Dakar. Previously, Ziguinchor had long been the center for collecting, processing, and selling this major export crop; in a good year peanuts may constitute 50% of the nation's primary sector exports. Rainfall has frequently been below average during the last two decades, leading to unpredictable agricultural production and further depressing the local economy. Emigration from the rural areas, primarily to Dakar but also to Ziguinchor, reaches 15% of the rural population every dry season and increases during years of poor harvest. The amount of return migration apparently slowed as the economy worsened. Not surprisingly, the number of women vendors doubled between 1983 and 1993.

Tensions between the provincial leaders and the central government caused by increasing central control and feelings of isolation were momentarily deflected during the 1980s, when the leaders of French-speaking Senegal and English-speaking Gambia proclaimed a short-lived confederation of Senegambia. Political unrest escalated in the Casamance from about 1983 onward after the central government introduced a policy of seizing land from subsistence families and allocating it to farmers who would increase its productivity (Hiltzik 1990). Unrest reached the level of a low-grade civil war during 1990; terrorist assaults on unarmed civilians and government brutality in rounding up separatist sympathizers had begun to affect the lucrative tourist trade (Noble 1991). The conflict exacerbated the country's downward economic spiral, affecting the Casamance the most.

With an estimated annual growth rate of 4.4%, the city had surpassed 98,000 people by 1983; its population had quadrupled since 1960. The city encompasses both a densely populated indigenous commercial center and a patchwork of urbanized villages and paddy rice fields. In order to accommodate this rapid urban migration, the government has been transforming traditional landownership rights by requiring registration of urban land. This process converts farm land to household plots, forcing subsistence farmers, primarily Diola, further from town. Traditionally, Diola women provide all the labor in the paddy fields once the men have prepared them, and grow vegetables for home consumption. As the distance to their rice fields increased, many women whose families could afford to buy rice stopped cultivating and turned to other economic activities (van der Laar 1989). Diola men primarily raise peanuts and other dry land crops on hilly land outside the municipal boundaries. In 1981 the Ministry of Urban Affairs estimated that 31% of the adult work force in Ziguinchor derived an income from agriculture or fishing; somewhat more women than men worked in agriculture, but only men fished. In addition, an unenumerated number of poor families survived by raising and consuming their own rice. Climatic variability over the last decade has seriously reduced rainfall in the region, affecting irrigation patterns as saline water pushes further up the river, and reducing rice yields.

The continued involvement of Diola women in agriculture is reflected in the reduced number of vendors selling foods during the rainy agricultural season. Because growing rice and vegetables is more cost-effective for the family, only older women in polygamous families have the freedom to become street traders (van de Laar 1989). In Posner's survey, only 16% of the street food venders were Diola, although they comprised 35% of the population of Ziguinchor. Posner notes that these Diola vendors were land poor and so lacked an agricultural option that was more culturally acceptable.

Domestic service employed more younger women in Casamance than either agricultural work or street vending. Young Diola women have been allowed greater access to education than girls from other more conservatively Islamic ethnic groups. Their ability to speak French prepares them to seek employment as domestics or clerks in Dakar. Although some do return to assist with the rice harvest, many families excuse their daughters from helping because their remittances have become ever more crucial in recent years.

Some young urban women had begun to engage in "commercialized courtships" in Ziguinchor, finding such relationships a more glamorous way of obtaining clothes, jewelry, and money than regular employment (van Oostrom 1989). But commercialized sex, while providing income, seldom leads to an advantageous marriage.[2] After a series of affairs, especially if they result in children, the women often end up becoming the second or third wife of older men. Among the street food vendors, 4% were unmarried mothers.

Polygyny remains the normal family type in Senegal at all social levels and among most religious groups;[3] the average family consists of eight children and four adults. Although the Islamic ideal requires men to support their families and to treat all wives equally, in fact women must contribute substantially to the household, although the activities assigned varies by ethnicity. Historically, the Diola agriculturalists, most of whom are not Muslims, maintained a strict sexual division of labor: men prepared the fields, and the women did all the farming. Urban Diola attitudes were influenced by the Manding, the second largest ethnic group (18%) in the city, whose beliefs accelerated "the spread of money economy on the one hand and Islam on the other" (Posner 1983, 29).

Two other ethnic groups are significant in Ziguinchor, whose distinctive cultural traditions affect their employment and involvement in the street food trade. The Peuhl (13%) were originally nomadic, their lives organized around their herds; urban Peuhl traders maintain a virtual monopoly on meat and yogurt. Wolof comprised only 10% of the population in the city but are the dominant group in Senegal itself. Their long association with the French in the north meant that many entered the administration; Wolof street vendors sell European-style doughnuts and bonbons, both made with wheat flour.

All ethnic groups subscribe to the ideology of the male provider that permeates the academic literature. In fact, a study in Dakar in 1981 found that the average male contribution to the family was approximately half of the amount required to live on (Achleitner and Ndione 1981). Women's income is an unacknowledged necessity for the household. Posner found that women were de facto heads in 59% of the households, yet even when a woman is the primary earner, she considers her contributions supplementary: her husband would support her if he were not too old, were not unemployed, or received too little from his pension.

In polygynous urban households, the husband provides each wife with staples and household money, usually once a month. This large single monthly outlay gives both men and women the sense that the man is the primary food supplier. The wife is expected to feed and clothe herself and her children with this contribution, meeting any shortfall herself. Women control their own income and do not usually tell either husbands or co-wives what they earn. Given the high divorce rate, women are prudent to invest in cloth or jewelry to sell in an emergency, and to provide gifts for her natal family that might smooth a possible return home. "In most polygamous households the woman's personal belongings are kept strictly separate. Every woman has her own suitcase with clothes, jewelry, etc. Kitchen utensils are jointly used but clearly initialed" (van de Laar 1989, 73).

The Survey

Responses to a consumer survey conducted as part of the street food study indicated that 71% of the men but only 25% of the women considered food to be their major expenditure. Clothing and house improvements, including furniture, were of more importance; yet an analysis of their actual expenditures showed that women's daily purchases of food when totaled over the month was comparable to the man's monthly contribution. Women purchased millet and sauce ingredients—oil, tomato paste, vegetables, and fish—to serve with rice. Overall, food consumed 80% of the total household budget. In addition, 6% of the women provided assistance to their parents and paid school fees, although only 23% of the families actually supported children in school.

To illustrate how families survive, Posner relates three case studies. Agate is among the most wealthy of the street food vendors in Ziguinchor. She sells marinated oysters at the market and also has a hired assistant who sells ices he makes in the freezer she owns. Her husband is a retired civil servant who gives her 15,000 francs (CFA; 400 CFA = $1.00 in September 1983) a month. At the time, 50 kilos of rice cost 5,500 francs. In order to feed her family of seven, Agate spends about 21,000 francs a month. In addition to her share of these food costs, which total 10,500 francs, Agate has to provide clothing and medicine for her children, two of whom come from a previous marriage.

Fatime is a Diola whose retired husband supplements his pension by cultivating two hectares of peanuts to sell and a hectare of millet to eat. These activities and the street food profits earned both by Fatime and her co-wife support nine other family members, five of whom are unemployed adults. They eat 150 kilos of rice per month, which costs 16,500 francs and is supplied by the husband; the co-wives share the cost of daily marketing and together spend an amount on fish about equal to the cost of rice. Vegetables for the sauce are grown in the family garden. The wives share other household expenses.

Nadou, a 51-year-old widow who sells yogurt at the bus station, is one of the poorest vendors. She lives with and is the sole support of her unemployed brother, his two wives, and their ten children; the wives lack sufficient capital to become vendors themselves. All Nadou's income goes to food, mostly rice or millet and a few vegetables. Necessities such as clothing or medicine are solicited from other relatives. Both this vignette and van de Laar's study of Diola traders underscore the fact that the poorest women are not vendors in Ziguinchor; women must have both time away from familial obligations such as agriculture or child care and some small amount of capital to become street food vendors.

Markets and Sellers

Most commercial activity takes place in one of the five open-air markets or along the streets; in the neighborhoods are small dry goods stores as well as ambulant vendors. St. Maur is the largest market, occupying 12,000 square meters in the densely populated town. The market is walled, with stalls lining the perimeter; the central area is shaded by hangar-like roofs. Although stalls are technically allocated by the municipality, those in good locations are passed down through families or sold in accordance with local custom, as they are in most African markets.

While nearly two-thirds of all types of vendors in the city are located here, only one-fifth of street food vendors are. They position themselves throughout the market, although the poorer women most often sit on the ground near the market entrances. The authorities had made no attempt to limit spontaneous expansion and the main market continued to spill further into surrounding streets. All vendors in the market area pay a daily location tax to the municipal agent, as do most other vendors in town, including those who cluster near the bush taxi center. Fees are based on the amount of space occupied: women on the ground pay 25 francs per day; the fee is double for those with tables and four times more for those with stalls. The tax collectors are friendly with the vendors and often overlook the fee for marginal sellers. This benign attitude may help explain why vendors felt no compulsion to organize, in contrast to Dakar with its citywide market association that includes vendors of all commodities.

Tax records provide a fairly accurate count of all vendors: 2,100 vendors paid fees in the dry season; the numbers fell to 1,365 in the rainy season.[4] The tax collectors kept track of the gender and actual fee paid by vendors of all products for a week in the dry season: women comprised just over half (53%) of the total of all vendors, but were the vast majority (68%) paying the 25 franc fee. Women were more dominant in the street food trade, representing 75% of the entrepreneurs in the sample. Twice as many vendors sold in the dry season than in the rainy season. Many of these seasonal vendors sold in the neighborhoods where they often paid no fee; both location and income suggested that these are marginal traders. In the dry season 59% sold outside the five city markets, in comparison with 41% in the rainy season. Among those in the study sample, 27% ceased vending to return to agriculture and only 60% of the vendors continued full-time selling. Demand is also less during the agricultural season, as customers are working in the fields and students are on vacation. Further, many ingredients are absent, while locally produced legumes and grains become more expensive.

This extreme fluctuation in the number of vendors was not characteristic of the trade in other cities studied, although seasonality was observed. As cities become more urbanized, vending becomes a full-time occupation; the casual vendor is more likely to be found in the periphery or in smaller towns. In Ziguinchor, most permanent vendors were landless, worked year round, and had higher profits. Most male vendors fell into this category; their income in the dry season was determined to be six times that of women on average.

Although the amount of money needed to buy ingredients for one day's sale is not high, women often had difficulty meeting higher costs when prices fluctuated. Because a woman's income was often so central to family survival, husbands or relatives might loan her cash. Rotating savings groups, called *tontines* in French or *naths* in Wolof, exist in the markets[5] and were utilized by 34% of the street food traders, mostly those who were full-time, year-round entrepreneurs. Formal credit was not available to most vendors, but men more often than women buy their ingredients on credit, paying for them at the end of the day. Among the Peuhl, who control the meat trade, young men selling *brochettes* (grilled meat and onions served on French bread covered with a spicy sauce) often make such arrangements with butchers who are often relatives, a practice which allows "newcomers to enter the sector with a minimum cash outlay. In effect, such credit channels make this an ethnically closed trade . . . the first rung in ascending the ladder towards increased economic stability" (Posner 1984, 31). Using profits from selling *brochettes*, these young entrepreneurs invest in permanent market stalls or small dry-goods shops that are also dominated by Peuhl.

The Foods They Sell

The numbers and varieties of street foods in Ziguinchor at the time of the study were limited; foods were mostly traditional and based on locally available products. Unlike the other cities studied, industrially made soft drinks and beer were not sold on the street because vendors did not own refrigerated coolers. Soft drinks were sold cold in the market from small grocery shops.[6] Beer and palm wine were sold in bars on the city periphery that presumably catered to the non-Muslim population. Locally made cold drinks made of ginger or *bisap* (a bright red infusion made from sorrel leaves that is reputed to have soothing medicinal properties) were more likely to be consumed during Ramadan to break the fast in the evening.

The types of street foods sold in Ziguinchor reflect its provincial and agricultural character. Most bureaucrats and students return home in the middle of the day for their main meal, which typically consists of rice and sauce. This meal is not available on the streets but may be purchased in restaurants. Evening meals are usually also eaten at home and may include rice or *couscous*, a millet-based pasta eaten with sauce or yogurt. The latter takes longer to prepare than rice and is sold pre-cooked in the market.[7]

Breakfast is the only meal widely available on the street. Two favorites are sold: the traditional millet porridge *monie* (often eaten with yogurt), and a French-style breakfast, *tangana*, consisting of coffee or tea served with condensed milk and accompanied by French bread with slabs of butter. Men both serve and eat the *tangana* in special stalls providing a place to sit located along commercial streets. The customers are men with a regular monthly income such as government employees, merchants, and workers in the peanut or shrimp processing plants. Market women prefer *monie*, and carry it with them to eat as they set up their own vending operation (Figure 6.1). The only light meal available in the city was *brochettes*. Because meat was too expensive to be part of the average diet, this food was exclusively a street food. Because meat was traditionally traded by Peuhl nomads, *brochettes* were only cooked by men, most often Peuhl (Figure 6.2).

Meal constituents, food that can be eaten alone but which is most often added to other dishes, include *couscous* and *petits poissons*, tiny dried and salted fish that are added to rice or eaten as a snack in bars. Yogurt is sold in the markets and by ambulatory vendors who follow a regular route; it is not made at home. Sixty percent of the yogurt vendors were Peuhl, in keeping with their pastoral background. Originally, women made yogurt from whole milk and brought it to their customers in town; this is the only type of vending allowed to Peuhl women by their husbands, who consider the marketplace unsuitable for women. With the wide availability of powdered milk distributed as part of the U.S. surplus food program, men began to purchase large bags of the milk to make a lighter yogurt. Women seldom have the cash for such a large sum; further they deride the "false milk" and the weak yogurt it produces. EPOC unsuccessfully proposed to both United States and European food assistance agencies that a pilot program be initiated that would supply powdered milk to women's groups at bulk prices as a way of increasing women's income.

Snacks in Ziguinchor include familiar street foods: peanuts, roast corn, boiled sweet potatoes, and fresh fruits, especially mango. Unusual tropical fruits are sold, along with cashew fruit and cassava. Fruits are minimally processed, often just peeled and sliced; peanuts are sold shelled and roasted or unshelled. *Sunduof*, a traditional

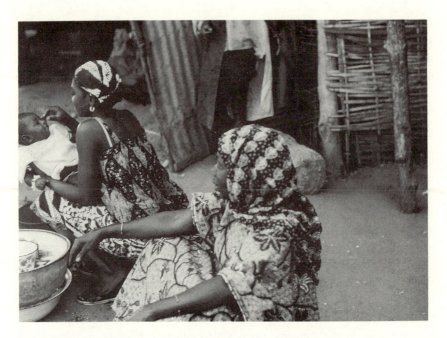

FIGURE 6.1   Women spend as much time making *monie* at home as selling this traditional millet gruel in the market place. *Monie* is a favorite breakfast food in Ziguinchor.

Wolof snack that consists of mounds of sweetened steamed rice or millet, is associated with funerals but is now eaten casually as well. *Acara* is a deep-fried cowpea fritter enhanced with a peppery sauce. Marinated boiled oysters are served in and near the local palm wine bars. Other popular snacks are adaptations of French foods that use wheat flour: fish or meat-filled pastries, hard cookies called *bon-bons*, and *beignets*, which resemble doughnuts. Ices are flavored with very sweet syrups made from commercial packets; local flavors such as *bisap* or the fruit of the baobab tree are also available.

Eating on the streets or even seated in a stall area is not considered quite proper by many customers, especially women. About half of all street food customers surveyed said that their purchases were consumed at home, a quarter ate the food outside the home, and another quarter ate the food in both places. Yogurt was almost always eaten at home, alone or with *monie* for breakfast, or in the evening as a sauce for *couscous*. Peanuts and *acara* were eaten along the streets or at home. Only *brochettes* were most often eaten at the place of purchase.

Limited though they are, the street foods consumed in Ziguinchor add significantly to people's diets. The five key foods—yogurt, *monie*, *petits poissons*, *acara*, and peanuts—are sources of both protein and vitamins. Children most often bought peanuts; the average amount purchased provided nearly two-thirds of their protein requirement. Older students, often boarding with relatives, were less frequent buyers of street foods than young children. Presumably they had to save their money for books and clothes.

FIGURE 6.2   Men of the Peuhl ethnic group sell the popular beef brochettes served on French bread with a liberal helping of hot tomato sauce.

National Policy and Local Vendors

Although the Senegalese government does not directly oppress street food vendors through police harassment, the vendors do suffer indirectly from various government policies. For example, food subsidies for importing rice and wheat, combined with agricultural policies neglecting millet—a crop well adapted to the arid Sahel—in favor of costly irrigated rice projects, have driven up the prices of basic street food ingredients. Millet shortages during the study forced most *monie* sellers to cease operations: 66 women offered this millet porridge in the markets in the dry season of May 1992; only 13 women vendors were selling *monie* that December. Reluctant to increase prices or reduce serving sizes, the sellers saw their profits decrease and then become negative as millet prices ballooned. One woman added subsidized rice to extend the millet.

National policies consolidating political and economic power in Dakar have also hurt the street food vendors. Unemployment has spiraled as civil unrest has escalated over the last decade. In the rural areas, women can no longer collect palm oil in the forest because of rebel operations. Lemon juice, an important flavoring, is hard to obtain; rural women used to squeeze lemons and take the juice, which lasts about three months without refrigeration, to Ziguinchor and Dakar. The difficult economic situation and the rival fighters have undermined law and order; trade is no longer profitable with the proliferation of *douaniers*, officials taking a cut. Families survive on remittances from Dakar, often sent home by transplanted street food vendors.

Because of the civil unrest in Casamance, the contemporary situation of street

Acara
Black-Eyed Pea / Cowpea Fritters

1 cup dried black-eyed peas
1 egg (optional)
½ teaspoon chopped chili pepper
¼ teaspoon cayenne

1 teaspoon salt
1 medium onion
1 large pepper or 2 okra (optional)
vegetable oil for deep frying

Soak black-eyed peas (or cowpeas) in water for about 10 minutes to remove skins. Drain, and blend or grind into a smooth paste; if a blender is used, add up to ⅓ cup water as needed. Then beat with a whisk or electric mixer until light and fluffy. This basic paste is used in a variety of recipes.

For fritters, add egg and spices and beat again. Thin paste with water as necessary to form a thick dropping consistency, like pancake batter. Chop vegetables, if desired, and add to bean paste just before frying. Drop spoonfuls of batter into hot and nearly smoking oil and cook until brown, about 1 minute. Flip once to cook evenly. Drain on paper towels.

These fritters are very popular throughout West Africa. Ingredients, spicing, and sauces vary. Acara are also called *kosai* in Nigeria.

Beef Brochettes

Marinade

2 pounds beef cut into 1-inch cubes
1 medium onion, finely chopped
10 sprigs of parsley, chopped
1 teaspoon salt
¾ teaspoon black pepper

2 teaspoons paprika
1 teaspoon cumin
1 tablespoon vinegar
1 tablespoon olive oil

Spicy hot tomato sauce

4 tablespoons tomato paste
2 tablespoons olive oil
4 tablespoons vinegar

2 tablespoons water
1 teaspoon salt
¼ teaspoon or more Tabasco sauce

Combine marinade ingredients into a large bowl and mix well. Let the meat marinate for at least 4 hours. Make the spicy hot tomato sauce by combining all ingredients, and set aside. Place four or five pieces of beef on each skewer and broil over a charcoal fire until done to your liking. Serve with French bread and the hot sauce.

vendors in Dakar gives some indication of changes over the past decade. As migrants flood Dakar, the squatter areas burgeon. Nongovernmental organizations working in the "bidonvilles," as the local shanty towns are called, note that the religious or traditional village organizations that encouraged male responsibility have not been replicated in the squatter areas. With little income, men find it increasingly difficult to provide for several wives, yet there is still a social expectation to marry and continue to support polygyny among all classes.[8] Before establishing projects to assist the poor in Dakar, Oxfam took a survey which found that 67% of the Dakar households were de facto headed by women, even though *all* are officially married. Heads of 26% of the households were widows or never-married mothers, while in the remaining 45% the husband provided less income to the family than the woman: in 27% of the households the man was a pensioner receiving little income, and 14% of the husbands were unemployed (Dem 1994). In Senegal, retirement is compulsory after 55 and the pension income, which has not kept up with inflation, has become worthless: a former high bureaucrat was receiving only 40,000 francs a month, while a room in a Western hotel at that time cost 36,000 francs per night.

Development organizations such as Oxfam that once worked only in rural areas have begun urban community development programs for women such as PROFEMU (Programme Pour les Femmes en Mileu Urbaine). Credit is offered through savings groups for individual income activities such as street food vending; once formed, the groups may also request training in literacy, health, and legal rights. The organizers consider these classes critical if women vendors are to survive in Dakar, where government regulations that require both a health certificate and a sales license are beginning to be enforced. A recent study of vendors in the capital found that 80% of them did not have the health certificate and 75% lacked the sales permit (Diouf 1992).

Of the 100 vendors studied, 80 were women. Only 8% of the group were educated, a figure consistent with the Ziguinchor findings when the sex ratio is considered. The food they sold included those found in Casamance, but because of the city's size most workers did not go home for the midday meal. Meal dishes were prominent: rice with meat, fish, peanut, and vegetable sauces; boiled eggs; fried fish; and soups with a meat or palm oil base. The vendors prepared food as they would at home. The researcher, expecting higher standards of cleanliness, was dismayed. Once cooked, the street foods are subject to environmental pollution from dust and automobile exhaust (Diouf 1992).

Improved facilities at existing markets, and the creation of smaller markets in the periphery, could immediately improve the conditions under which street foods are sold. Attention to the backward linkages to agricultural producers seems particularly important for the secondary cities in Senegal and will be critical as Casamance emerges from its current problems. Assisting women to operate stalls where they could serve traditional foods not available at the *tangana* would help them increase their profits and diversify the foods sold. Women in Dakar have for some years prepared food on contract for factory workers; perhaps contracts with government workers or schools could be tried in Ziguinchor. Clearly, the street food trade continues to be a critical activity of the urban poor in Senegal, essential not only to produce income but also to provide cheap and convenient foods for urban workers.

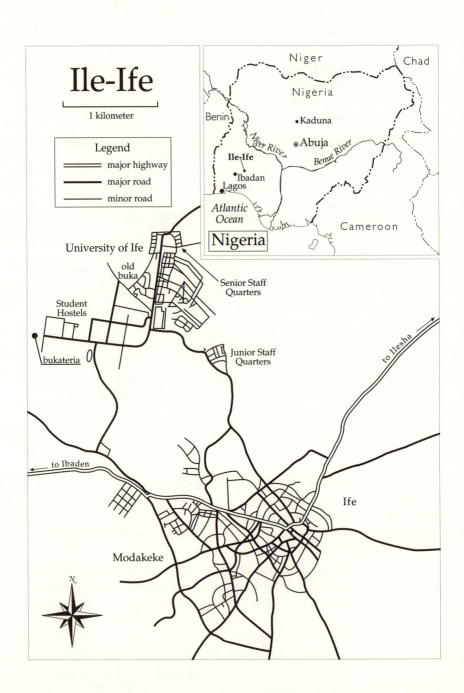

CHAPTER SEVEN

Ile-Ife, Nigeria

Ile-Ife is an ancient town, and its inhabitants have a long tradition of eating food on the street, which is sold predominantly by women who are culturally bound to support their own children in this land of non-pooling household budgets. In the decades since independence from British colonial rule, however, a combination of rapid urbanization and the spectacular boom and bust of the Nigerian economy has fueled the growth of the street food sector, as well as its conflicts with the military governments. In few other countries has a modern state waged such a destructive "street cleaning" campaign against its street food vendors, in the supposed interests of public health and civic order. The stalls of many Ife vendors were destroyed while the research study was in progress; the staff was able to document the immediate impact.

This chapter documents the troubled contemporary history of vendors in Ile-Ife, as well as in the larger Nigerian cities of Ibadan and Lagos. Central government actions have been particularly focused on vendors in Lagos, where, perhaps more than in other countries, sellers of food (and just about everything else) have contributed to massive urban congestion. Local scholars, activists, government officials, and vendors in Lagos have been meeting in an effort to reach workable compromises between excessive regulation and urban chaos. In contrast, many local government officials outside Lagos have been sympathetic to vendors and have supported efforts to train them in safe food handling procedures. Universities in Ife and Ibadan built serviced facilities and rented them to vendors who cater to students and faculty.

Local Context

Ile-Ife, a major regional town with a long urban history, is located in Oyo state, in the forested cocoa-farming zone of southwestern Nigeria; the town is an hour's drive northeast of Ibadan, the largest Yoruba city, which is itself about two hours north of Lagos. Ile-Ife epitomizes Yoruba culture and is regarded as the cradle of the Yoruba people: Ile-Ife means birthplace of the Ife.[1] Traditional leaders continue to play an important role in local society, and the Ooni of Ife remains the spiritual leader and a paramount *oba*, or king of the Yoruba.

Yoruba cities date back to at least the sixteenth century (Sudarkasa 1973). These ancient cities resembled large villages; walled compounds of thatch and mud buildings lined broad straight streets leading to the palace and central market. In Ife today, the traditional neighborhoods of the two indigenous groups of Yoruba—the Ife and the Modakeke—form the urban core. These congested areas are linked by narrow crooked lanes, but the cocoa money has allowed farmers to build modern-style two-story houses, often with a shop on the first floor (Gugler and Flanagan 1978). The core is surrounded by established commercial and residential areas filled predominantly with migrants. Contemporary Ife supports two large daily markets, two biweekly market centers, and a number of smaller neighborhood markets.

Like other urban centers in Nigeria, Ife has experienced extremely high rates of growth since independence in 1960. The establishment of the University of Ife in 1967, now called Obafemi Awolowo University, attracted other institutions of higher learning, making the city a major educational center. The low buildings of the traditional town contrast with the modern concrete high-rise buildings of the spacious university campus, set amid farmlands about four kilometers from town. Planned under the British government, the architecture reflects the early 1960s European style adapted to the tropics: odd-shaped cutouts and brightly painted geometric figures relieve the monotony of concrete buildings. Residential estates were set up in the periphery of town to cater to the influx of a more Westernized and higher-income clientele. Types of street foods consumed in these areas and on campus differ from those in the traditional areas of town.

The census of 1963 recorded a population for Ife of 135,000; in 1983 the population was estimated to be 617,296, or nearly four times the 1963 figure![2] Rural urban migration was intensified by the oil boom of the early 1970s: work and educational opportunities expanded in the cities, while agriculture was neglected. At the time of the Street Food Project study in 1984, a recession had hit the country. This downturn of the economy had a clear impact on both street food vendors and their customers.

The origins of the city predate the colonial period. Unlike farmers of most other ethnic groups in West Africa, Yoruba farmers usually live in towns and commute four or five miles daily to their fields; those with lands farther away may return to the town for the weekend. Such urban clustering facilitated women's trading activities and may help explain their relatively low participation in agriculture relative to other ethnic groups in the area. A 1951 study in the cocoa belt showed that women did only 7% of the agricultural work while male family members and male laborers did 93% of the work (Boserup 1970, 23, 72). The presence of farm laborers, many from tribes to the north, was cited to explain why many male land owners pursue an additional economic activity in town such as carpentry, tailoring, or bicycle repair.

Ethnographic descriptions suggest that women spent more time on agricultural tasks in precolonial times than they did in 1952, perhaps because the fields were closer to town, or even within the city itself. However, recent studies challenge these data concerning women's contribution to farm work. Afonja reports that in 1986 *all* women in the cocoa growing areas near Ife "worked regularly on their husband's farm planting, weeding, harvesting, and carrying the harvests during the peak of production. Less than 1 percent had personal access to land, but the majority did not classify themselves as farmers, in spite of their heavy labor input" (1990, 207). Apparently women consider their farm work as part of their marriage contract; their income is derived from trading.

Women Traders

Yoruba women are renowned for their trading activities, both in urban markets and as intermediaries between urban and rural areas (Trager 1981). As early as the fifteenth century, Yoruba women were observed participating in long-distance trade, but the majority of women traded locally or produced crafts or food for sale (Afonja 1981). Much Western literature celebrated the business acumen of the autonomous West African woman trader.

In contrast, Afonja argues that this apparent autonomy masks the continued subordination of Yoruba women in the domestic domain. Women are typically not remunerated for work on their husbands' farms, yet they are expected to pay for most (if not all) food and other basic needs for themselves and their children.[3] Consequently, they must pour their profits from petty trading into household expenses and school fees rather than into their enterprises. Lack of working capital limits the ability of street food vendors to invest in improved food handling or more sanitary establishments. The need for women to earn a separate income makes for a very long workday, whether they alternate farm and market work or concentrate on their entrepreneurial activities. Constrained for time, women frequently buy whole meals or portions of meals to feed themselves and their families.

Street food selling was observed in the region as early as 1857; foods were sometimes left unattended along the roadside "with a mark to indicate the worth of the wares" (Akinyele 1989, 2). In the 1930s, a detailed study was made of traditional Yoruba foods, most of which were available for purchase on the street (Bascom 1951). Anthropologists have speculated that this widespread availability of cooked foods reflects the tensions of polygynous marriages: mothers were afraid to allow their co-wives to feed their children. When the mother could not prepare a meal, a street food seller who sold to the public was preferable and safer than a co-wife (Mabogunje 1958). This view contrasts with a portrayal of the Yoruba polygynous households as sites where "mutual assistance was common among women, interweaving the generations, and networks were dense" (Pearce 1992, 5).

Whatever the historic or cultural reasons for women becoming entrepreneurs, women dominate the street food trade throughout southern Nigeria, particularly among the Yoruba. Street food vendors cluster along the streets leading to the marketplaces where agricultural products and cloth are sold, or along major highways.

FIGURE 7.1   The old *buka* behind the science buildings is still a favorite of Owolowo students. The only water source is this tap from university lines.

Many vendors rent or build stalls called *buka*; these structures, whether constructed of unpainted rough boards or plywood or vividly decorated log planks, all provide a covered area with tables and chairs where the vendors serve their customers. During the economic expansion in the 1970s, mobile vans serving hot meals and run by men appeared in several major urban centers; four were noted in Ife during the study (Pearce et al. 1988). Like restaurants, the vans serve more expensive food than vendors do, and so do not yet offer serious competition to the *buka*.

Street Foods in Ife

During the construction of the university, vendors moved out from the town to feed the workers and erected a colony of *buka* on the campus adjacent to the biology complex. When the students arrived, they also patronized these *buka* for their cheap traditional foods. The *buka* are built in two rows up a steep hill; rain has carved a deep wash between them, making access difficult even in the dry season. One nearby pump, provided by the university, provides the only access to water for the dozen or more *buka* clustered here (Figure 7.1).

After the vice chancellor of the university observed students patronizing these street food vendors, he decided to create a more suitable eating area where each *buka* would be supplied with water and electricity. This improved *bukateria* was erected at

FIGURE 7.2   Students in Owolowo University in Ile-Ife frequent the *bukateria*. Note the water faucet for washing hands is blocked by cases of soft drinks.

the end of a campus road that runs past the student hostels. Walking from campus, students pass through a cement arch and past a security guard to reach the spacious arrangement of two long rows of *buka*. Constructed of cement with a tin roof, a covered walkway shelters customers from sun or rain. The individual stalls are separated from the walk by low walls, allowing the eating area to remain open to the breezes. Each stall is supplied with an interior sink for washing hands in the eating area; behind a serving counter is a small covered cooking space. Spilling out onto a rear concrete strip behind the stalls are piles of firewood, spices drying on wooden panels, and cooking pots being washed or dried. Almost every stall supplements the small kitchen area by setting out pots to cook on charcoal braziers or over firewood in this rear area.

The two rows of *buka* face a well-landscaped and terraced green, in the center of which is a round open pavilion where male students gather in the evening to talk and drink after eating; women students generally buy food and take it back to their rooms to eat. The food is reputed to be "gourmet" compared to the traditional *buka* settlement. Together the two *bukaterias* feed a majority of the students, who prefer the variety, convenience, and low cost of street foods to the university's dining room fare (Figure 7.2). By 1994, all but one or two of the university dining rooms had been closed; students reported at the time that eating in the hostel was three to four times more expensive.

Boli and Dada
Plantains Baked or Fried

Boli

Trim ends of four large green plantains. Slit carefully and free plantain from skin; then replace in skin for steaming over coals or in the oven. Boli is cooked when the skin changes color and the fruit shrinks a little. Serve with roasted peanuts.

Dada

Remove the skin carefully by cutting plantain lengthwise. Cut plantain into even slices. Heat oil in a deep pot, and when the oil has just begun to smoke, lower slices into the oil slowly, to maintain the temperature. After 2 minutes, reduce the heat and continue to fry until light brown. Remove and drain. Serve hot or cold.

Moyin-Moyin
Steamed Black-eyed Pea / Cowpea Paste

1 cup black-eyed peas / cowpeas, dried	1 teaspoon cayenne
2 tablespoons chopped onion	1 teaspoon fresh ginger, chopped
2 tablespoons palm or peanut oil	1 egg, beaten (optional)

Prepare paste from 1 cup dried black-eyed peas or cowpeas. Soak peas in water for about 10 minutes to remove skins. Drain, and blend or grind into a smooth paste; if a blender is used, add up to 1/3 cup water as needed. Then beat with a whisk or electric mixer until light and fluffy. Add onion, oil, seasoning, and egg.

Wrap seasoned paste in leaves or pour into molds, three-quarters full. Steam, tightly covered, for 60 minutes. Meat or fish such as crayfish, corned beef, chopped ham or liver, is often added to the seasoned paste before steaming. Moyin-moyin is traditionally served with ogi (cornmeal porridge) or eko (cornmeal loaf).

Choices of Foods to Eat

The study recorded 74 separate combinations of foods for sale on the streets of Ife: 39 types or combinations of a starchy base, nine varieties of meat or fish, six different stews or sauces, and 20 foods classified as snacks but which, in combination, were often considered a meal.[4] The most popular meals served by street food vendors consist of one form of gruel or dough served under a sauce or stew of vegetables; meat or fish, and sometimes chicken, might also be added. One of the attractions of buying from street vendors is that each customer can select, according to taste and available cash, a variety of sauces and meats, each purchased in individual and inexpensive portions wrapped in leaves or paper (Pearce 1984; Kujore 1985).

The starchy base comes from tubers, legumes, or corn, processed in an astonishing variety of ways. Yams are boiled or mashed as *iyan*, while yam flour is cooked into porridge or the doughy local specialty *amala*. Treating and producing cassava flour is particularly time-consuming; it is served as porridge or as dough called *eba*. Corn (maize) is boiled or roasted; corn meal is served hot as a breakfast porridge (*ogi*) or cooked into a white gelatinous loaf called *eko*. Beans of several types, including cowpeas, are steamed in banana leaves for *moyin-moyin*, made into fritters (*akara*) or mixed with rice or corn. Even plantains are reduced to a flour and used to make a form of *amala*; more often they are either roasted (*boli*) or deep-fried—both green (*ipekere*) and ripe (*dodo*)—and eaten as a snack. Recently, bread has become a major staple, and it is usually eaten alone with tea or combined with more traditional starches and sauces.

Vegetable sauces give flavor to the starch base. Six styles were commonly served; one favorite uses okra with seasonings similar to Creole cooking in Louisiana. Meats most often served include beef from the northern part of the country; snails; frozen, dried, or smoked fish; or animal skin. Also available are wild bushmeat and chicken.

Puff-puff, a sort of donut, is the most popular snack; but biscuits and cake are favorites on campus. Melon seeds, peanuts, and deep-fried pastry are widely consumed. Seasonal fruits are more popular in the traditional neighborhoods than elsewhere.

Training Vendors

In order to claim space in the *bukateria*, vendors are required to hold a certificate showing they have completed a two-week-long course in nutrition and food handling taught by the nursing services in Oyo state and supervised on campus by members of the department of nursing, including Olufemi Kujore, who became the project leader for the Street Food Project study in Ife. Vendors in the traditional *buka* area also needed the certificate to sell on the schoolgrounds. City vendors, seeking the legitimacy such a certificate confers, had begun to ask for a course as well. Because customers had more trust in vendors with the certificate, many establishments, such as banks, had begun to require vendors to take the course if they wished to sell within the company compound.

In theory, street food vendors are supposed to be regularly monitored by a health inspector. The colonial government first instituted street food inspections in 1917. The inspection ordinance emphasized food safety and allowed for the analysis of any food that customers or government officers thought might be contaminated. In 1957 the powers of inspection and control of street foods were specifically lodged in government health services; in addition, the venue was expanded to include the place of preparation. However, the numbers of public health inspectors did not expand as quickly as the population in most cities during the 1960s and 1970s; for this reason, "virtually no rigorous inspection of the premises of street food vendors" took place (Akinyele 1987, 4). Uncovered food, unsanitary practices, and sick or diseased employees increased the dangers of epidemics, such as a deadly 1972 cholera epidemic in Ibadan (Akinyele 1987).

In 1979 Kujore initiated a study of 120 children in primary grades in Ile-Ife to assess the importance of street foods to children's nutrition. The results were startling: 96% of the children bought breakfast daily; further, 76% of the children purchased two meals a day on a regular basis. A larger study of 780 students done in 1984 confirmed the importance of street foods in children's nutrition: 60% bought breakfast, 76% lunch, and 87% dinner! Concerned with the health risks that unsanitary food might pose to children because few of the town vendors had health certificates, Kujore sought a way to offer training to the market vendors.

Meanwhile, EPOC was searching for a Street Food Project site in West Africa; they contracted with Lillian Trager to visit major Nigerian universities and discuss the project during her 1983 field trip to the country. Trager found widespread interest in studying street food vendors but some hesitation about linking to action projects. Encouraged by Trager, Kujore and her colleagues at Ife submitted a proposal to the Ford Foundation in Lagos that combined both research and action. Trager returned in 1984 as EPOC's consultant to the project; during her subsequent tenure as project officer in the Ford-Lagos office, she approved a second project to develop a model training program for market vendors.

The Ife Street Foods Project

Medical sociologist Tola O. Pearce of the department of sociology and anthropology and V. Aina Agboh of the department of community health and nutrition joined Olufemi Kujore to carry out the study. From the beginning in October 1983, the team planned to utilize the study data to refine their training model for vendors and then to conduct sessions for vendors in Ile-Ife and perhaps also in the larger neighboring city of Ilesha. All public hospitals in both cities are part of the University of Ife Teaching Hospital, and the two cities form the centers of the Ife-Ilesha Zonal Health Board.

The team felt that university students might not be appropriate for interviewing vendors given the social distance between the two groups. Therefore, they recruited as interviewers seven young women who had not yet been accepted into post–secondary school training programs and were waiting to retake entrance examinations. This decision caused problems during the project: attrition rates were high, and the women needed considerable supervision because they were untrained in interview techniques.

The worsening economic situation in the country affected both the vendors and the study itself. Some vendors included in the census had ceased operation by November 1984. Others prepared less food as ingredient prices rose and they were forced to spend more time buying smaller quantities of supplies. Kujore reported that the chemical and microbiological analyses could not be carried out in a timely fashion because the requisite reagents were unavailable at the time in Nigeria.[5]

The new government of Major General Muhammadu Buhari took power through a miliary coup on December 31, 1983. Known as the "iron man," Buhari launched his regime by proclaiming a War against Indiscipline (Street Trading and Illegal Market [Prohibition] Edict 1/84).[6] Supporting the campaign, a local television station in Ibadan ran a film in March 1984 documenting the polluted conditions characteristic of *buka* in the city. Kujore wrote that the documentary tallied closely with what had been observed in Ife. The film showed heaps of refuse, open latrines, dirty gutters, and flies galore. Clothing of the sellers was dirty, as were utensils used for cooking. Crockery and cutlery were left unwashed for long periods of time; when they were washed, dirty water was used. Street food sellers either let their waste water run into the streets or threw it into an open gutter (Kujore et al. 1985).

In July 1984, the army and police implemented an old law forbidding structures within a set distance from the middle of federal highways, and they began demolishing *buka* and stalls around the country. In Ife, the local authorities razed all structures built too close to the three highways both in the town and on the outskirts (Pearce et al. 1988; Trager 1992). The local newspaper, the *Daily Times*, supported the action in an editorial on November 13, 1984, entitled "Proper Care for Food:" "Although flies, mosquitoes, and rats may spread the diseases that are detrimental to public health, perhaps the most serious threat to peoples' well-being is the unhealthy condition under which food is sold in this country."

Project interviewers searched for those vendors whose *buka* had been destroyed; they were able to find and interview all 65 of the displaced entrepreneurs soon after the "road clearance" (Kujore et al. 1985/7). Eighty percent of the demolished *buka* were along the highways leading out of town: 23 along the Ife-Ibadan highway, 17 along the Ife-Ondo road, and 12 along the Ife-Ilesha road. The other *buka* had been set up within the town, seven on the road to Ondo and six on the road to Ilesha. All but one of the women continued in the trade in some fashion, either by hawking goods or by serving meals in front of schools or from their own compounds. All experienced loss of profits; 58 of them, or 90%, said they only made half their usual profits, a serious problem, since all said food selling was their only source of income. A third of the sellers said their customers refused to eat in the open and so went elsewhere; another third lost customers because some had not yet found the vendor's new location or had decided it was too distant. Five women said that the mechanics they had fed regularly had also had their sheds demolished. The campaign not only affected the street food sellers and their customers but also had ripple effects on women traders in the market because the vendors bought fewer supplies. It also decreased employment of assistants in the larger street food enterprises: three-quarters of the group employed assistants before the raid, but only one-quarter could afford to do so afterward. With carefully chosen words, the team concluded: "Whilst one recognizes and appreciates the government's efforts in promoting environmental sanitation, some information has emerged from the study which makes it necessary to call the attention of policy makers to the wider issue of the welfare of the citizens" (p. 14).

Final Seminars

Results from the study were presented in separate seminars in both Ife[7] and Ilesha to faculty members and health personnel from both the university and from the teaching hospital. The broad implications of the study encouraged attendance by representatives from the Ministries of Health, Trade and Industries, Works, Social Welfare, and Local Government. The seminar helped create a group of sympathetic officials who appreciated the vendors' perspectives and helped moderate further attempts at street cleaning.

The dean of the faculty of health sciences, Professor Femi Soyinka, opened the Ife seminar, identifying with the vendors:

> "Personally, many years ago I was actively a street food vendor. I sold akara and puff-puff to augment my parents' income as they took care of our schooling and feeding. I also patronized street food vendors for a period of ten years while in primary and secondary schools. Street food vending and consumption are a way of life in the Nigerian community, and many of us have been sustained by both activities. However, thousands have also died through street food vending or the consumption of street foods. . . . We know that the street food is a way of life for us. But rather than say "Do away with them" we have a group of people who now would tell us how best we can utilize them. (Kujore et al. 1985, 1).

Government versus the Street Vendors

Government raids continued, though with less frequency, after then Major General Ibrahim Babangida overthrew Buhari in August 1985 and headed the government until 1993. Elimination of street sellers from one area only pushed them to another; clearly the surge of vendors in urban areas throughout the country required some form of more positive response. The spiraling numbers of street vendors was directly related to the extremely high rates of population increase and rapid urbanization in the country since independence in 1960. The total population of Nigeria in 1950 was only 32 million; by the end of the century the population is projected at about 132

FIGURE 7.3   Street food vendors cooking chicken to serve with *akara* in the government complex in Lagos. High inflation encourages more middle-class people to eat street foods.

million, a four-fold increase in half a century! Although the most recent census of 1991 gives the official total as 88.5 million, the United Nations uses an estimate of 109 million. The percentage of persons living in urban centers with over 750,000 people was not quite 4% in 1963; the number had risen to 9.3% by 1995. Lagos is the commercial center of the country and was the capital until 1991, when the new capital of Abuja was sufficiently completed to begin moving government agencies inland. Lagos is today the largest city with 1.10 million residents; it surpassed Ibadan only in 1973. Migrants crowd into the older sections of town; today 48% of the population of Lagos State lives on Lagos Island, which is only 2% of the area of the state (Adalemo 1994). Ibadan, with a current population of 1.06 million, remains the largest indigenous—as opposed to colonial—city in all West Africa; densities reach 3,245 persons per square kilometer in the traditional sections of town (Akinyele 1991). Both cities are hampered by inadequate transportation systems that connect the new suburban areas to the commercial centers where middle-class women and men work. Long hours of commuting leave little time to cook, which contributes to the huge demand for inexpensive, convenient food near schools and workplaces (Figure 7.3).

Extravagant government spending and falling oil prices led to an economic downturn in the 1980s; reduction of government spending and the devaluation of the currency propelled even more people to the cities to eke out a living, often selling on the street. A UNICEF study found that 52% of household income in Nigeria was spent on food between 1980 and 1985 (UNICEF 1991). The subsequent imposition of a Structural Adjustment Program in 1986 "increased the number of consumers of street foods including school children, private and public sector workers, traders, and many families. . . . Changes in the economic situation of many people . . . resulted in a reduction of the number of meals consumed daily from three to two or only once. It was thus cheaper for many families to purchase street foods than prepare similar dishes at home" (Akinyele 1991, 1).

The proliferation of street vending, particularly in Lagos, has created problems the local authorities could hardly ignore. Haphazardly constructed shops and stalls were so ubiquitous before the demolitions that they often blocked the entrances to modern commercial buildings. Shacks also crammed into spaces under the freeways that circle the islands on which Lagos is built. *The Guardian* (6 November 1983) reported on the newest form of traffic congestion, fast food vans: "Often in convoys, [they] attract smartly dressed ladies in frocks and suits, trendy clothed men in two and three piece suits, who move about in the sweltering Lagos heat clutching fast food packs of different sizes and colours." A restaurant owner complained: "Hardly can our customers move along the sidewalks without bumping into the hawkers or people with greasy hands. I mean those people who eat fast foods."

As the temporary shops were removed and hawkers' carts destroyed, the vendors invaded the highways, selling goods in the midst of the automobiles as they inch along in the daily traffic jams. Vendors would often hop on the slowly moving buses and harangue the passengers. School-aged children as well as adults converge on cars at stoplights, selling everything from candy to razors, sodas to neckties, to music tapes and newspapers. After a number of children were killed while vending in traffic in 1986–87, the government responded with edicts imposing fines on both vendors and motorists (Adalemo 1994). But of course the vending continues.

During Babangida's rule vendors began to protest the raids. In 1985 a raid at a Lagos bus stop resulted in the destruction of several government vehicles during the arrest of 150 vendors (Trager 1992). In Oshodi in April 1988, the market women staged a traditional form of protest by removing their blouses and wrappers in a confrontation with army and police (Adalemo 1994). Protest marches were reported in several states; a market vendors' association in Lagos State actually ran an advertisement in a major newspaper complaining to the governor about the treatment of the vendors (Trager 1992).

Media in the country have generally supported the restrictions on street food vendors, but now have begun to question the abuses associated with this policy. An editorial in *The Guardian* (12 March 1994) notes that measures have helped "bring sanity and restore acceptable standards of normalcy in society." The editorial agrees that traditional preferences for open markets must be checked in the city. "But what cannot be justified is that those charged with enforcing order often make it their business to loot the wares of these traders." Lillian Trager observes that the policies against street vendors produce not only these private spoils but also generate considerable revenue for local governments (1992).

In the Lagos markets the traders have recently initiated an early warning system to minimize the effect of police raids. Shopkeepers on the periphery warn traders deeper in the market whenever army or police invasions are imminent. Such advance notice gives most sellers time to remove or hide their goods and so minimize their losses. In some cases the market associations help fund the replacement of inventory lost by the more vulnerable shops. During the election campaigns and interim governments of 1993, enforcement was minimal; after the military took over under General Sani Abacha, however, control was reasserted and demolition of shops was renewed.

Nigerian policy toward street food vendors exemplifies the contradictory attitudes of government officials toward the activity. On the one hand, the army and police continue to engage in cleaning the streets of all vendors; on the other hand, the government proclaims its support of self-employment as part of private enterprise (Trager 1992). Caught between these conflicting approaches of support and removal, the vendors find their position remains precarious; not surprisingly, this insecurity makes them unwilling to invest in new stalls or equipment that would improve their food-handling practices. Sympathetic observers note that the unsanitary practices generally reflect community practices and that the lack of available water and refuse collection is hardly the fault of the vendors. In Ife, Ibadan, and Lagos, groups with very different approaches are trying to work both with government and vendors to reach some sort of accommodation.

Helping Street Food Vendors in Ife, Ibadan, and Lagos

The impetus to work with street vendors in both Ife and Ibadan came from university teachers who had long been concerned with the safety and nutritional value of the foods sold. In Ife, Olufemi Kujore approached the problem with the eye of a public health nurse determined to train vendors in improved food-handling practices; Tola Pearce, with her focus on medical sociology, probed their health practices. Isaac Olaolu Akinyele from the department of human nutrition at the University of Ibadan had also been involved in training vendors before the government crackdown began; he decided that data collection using the EPOC model would provide him with better information for planning fundamental changes in the street food trade. Recognizing that demolition only exacerbated the situation, these scholars used their contacts with the vendors and with local government officials to search for alternative solutions.

In Lagos, the politically charged atmosphere had created a confrontational situation between street vendors and the government; any search for alternatives to the government's demolition approach required more immediate policy dialogue than scholarly research. Clara Osinulu, director of the African American Institute in Nigeria, designed two complementary projects that would involve a wide range of scholars and activists in collecting information and convening a policy forum. The impact of these three programs are analyzed next.

Ife: Health and Training

Environmental sanitation was shown to be a critical problem that affected the cleanliness of food in the Ife Street Food Project. Olufemi Kujore and Tola Pearce sought funds from the Ford Foundation for a second phase of the Street Foods Project that would investigate health practices of all types of market women regarding their families, their community, and themselves as they are "faced with choices of both indigenous and western patterns of health behavior" (Kujore and Pearce 1992, 2).[8] The twin objectives of the study were, first, to design and test a comprehensive training program for street food vendors, and, second, to draw up recommendations for local government on ways to improve primary health services for all market sellers.[9] In return for participating in the study and training, the women vendors in the Odo-Ogbe market in Ife expected help in prodding the government to improve the market conditions. They understood clearly the need for public toilets, piped water, regular refuse collection, and paved pathways in the markets; without such services, creating a cleaner environment was virtually impossible. The vendors also asked for a health clinic: health costs for their families and themselves was their third spending priority after food and enterprise costs. Kujore was actually able to secure funding for a health clinic in the market from local donations through the Ife chapter of Soroptomist International; continued economic difficulties in the country undercut this charitable effort. Also responding to Kujore's entreaties, the local government paved the main path in the market (Kujore 1991).

The model week-long training program for street food vendors was tested on three successive groups, for a total of 64 women. To assess the usefulness of the training, both the sanitary practices at the place of business and the vendor's attitudes toward health-related issues were investigated before and after the training. Further, each woman was given a medical examination. None had previously had one, although the 1957 Foodstuffs Ordinance clearly states that no one with infectious diseases shall be employed in food selling (Akinyele 1987). In fact, the stool examinations found that 62% of the women had one or more of six types of parasites that cause worms or diarrhea; all are easily transmitted when hand washing is inadequate. The strain of providing for their families and keeping their enterprises going during the time of economic instability and government harassment was having an impact on women's health as well: of the vendors tested, 42% had high blood pressure; one person's reading was serious enough that it led to hospitalization (Kujore 1991, Pearce 1992).

To add value to the training program, certificates were awarded to the women during an impressive graduation ceremony in December 1991. Dignitaries from local government and the university attended, along with nurses from the primary health centers in the city and active local citizens. Program graduates used a specially designed demonstration *buka*, designed and built for the training program, to prepare *akara* from recipes learned during the training. Such ceremonies are essential to the ongoing success of new activities by "welding together . . . different groups of people, both in the Ife township and the University, who have either personal or official interest in the health and economic dimensions of food vending" (Kujore 1992, 7).

In recognition of her dedicated efforts to help market women, Olufemi Kujore was appointed to the Health Committee of the Oranmiyan Local Government Council in Ife (Pearce et al. 1988). Her training program was adopted by the municipality and was taught to nearly 100 vendors over the following year under the supervision of G. A. Awotidebe, public health coordinator in Ife. Due to the instability of the government during much of 1993, no senior officer was appointed to head the council and therefore no graduation ceremony could be held (Awotidebe interview, 11 January 1994).

Pearce analyzed the data on the Odo-Ogbe market women for information on how the women cope with their family responsibilities in the face of reduced earnings. She argues that in Nigeria, as elsewhere around the world, the stress of structural adjustment hits women hardest. While in many countries the reduction of governmental social services forces women to undertake new duties, Pearce finds the breakdown of traditional household support networks that formerly provided a cushion for mothers is creating similar pressures. Over half of the families studied lived in nuclear households, split evenly between polygynous and monogamous marriages; 21% were households headed by women. Only 4% of the market women lived in a traditional polygynous family compound. Nonetheless, the custom of fostering children within kinship networks continues (1992). In the original street food study, 85% of the mature women had children from other families living with them; of these women, two-thirds cared for only one extra child, but one-fifth took care of two to four children while 12% had two to seven extra children to feed (Kujore 1984).

Most women were having problems paying school fees for their children; whereas a few husbands increased their assistance in paying fees, others reduced this support to buy basic food items. Over half the sample (52%) faced difficulties in getting enough food for the families, even though most traded in raw or cooked foods. The seriousness of this problem is reflected in a report issued in 1990 by the Ife-Central Local Government that recorded increased evidence of widespread malnutrition. Clinics note the increase in underweight babies: "On the average 30% of the children die before the age of five" (Pearce 1992, 16).

Another major problem faced by these women entrepreneurs was transportation: fares locally had tripled in the previous three years, and the number of vans and trucks still running diminished in response to higher prices for fuel and replacement parts (Pearce 1992). The women indicated that they used their available money "on food, their business, health activities, family functions,[10] and school fees, in that order" (Kujore and Pearce 1992, 12).

Ibadan: Training and Organizing

Isaac Akinyele says his interest in street food vendors was sparked by his love for eating on the street and by his concern that the food was not very clean. In 1982 he initiated a pilot program to train 54 women street food vendors in health education, in cooperation with the health department of the Ibadan municipal government. As a result of a proposal to expand the training program that he submitted to the Food and Agricultural Organization (FAO), Akinyele was invited to Rome to discuss the idea and to read materials in the FAO library. Staff of the Food Quality and Consumer Protection Group directed him to the first two EPOC street food studies on the Philippines and on Senegal as a possible model for his design (Akinyele interview 11 January 1994). Using EPOC's definition and the terminology of "street foods," Akinyele subsequently studied the "characteristics of food vendors and consumers" in Ibadan in 1986 with FAO funding; in 1991 he carried out a comparative study in Nigeria's three largest cities: repeating Ibadan and adding Lagos and Kaduna. The comparisons among the three towns, when added to the Ife data, provide a unique and thorough picture of street food trade in Nigeria and provide indicators of how it might change.

For example, Akinyele's studies provide details on the varieties of shops the vendors rent or own. Among the permanent vendors, most sell in a fixed place; 68% in Ibadan, 79% in Lagos, and 87% in Kaduna pay rent. Such data would suggest that a majority of vendors in these large cities have forsaken the casual, self-built *buka* for more complex structures. The Oyo state government built a concrete *bukateria* for vendors servicing the state secretariat that, like the lavish structure on the Awolowo University campus, is probably too expensive for wide-scale replication. A less elaborate *bukateria* was built from plywood and bamboo on the campus of the University of Ibadan. Shaped like an arrow, *buka* lined all sides and faced inward toward an open space; a gate and a security guard protected both entrepreneur and customer. This construction is still too expensive for most vendors to build, even as a collective. Rental fees of *bukateria* owned by the university or government may be subsidized, but owners of the other rental stalls presumably build them for investment and charge market rates. Akinyele is promoting more modest food centers that can be self-built by organizations of vendors who would be able to secure credit for construction costs (Interview 11 January 1994).

These data, plus information on the availability of fuel, water, and refuse services, both at home and at the place of business, increase our understanding of the conditions under which food is prepared. The scope and methodology of these studies, as well as data on vendor characteristics and income, closely resemble the EPOC studies; salient findings that expand or challenge previous conclusions are included in the analytical sections in Part II.

While supervising these studies, Akinyele continued to conduct training programs. Instruction was given for six hours twice a week for four weeks; certificates of completion were awarded the vendors to encourage their attendance. Between 1982 and 1986, some 3,184 women and five men were trained; by then the course had become so popular that some 1,000 women would regularly apply for the 250 places available each time the course was offered. Akinyele was delighted when his training graduates formed the Ibadan Women Food Vendors Association in July 1985, because such an organization provides "a forum for the continued re-education of the vendors. It also constitutes a unit that can be recognized by government . . . for community health development. The women can at the same time work cohesively and supportively to enhance their individual and collective growth in the business of food vending" (Akinyele 1987, 9).

All trainees receive a medical examination. Among the 1,237 trained in the second half of 1986, four women were diagnosed with tuberculosis and advised to accept treatment before resuming their vending (Akinyele 1987). A higher percentage of the women were found to have parasitic infection than in the Ife study, 83% versus 62%, but there was a much lower incidence of hypertension, 17% versus 42%. The increased stress in the later Ife study, for which data were collected between September 1988 and March 1989, may reflect the worsening economic conditions in the country.

With encouragement from FAO, Akinyele expanded his training efforts to the rest of Nigeria, presenting a week-long program for government officials at the state and municipal levels, all of whom happened to be women (Akinyele 1989). He convened the workshop and has conducted subsequent research through Food Basket Foundation International (FBFI), a development NGO that he had set up outside the university to facilitate working with the vendors.[11] Having an NGO encourages faculty and townspeople to volunteer their services for the various vendor projects and also simplifies accounting procedures with FAO or other foreign donors.

At the conclusion of the national training program, Akinyele decided that he was focusing too much on the problems of vendors and not enough on the solutions. Since then he began to concentrate on working with the Ibadan vendors (Interview 11 January 1994). In 1992–93 he initiated what he calls "action training" for municipal environmental health officers by including them in a new form of training for vendors. Faced with increasing difficulty in getting funding for training, Akinyele is now working with representatives from area associations. This method of training is less costly since it relies on trained members to voluntarily provide information from the course to other members of their groups.

Getting the associations involved has required attention to the variety of existing market associations. For years there has been one food association for all of Ibadan. Originally set up for social support, the organization is controlled at the center by leadership, invariably male, selected at an annual meeting. In 1990 the city was divided into five local government areas, but Akinyele finds these areas still too large to provide members with a sense of community. He is encouraging the vendors to set up ward units so that there can be more real participation by the ordinary members.

Akinyele believes that many problems of both the vendors and the government will be more easily addressed through collective action: creating designs for new *bukateria* and obtaining credit to build them; providing yearly medical examinations; offering training in business practices and health aspects of the enterprise; and warning against adulteration of foods. He would like to see the vendor groups, as well as consumer groups that ought to be created, involved in developing regulations for street vendors. Akinyele also expects the vendor groups to assist in enforcement among their own members.

Finally, Akinyele urges the provision of child care for vendors. Not only do children distract the vendor when cooking, often leading to unsafe food handling, but also young children are themselves a source of contamination "since the women normally took care of the mucus, faeces, and urine passed by these children in the same environment where the foods are prepared and served" (Akinyele 1987, 44). In conclusion, Akinyele urges the government at both federal and state levels to "be more concerned with the vital but uncoordinated sector of the economy" and to support it (1991, 96).

Lagos: Influencing Policy

While local government policy toward vendors appears to have softened from confrontation to cooperation in Ibadan and Ife, in Lagos, where congestion problems are far more severe, the policy remained punitive. Additional bridges and traffic controls have eased the situation, but chaos is a daily part of living in Lagos. Vendors evicted from entrances to commercial buildings or the restriction on hawking among cars on the elevated highways simply relocated to the already crowded city markets and surrounding streets. The Better Life Movement, led by Maryam Babangida, wife of the former president, sponsored the introduction of weekend and night markets; although widely patronized, these did little to relieve daytime congestion in the market areas.

The conflict between government and vendors was becoming increasingly polarized as the economy worsened and the poor became more desperate, even as the government task forces confiscated vendor supplies for their own purpose. Noting that the targets of harassment were often women, Clara Osinulu proposed that the African American Institute sponsor a forum to examine all sides of the conflict and to produce a policy paper. In 1988 she took the idea to Lillian Trager, then a program officer at the Ford Foundation, who enthusiastically endorsed it as a logical expansion of the Ife street food action research. Two distinct projects emerged from these discussions: the first produced recommendations for the government based on hearings and field studies of street and market vendors generally; the second focused on women's market organizations.

A "working group on urban regulatory policy towards informal sector employment" was set up under Ayinde Adalemo, a geography professor at the University of Lagos, to design studies and to plan public hearings with everyone from magistrates to vendors. Members were men and women drawn both from the university and from Lagos professional circles and included a lawyer, a city planner, and a journalist. According to Adalemo, the heart of the problem seemed to be that although street vendors embody the ideal of rugged independence, their aggressive selling methods run counter to the Nigerian military government's efforts to maintain smooth traffic flow, uncluttered walkways, and a healthy urban environment. The goal of the working group was to create "a machinery or economic system which will offer a reasonable solution . . . with an African character" to this conflict (Interview in Lagos 13 January 1994).

The working group conducted a survey of the 1,148 street vendors in Lagos State located in alleys or garages, along streets, on street corners, under expressways, and around markets. Most were street food sellers, but others sold unprocessed foods, non-food durables, and non-food non-durables such as clothing. Eighty-nine percent of those interviewed were self-employed; most had been in business between two and six years, and 60% were Yoruba from out of state. The findings reflected a great range of income and investment since food vending, processed or not, usually has a lower profit margin than dry goods and manufactured products: about half of all vendors made less than 10 naira per day. Still, an income of 10 naira per day was comparable to the legal minimum monthly wage, even after it was increased from 150 naira per month to 250 naira in January 1990. Fascinating data resulted from questions about commuting: half take the bus, while a third walk to work; distances are less important than time: walking might take 20 minutes, but some bus trips took an hour each way (Adalemo et al. 1994).

As in many countries, commerce is often divided along both ethnic and gender lines: Yoruba women dominate the food sectors; Igbo men sell electronics and spare parts; Hausa men deal in textiles, meat, beans, oil, and foreign exchange. Both women and men trade in used clothing and shoes south of the Niger; north of the river such commodities are reserved for male enterprise. These specialties were reflected in the public hearings that AAI held to allow representatives of vendor's organizations to comment on the working group recommendations: men represented associations for sellers of shoes, used clothing, and electronics, whereas Yoruba women spoke for food vendors.

Market areas were the focus of group's recommendations, since markets are built by local government, which then rents out the stalls. The studies documented two recurrent problems: the tendency of stall owners to treat rental rights as an asset that can be inherited or sold; and the penchant of rent collectors to steal the rents. Also, stall owners apparently often instigate raids against the street vendors squatting at the entrances of the markets or in front of their stalls, who, because they pay no rent, tend to sell at lower prices. Covered markets were criticized as hot and confining, especially those made with concrete; most women preferred open areas. Given these observations, the group recommended building more markets and providing adequate parking space for customers. Markets should all be surrounded by a wall but not totally enclosed; interior open spaces along the walls should be rented to those who dislike selling from stalls. The walls would exclude the squatter seller and presumably reduce conflicts with renters. Walls would allow closing of the markets at six o'clock unless the area is lighted, in which case the closing time could be eight o'clock. The report also suggests that vendors infringing on regulations should not both be fined and have goods confiscated, and it proposes that community service might be considered in lieu of fines. Finally, the report urges discussions between government and vendor organizations to negotiate the implementation these recommendations (Adalemo et al. 1994).

Given this report's emphasis on vendor associations, along with the realization that women's groups seemed less well organized than men's, the second study focused on women's groups in several major markets. This study found that existing market organizations conform to traditional forms: they are based on commodity and area; their activities address the personal, by providing social interactions, emergency funds, and conflict resolution, and also the economic, by serving as the unit for revolving savings or *esusu*, and by agreeing on prices to avoid immoderate competition. Market organizations hire someone to keep the market clean, especially the toilet; vendors each pay a fee for this service that is collected daily by a man, because women assume robbers would be less likely to steal from a male (Osinulu interview in Lagos 14 January 1994).

Clara Osinulu, who supervised the project, hopes that the study will result in stronger organizations capable of negotiating with local government. In common with all the vendors, women's organizations need to press for improved market infrastructure and services. But women vendors also need child care centers in the markets to provide better care for their children. To improve their profits, Osinulu hopes that these organizations can take on stronger economic functions such as group purchase of commodities. However, Osinulu emphasized that these organizations exist only in the markets, not on the streets, and so do not address the problems of Lagos street vendors (Interview in Lagos 14 January 1994).

Supporting Vendors

These efforts in Ife, Ibadan, and Lagos have their roots in the original EPOC Street Food Project. By documenting the contributions of street food vendors in providing food for the general public and in stimulating income throughout the economy, EPOC legitimized action research projects with the donor community. Staff at FAO encouraged Akinyele to expand his training programs to consider the lives and needs of the vendors themselves. When Kujore and Pearce in Ife wished to include all women market vendors in their health survey, and when Osinulu suggested studying the all street vendors in Lagos, Trager at the Ford Foundation in Lagos supported the projects.

The research and recommended actions that flow from these projects take account of the diversity of vendors and emphasize how policies affect different categories of vendors differently. Food vendors are a distinct category because of the health and sanitary implications of their products. Reports from all three cities call for improved market infrastructure from paved walkways to public toilets, and for improved water supply, garbage removal, and market cleaning. Child care was justified on both health and developmental grounds. Recommendations went further in Lagos, and called for enlarging and improving existing markets and for building new markets better adapted to the climate and vendors' needs.

Vendor organizations were considered essential by Adalemo and Osinulu to ensure that the views of the vendors will be represented to local authorities and that vendors will accept negotiated decisions. Similarly, in Ibadan, solutions proffered by Akinyele emphasize more hygienic food centers, organized and self-policed by local vendor organizations. The present absence of market associations in Ife are probably a reflection of economic hardship; sporadic efforts to form them need to be strengthened. These recommendations chart a course for local action regarding vendors with fixed premises.

More difficult to solve are problems related to mobile and semi-itinerant vendors, who are more difficult to organize and regulate. Mobile sellers can move away quickly, while the roadside sellers have usually made a smaller investment in their business and so have less to lose by flouting regulations. In particular, the children rushing through Lagos traffic selling goods on commission are a perplexing problem, as they respond to poverty and seek excitement by challenging police and dodging automobiles.

Approaches to studying and working with the vendors varied across the three cities, reflecting the size and socioeconomic characteristics of each urban center, as well as the interests of the leadership involved in the projects. In Ife and Ibadan the original concerns focused on food safety for consumers, whereas the primary aim in Lagos was to define a legitimate role and place for vendors' own entrepreneurial activities. Traditional market organizations already existed in both Ibadan and Lagos; they provide access to the vendors for the NGOs, who offer to play the role of intermediary between vendor and state. In Ife, efforts to form market groups have not succeeded; lacking a constituency organization, Kujore sought to influence the local council directly from her position as a member of the health committee. The advocacy of both Kujore and Akinyele has been instrumental in changing the attitudes of local government officials in Ife and Ibadan. In the more contentious climate of Lagos, similar efforts have begun to influence the debate, but have not yet had positive results.

PART II

THE STREET FOOD PROJECT: INFLUENCING DEVELOPMENT THEORY AND PRACTICE

Assumptions about the reality of microenterprise clouded the perceptions both of scholars and practitioners as they began to address informal sector employment in the mid-1970s. Generalizations about women's domestic roles based on U.S. and European models resulted in inappropriate programs and ethnocentric theories. Urban planning models similarly misled government officials in developing countries, as they tried to clean the streets of vendors or impose unattainable standards on sellers of street foods. Research findings of the Street Food Project provide a reality test for these three distinct discourses on the informal sector, women's roles, and food safety in both their theoretic and applied modes.

Socioeconomic data from the seven EPOC Street Food Project studies are aggregated in Chapter 8 and supplemented by additional studies of street foods to provide a basis for challenging many of the assumptions undergirding these discourses. These robust findings delineate the vendors by gender, age, education, marital status, family size, and birthplace; other variables such as ethnicity or religion are noted in some countries. The functioning of the enterprise and its profitability illustrate the spectrum of street food vendors—from the woman hawking peanuts seated by the dusty road to the screened *caranderia*, a closer approximation to the old ready-to-eat Horn and Hardart cafeterias than to the cooked-to-order fast-food establishments now proliferating worldwide.

Stressed throughout the chapter are the differentials between women and men regarding dominance in the trade, types of enterprises and of food sold, and income derived from street foods. Women's involvement, influenced by culture and religion, varies widely across the countries. A second theme is how government attitudes toward vendors strongly affects the enterprises and their profits. National regulations and frequent street cleaning campaigns contrast with more benign approaches by provincial officials toward enforcement.

Street foods themselves are featured in Chapter 9; it covers their fantastic variety, their safety, and their nutritional value. An analysis of customers reflects stages of urbanization, the economic health of the country, and cultural traditions. Details are provided of the efforts by international food safety establishments, as well as national and local governments, activists, and teachers, to improve food handling.

This section begins with a presentation of the foods themselves and how they are made. Because street foods are often produced and traded by vendors, the distinctions between service and production activities are obscured, thus confounding attempts to categorize the activity. The product that street food vendors sell, namely food, sets them apart from other hawkers and vendors because of the related questions of nutritional value and food safety. Chapter 9 explores these fundamental issues as perceived by customers and the international food safety establishment. These sections on nutrition and food safety are preceded by a description of the varieties of foods sold on the street and the methods by which they are produced, often by the vendors themselves. The second section draws on the EPOC case studies to analyze the demand for street foods: Who are the customers? When do they buy street foods? What type of food is eaten on the street?

The sections on nutrition and food safety delineate the crucial role played by the Food and Agricultural Organization (FAO) in addressing these intrinsic aspects of street foods. Their initial interest in the project expanded to a global series of studies on street foods which adopted both the EPOC term and our insistence on the economic importance of the trade. Members of both EPOC and FAO research teams initiated programs to improve the nutritional value of street foods; efforts to fortify foods, especially those eaten by schoolchildren, are recounted.

Initiatives to train vendors in improved food handling techniques were central to many projects. In order to reach the vendors, the researchers utilized existing organizations or promoted new ones. The differing perceptions of vendors' needs by themselves and by the middle-class researchers resulted in several distinct types of nongovernmental organizations. These efforts may provide models for organizing other types of activities aimed at poverty alleviation.

Early efforts by local health officials to enforce international food safety standards supported by the FAO and World Health Organization tended to result in harassment rather than more hygienic conditions. A decade of research on street food vendors produced a series of international workshops where the recognition of the importance of street foods to the urban diet and as a source of income stimulated a reexamination of older regulatory policies. Today, both organizations urge local governments to work with street food vendors to ensure that customers are offered reasonably safe food at affordable prices.

In chapter 10, data produced by the street food study is utilized to challenge many prevailing assumptions about enterprise and informality in developing countries within the scholarly discourse. Specifically, three discourses are engaged: the competing views within economic development toward the informal sector/small- and microenterprise, women's status and economic attitudes within the family and community, and urban planning standards and goals. These themes are also interrelated: gender analysis is imperative in all development programs; the growing importance of the civil society encourages partnerships between governments and NGOs to provide services and training for street food vendors; and shifts within the global economic system affect not only funds for programs but the products vendors sell and the income they earn.

CHAPTER EIGHT

Vendors and the Economics of Their Enterprises

The comparative statistics and information collected in the seven preceding case studies provide a rich and unique data set about an activity found in almost every country around the world: the street food trade. This chapter aggregates and analyzes the data about the vendors and their microenterprises drawn from the seven EPOC studies in the Philippines, Indonesia, Thailand, Bangladesh, Egypt, Nigeria, and Senegal, and adds to them information collected in similar research in India and Jamaica, where research centers utilized the EPOC methodology. Where appropriate, data are included from subsequent street food studies that were often stimulated by the EPOC work.

Principal conclusions include the following: street foods are ubiquitous and a growing phenomenon in urban areas in developing countries; wide variations in the numbers of vendors and their gender roles exist; family and kin support is central to most street food enterprises; stability and profitability characterize a high proportion of the trade, but failure is also frequent; most vendors are microentrepreneurs, rather than dependent workers; harassment by local officials, not credit, is the major impediment of the trade; vendors' average income is generally higher than the official minimum wage and many vendors earn as much as schoolteachers or government clerks.

Size and Seasonality of the Trade

Table 8.1 lists the seven cities by total population and presents the number of street food establishments counted throughout each city in both high and low season. No direct relationship between city size and the number of street food vendors is reflected, despite the intuitive expectation of finding more vendors as cities become larger and more congested. When workers and students travel further each day through clogged roads on overburdened public transport systems, returning home for a midday meal is no longer possible. Nor are women necessarily at home to cook: pressures on women's time as they juggle income-producing jobs with household

TABLE 8.1   Cities by population, vendor enterprises, and survey samples in the Street Foods Project

City	Urban population at time of study	No. of Enterprises (census)		No. of survey samples	
		High season	Low season	Vendor	Customer
Manikganj, Bangladesh	37,996	550	308	159	435
Chonburi, Thailand	46,862	1,370	948	219	249
Ziguinchor, Senegal	98,295	1,534	748	188	250
Minia, Egypt	179,060	784	NA	174	NA
Iloilo, Philippines	244,827	5,100	4,729	135	246
Bogor, Indonesia	248,000	17,756	16,866	235	470
Ile-Ife, Nigeria	617,296	2,603	1,796	255	60

NA = not available.

responsibilities make street foods an attractive alternative to cooking at home. Migrant workers, often without family, find street foods cheaper than setting up a kitchen. Yet our data do not support these propositions.

One explanation is the absence of any consistent definition of *urban*. Official government boundaries were used to delimit the area of study; yet these lines seldom relate to population density or land use. The countries in the study all have highly centralized governmental systems that allow expansion of municipal boundaries for purposes of planning or taxation without input from local interests. Or the center can oppose local initiatives, as it did in Thailand: the national administration preferred to keep the peri-urban areas of Chonburi outside the city, where lower taxes encouraged industrialization. As a result, of the cities studied, only Chonburi appears consistently urban. In Bogor, villages have been engulfed by the city, their housing intensified; even steep ravines and riverbanks have become housing sites. These two cities report the largest number of vendors per population, with Bogor recording an amazing figure of one vendor per fourteen inhabitants. Ziguinchor, Ife, Iloilo, and Manikganj have expanded their earlier boundaries to incorporate agricultural areas that are interspersed with villages.

Persistent rural poverty unalleviated by economic transition is another obvious reason for lower consumption of street foods. Villagers in poor peri-urban families consume their own products and limit street food purchases to market days, when they tend only to purchase snacks. Thus in Bangladesh, where rural areas are so close to the small town of Manikganj that 45% of the vendors live in the district, customers are the slightly better-off travelers or visitors to the courts. In Ziguinchor, women agriculturalists flock to city markets to sell peanuts during the off season, but buy little themselves. As the economy becomes monetized, poor urban workers, from pedicab drivers to office guards to laborers, are paid in money and often subsist on street foods. Higher-skilled jobs encourage schooling that, in turn, usually provides more street food customers.

Neither explanation accounts for the low ratio of establishments to city size in Ife or Minia. Two factors may contribute to low consumption in Minia. First, the traditional diet of flat bread and cheese is not onerous to make or buy at the store, and bread is highly subsidized. Second, we have noted that the income of the government officials in Minia is not appreciably higher than some vendors, although their lifestyle may be different. Since saving preparation time is not an issue and discretionary funds of the middle class are minimal, regular consumption of street foods is left to visitors at markets or hospitals and to workers and schoolchildren at midday. In contrast, vendors in Ife serve many meals each day and so may service more customers than the ratio suggests, since the town limits encompass much rural land. Further, government harassment may have discouraged some vendors, while poor economic conditions, which depressed markets while increasing the cost of many ingredients, could have made vending a poor investment of time and money.

Seasonal fluctuations in the number of establishments reflect local holidays and agricultural cycles. Nearly 25% of vendors in Manikganj and 5% of vendors in Bogor left the trade when agricultural labor was in high demand. Conversely, agricultural cycles also account for the influx from rural areas of vendors who often specialize in seasonal foods such as corn or fruit. Many full-time vendors switch merchandise seasonally, but totals are not affected. School terms do affect totals, however. Many vendors in Ife stopped selling during vacations, when their university customers went home and the schoolchildren were sent to visit kin; the women are not idle, but spend their time farming, sewing, or trading. The fasting month of Ramadan altered the types of food sold and the time of sale, especially in Bangladesh; in Indonesia many vendors chose this time of year to return to their villages. In contrast, Christmas brought additional vendors to the streets of Iloilo.

Besides the number of establishments drawn from the census, the sample of vendors selected for inclusion in the socioeconomic survey and the number of customers interviewed are also given in Table 8.1. Most data in this chapter are based on these intensive surveys rather than on the census; the repeat censuses, which also recorded number and gender of vendors at each establishment and the type of food sold, were based on observation, not interviews. Some discrepancies between the two sets of data, such as the percentages of women vendors, sometimes occurred because of the factors used in selecting the sample. Customers selected for interview were buying from street food vendors included in the economic survey.

In five of the towns, the sample of vendors to total census of establishments was at least the 10% suggested in the EPOC design. The size of Iloilo and Bogor and their high vendor population resulted in different approaches for obtaining the sample. In Iloilo the intensive study focused on Iloilo proper, the city before expansion, in addition to the commercial and market area of La Paz that borders the city. A census of this area, with a population of roughly 55,000, was taken four times; the

1,350 vendors remained fairly constant, but roast corn sellers appeared and added 110 vendors in season. The survey was 10% of the stable vendor group. Projections of total vendors within the current city boundaries were based on counts in business areas of surrounding districts and on the Iloilo household survey. The census in Bogor, with about the same total population, was based on a complete counting at different times of the day in the three major and 10 minor markets of the city and in the two major business strips. Because the neighborhoods were too extensive and official permission to count them difficult to obtain, the research team obtained a count of neighborhood vendors based on a cluster sample of 20% of all neighborhoods and enumerating 20% of the districts in those areas.

Involvement of Women and Family

The proportion of women-run establishments varied enormously between cities: from 96% of all establishments in Ife to a mere 1% in Manikganj. In enterprises with both husband and wife present, deciding who controlled the firm was difficult. Repeat interviews or later studies suggest that in many instances when a man was listed as owner, the couple or the wife should have been credited; but local cultural practices meant that either the respondent or the interviewer gave preference to the man. Even more crucial to an understanding of the trade as an economic activity for the poor is women's *involvement* in some of the many of the aspects of producing street foods, even when they are not the primary seller. Spouses support each other's enterprise through unpaid assistance in most, but not all, countries. A larger circle of family/kin labor is critical to the functioning of street food vending in all countries: this usually unpaid labor is predominantly, but not exclusively, female.

Demographic data on vendors produced several unexpected results: the low numbers of migrant vendors; the career nature of the trade; the variation of vendors ages by gender and life-cycle; and the high levels of education in some countries, which is less surprising when the profitability of the trade is considered.

Women Vendors and Workers

Documenting women's participation in the street food trade was a major goal of the project; comparative results are shown in Table 8.2. Women's roles in the making and selling varies by country due to cultural and religious reasons (Tinker 1993a). In Ile-Ife and Iloilo, women account for some 90% of all street food vendors, but their mode of work is directly opposite. In Ile-Ife the women work alone and keep their income separate; in Iloilo, where 63% of the enterprises are operated by women alone, most of the 27% of firms listed as couple-owned had been started by women. As the wife's earnings rose, her husband would quit his formal sector or casual labor job to assist in the increasingly profitable effort. Barth recorded that Philippine women dominated the street food trade by making some 83% of all business decisions, either by themselves or jointly with their husbands.

TABLE 8.2   Street food enterprises by women's involvement (%)

City	Owner *or* operator			Enterprises with female assistants		Enterprises involving women[a]
	Women	Men	Couple	Paid	Unpaid	
Manikganj, Bangladesh	1	99		10	25	37
Chonburi, Thailand	78	22		13	31	88
Ziguinchor, Senegal	77	23		0	25	77
Minia, Egypt	17	83		1	34	52
Iloilo, Philippines	63	10	27	4	11	92
Bogor, Indonesia	16	60	24	5	33	62
Ile-Ife, Nigeria	94	6	0	19	15	94
Kingston,[b] Jamaica	44	46	10			54
Pune, India	13	87		33	51	53

a. Involvement means that women are involved in some of the many of the aspects of street food production or sale even when they are not the primary seller. Enterprises may have both paid and unpaid female assistants who may be wives, daughters, relatives, or hired help. Women vendors also have help from women and girls. Thus total involvement is not a numerical addition of previous figures.

b. Street foods studies done in Jamaica and India utilized EPOC methodology and background materials but not EPOC staff. Results from these studies are used in the analytical chapters, but the countries are not profiled.

In Ziguinchor and Chonburi women constitute over three-quarters of the vendors; in both cities, as in Ile-Ife, women and men vendors sell separate types of food; they never work at the enterprise together in Ziguinchor, but women are unpaid help in many male-run enterprises in Chonburi. In all four countries women have traditionally made important monetary contributions to the household. In West Africa women are expected to help feed the family, though men are responsible for providing staples. Women in Thailand and the Philippines have traditionally managed the household budget and supplemented their husband's income as needed.

The dominance of women as street food vendors in these areas of West Africa and Southeast Asia had been anticipated; thus the findings in Bogor surprised us. Previous studies in Central Java had recorded a substantial majority of women vendors; the census in Bogor counted men as 60% of vendors, women as only 16%, and couples as 24%. West Javanese culture with its greater internalization of Islam, explains much of this discrepancy between findings in two contiguous areas of Java and provides a cautionary tale against overgeneralizing socioeconomic data from one area to another.

Studies in the two other Islamic countries of Bangladesh and Egypt illustrate even more clearly the social and cultural influences of religion and their differential application; in both countries, minority religions prescribed analogous social customs. In

Manikganj, the only women working in public were destitute and had no male kin; only under these circumstances was it acceptable for women to break seclusion. Only six street food vendors, or 1%, were observed selling foods, and one of these vendors only occasionally sold bananas from her own trees. A seventh woman entrepreneur frequented the market as a trader selling the snack *canacur* to vendors and shopkeepers. Half of these women were widows; two of the spouses were drunks and abusive, while one, an asthmatic, was a dedicated househusband, a unique role in Bangladesh.

Census figures from Minia show women operating only 17% of the vendor enterprises, but they were also visible assistants in others. The problem of ascertaining who is the operator and who the assistant was underscored in a 1993 vendor survey that recorded 32% of the members of the Street Food Vendors Organization of Minia as women. The distribution of women vendors showed the highest numbers in the peri-urban villages and the lowest in the central city. Similar conservative cultural practices, in this case Hinduism, clearly influenced the low numbers of women street food vendors in Pune.[1]

Deciding who was in fact the primary operator of permanent enterprises was often difficult. In Jamaica, the census count ignored the idea of a couple running an enterprise and recorded nearly equal numbers of men and women vendors; based on detailed interviews of vendors in the survey, they revised their figures to reflect 10% couple operators and slightly more single male operators than female.

Family Enterprise

These observations on couples jointly operating their enterprise underscore the critical fact that *in most countries the street food trade is a family enterprise*. Women's roles as entrepreneurs are shaped by their family responsibilities: usually they work shorter hours, invest less money, and earn lower returns. They also benefit by family and kin support in varying measures across the widely divergent cultural patterns in the countries studied.

Most vendors, women as well as men, had family help in their many trade activities: buying ingredients, preparing the food, cleaning utensils, moving the cart into place, selling, even eating leftovers. The figures of women's involvement, as shown in Table 8.2, are probably too low since household tasks, such as cleaning utensils, may not always be reported. Family help, particularly female help, was seldom compensated; in no country were spouses paid. But in Chonburi, young women as well as men might receive a small stipend as they learned the trade. Minia reported that more male spouses helped their wives (17%) than wives helped their husbands (11%) in preparing the food; this point is then modified by saying "if the wives do not help in the enterprise, they at least wash utensils at the end of the vending day" (Loza 1985, 16). This ambiguity about the nature of unpaid family assistance is illustrated in case studies collected in Ziguinchor: some 25% of the women vendors were assisted at home by their daughters or other female relatives. Besides performing some of the more tedious tasks in food preparation, such as mixing cowpea batter for *acaras*, or pounding and winnowing millet for porridge, these daughters and female kin also took over household work to free the vendor for her enterprise. Only 20% of the women vendors themselves cooked meals for their families on a daily basis.

Paid female workers were usually not relatives. In Manikganj, assisting street food vendors by carrying water or cleaning up was considered by local cultural standards to be less degrading than being a vendor and selling in public. That monetary need was the primary motive is underscored by noting that the average age of paid female assistants working at the shops was 32, compared to 17 for unpaid female helpers, who were primarily daughters. Similar motivation seems to account for the fact that in Pune, where 8% of the vendors employed paid help, 70% of these employees were female: they were paid even less than children. In Ife, mature women sent younger female kin off to sell in another site; the census sometimes recorded them separately, but interviews revealed that many of them were apprentices.

Women's involvement in the street food trade is clearly much higher than the figures for women vendors would indicate. Table 8.2 shows the percentage of enterprises with some female help. These numbers should be taken as indicative of the importance of the street food trade for women; as composite figures they include women who are single operators; women who run a joint operation and are presumed to be the decision-maker; and women who assist male operators, either at home or at the place of sale. If a woman who washes up at home is not reported by the vendor as an assistant, she becomes invisible unpaid family labor.[2] The fact that participation in Ziguinchor and Ife is the same as the number of vendors reflects the division of labor that coincides with separate budgets. In Chonburi, those family members working for male operators were mostly children in the larger Chinese street food establishments, but family members working for Thai female vendors were usually paid. Three cities display a large number of couple-operated enterprises. Minia did not record this type of operation in the original study, but later research suggests that couples do operate some enterprises there as well. Only in the two South Asian cities does women's involvement fall below half of all enterprises. But the rise from 1% to 37% in Manikganj shows both the importance of women's support and the effect of seclusion; Pune's total for women's participation in the trade records a similar increase from vendor to involvement.

Basic Data on Vendors

Across the countries, the average age of vendors was between 35 and 40 years of age. Most women apparently wait until their mid-20s, after their childbearing years, to start working, and retire or work less after age 50; they have presumably fulfilled their responsibilities of feeding their families and paying school fees for their children. Men often start young and may use the income as a stake for other work. Career male vendors continued working later in life than females: 10% of the male vendors in Manikganj were over 56 years old, and 12.5% of male vendors in Chonburi were in the 50–65 age bracket.

Young children, especially girls, were observed selling street foods; but because UNICEF defines anyone under 18 years old as a child, most teenagers fall into this category. In areas with high school attendance (Iloilo, Bogor, Chonburi, and Minia) children turned up in the markets in the afternoons. In Bogor, Ibu Sidik's two children, aged 15 and 17, often took over her stand in the afternoon so that she could go home to cook the family meals and collect ingredients for the next day's sale of deep-fried snacks. In Manikganj, Ife, Ziguinchor, and Pune, school attendance is not compulsory, and poverty often dictates that children begin to earn money as soon as possible. Few people in Manikganj knew their date of birth exactly; the staff estimated that 5% of the vendors appeared to be below the age of 16. In addition, children assisted parents at 31% of the enterprises; another 10% of the vendors utilized help from children at home. In Pune, 10% of all assistants to vendors were children, two-thirds of whom were female.

Among the vendors counted in the Ife census, 9% were under 16 years old, including one under 10. In contrast, Akinyele's study of Ibadan, Lagos, and Kaduna found that a majority of vendor's children attended school and did not assist in the trade. Since his data also showed that a major reason women work is to pay school fees, investment in their children by freeing their time to study is logical. Only in Ibadan did it appear that some children both attended school (74%) and helped at point of sale (31%). Of those working, in Kaduna and Ibadan three-quarters were girls, but in Lagos this dropped to 60%.

Ethnic and religious differences in the countries had some influence on the types of foods sold and who sold them. In Ziguinchor, for example, the nomadic Peuhl dominated the meat and milk trade. The largest ethnic group in the area, the Diola, were substantially underrepresented in the trade because of their women's responsibility for rice cultivation during the wet season. In both Bogor and Chonburi, ethnic groups from other parts of the country enticed customers with their distinctive cuisine. Southeast Asia has long been influenced by Chinese foods: in Bogor, Chinese continued to dominate the noodle trade, while in Chonburi, where most male vendors were Chinese, they specialized in steamed breads and food with drinks. Only two Chinese vendors were enumerated in Iloilo, and neither family spoke a Chinese language at home; but many foods sold on the street are derivatives of Chinese food. In Manikganj, which has a 20% Hindu population, 24% of the vendors were Hindus; they owned all the sweets shops that sold foods traditionally made by certain Hindu castes, as well as about half the dairy-based enterprises and tea shops. In Pune, the caste of the vendors is correlated with income, with 80% of the kiosk holders being high-caste Hindus; 15% of the street vendors belong to the scheduled castes. Muslims and lower-caste Hindus are both cart and street vendors. Since the bulk of street foods in Pune are snacks, the caste background of the vendor is not as critical as it would definitely be if meals were sold.[3] In Minia, the Coptic minority has little representation in the trade, and those Coptics who do sell are indistinguishable from the rest.

Ife had a vendor population only one-quarter Muslim compared to nearby Ibadan, where 57% of the vendors were Muslim and 43% Christian. Akinyele suggests that the lower educational levels among Muslim women allow them few alternatives and results in their overrepresentation in the trade.[4] In Ibadan the Muslim vendors are indistinguishable from the Christians, except that they do not sell pork (Akinyele 1987). In Kaduna, few Muslim women sell on the streets, compared to non-Muslim women. They do, however, frequently prepare street foods for their children to sell on the streets (Akinyele 1991). Christian vendors in Ife were divided into 47% Pentecostal or Evangelist, 14% Catholic, and 10% Alafura or African Christians; the remaining women adhered to traditional beliefs. These distinctions had no impact on their work as street food sellers.

Marital Status

It is unusual for mature women or men in most developing countries to be unmarried; single vendors enumerated in the censuses were usually very young; vendors in their early 20s were predominantly men, since most women were bearing children. The highest percentage of unmarried vendors, nearly two-fifths of all vendors, was recorded in Jamaica. Young men were the largest segment of unmarrieds. Overall, 27.5% of the vendors lived in legal unions, while 35% were in some form of common-law union.[5] Figures from Ziguinchor do indicate that 4% of the women vendors were unmarried older women who considered themselves self-supporting; another 4% of all women were unmarried parents, a phenomenon discussed in the Ziguinchor study. Many of the women vendors are widows, including 24% in Minia and 14% in Ziguinchor. Five of the six women vendors in Manikganj were also widows.

Only in Ziguinchor and Ife were many women living in polygynous marriages. In Ziguinchor co-wives lived together in apparent harmony with younger wives, doing housework to enable older women to vend; the average household had three adult earners and a size of 9.5 persons. Fifty-nine percent of the women in that city were the primary supporters of the family, with a husband either unemployed or on a pension. In Ife, where 54% lived in polygynous marriages, co-wives do not usually cohabitate; nonetheless, when women vendors were asked in 1988 to whom they might turn for help in a crisis, 13% mentioned co-wives. Husbands were considered supportive by only 17% of the women, but relatives and children, at 20% each, were considered the most helpful. The women themselves were often helping take care of other people's children; while vendors had an average of 4.5 children, 30% of the vendors in the 1988 study were caring for five to eight children (Pearce 1992).

Education

The educational levels of vendors varied significantly across the countries (see Table 8.3). Illiteracy, often associated with street vendors, indeed characterized women in a majority of the cities: 93% in Minia, 80% in Ziguinchor, 60% in Ile-Ife,[6] and all six

TABLE 8.3   Vendor's educational levels

City			Schooling		
	Illiterate	Primary	Secondary	Vocational	University
Manikganj, Bangladesh	32	34	27	7	
Chonburi, Thailand	9 female 8.5 male	89 female 63 male	17 male		4 female 11.5 male
Ziguinchor, Senegal	80	16	4		
Minia, Egypt	93 female 53 male	7 female 29 male	17 male		
Iloilo, Philippines		47	33		20
Bogor, Indonesia		80	7	13	
Ile-Ife, Nigeria	60	30	10		
Kingston, Jamaica		70	30		
Pune, India	32	47	18		3

women vendors in Manikganj. In contrast, in Manikganj only one-third of the male vendors were illiterate, and another third had completed more that six years in school. Although more than half of the male vendors in Minia were illiterate, 17% had graduated from secondary school. In Ziguinchor the men could read and write in Arabic, but no one kept written records. The Pune study correlated education with vending types: nearly half the street vendors, including all the women, were illiterate, as compared to a quarter of the kiosk or cart sellers. Educational levels of Nigerian vendors were higher in Ibadan than in Ife: only 27% were illiterate, compared to 60%; further, over 30% had completed secondary school or higher levels. In Kaduna and Lagos less contrast was recorded; illiteracy was 20% in Lagos and 27% in Kaduna, but a majority of vendors in those cities had not completed secondary school. These data suggest that the educational level of vendors rapidly changes in response to socioeconomic change, from a level below the city average to one that reflects the overall educational attainments of the city inhabitants.

Illiteracy was not a major problem in the other countries. Chonburi recorded that 9% of all vendors were illiterate and that more women (89%) than men (63%) had only primary school education; 4% of the women and 11.5% of the men had attended the university. Vendors in Bogor and Kingston (80% and 70%, respectively) felt that having only a primary education limited alternative activities. Vendors in Iloilo were the best educated: 20% had some university education, and 30% had completed secondary school. Since Iloilo, like Ibadan, is a university town, the presence of vendors with university degrees is not too surprising; many of these vendors paid their college fees by assisting street food vendors, and they found that their income in this occupation is higher than most low-level governmental posts. The mayor of

Iloilo in 1994 told me how he had worked first as an assistant, and then as an independent vendor during his college years.

Rapid modernization tends to increase pressure on parents to keep their children in school, even though school systems seldom prepare students for available jobs. In most countries studied, paying school fees was a major reason women vendors worked. A follow-up study of vendors in Ife conducted after the Structural Adjustment Program had been initiated in Nigeria found that paying children's school fees was considered a problem by 98.4% of all respondents, while 52% were concerned with providing sufficient food for their families (Kujore and Pearce 1992). In most countries, swollen government bureaucracies can no longer absorb graduates; microenterprise is becoming a career of choice for many educated people.

Migration Patterns

Street food vendors are not predominantly new migrants in any of the cities studied: as shown in Tables 8.4 and 8.5, a majority of vendors in Manikganj, Ife, and Minia and some 45% in Bogor and Iloilo continue to live where they were born. Only Bogor, Ife, and Kingston recorded significant numbers of vendors who had been in the city fewer than 10 years. These patterns of migration relate to the speed and timing of economic transition, urban definition, and local political factors.

In Minia and Ife a majority of vendors, 55% in each, were born in the city. Today all vendors live in Ife, including the 20% who arrived within the last 10 years. In contrast, only 69% of the vendors live in Minia itself, while 28% continue to commute from other urban areas in Minia Governorate, a unique situation not replicated else-

TABLE 8.4   Birthplace and residence of street food vendors (%)

City	Birthplace					Residence		
	City	Village/ peri-urban	Region/ state	Country	Foreign	City	Village	Region
Manikganj, Bangladesh	37	45	18	0	0	55	45	
Chonburi, Thailand	36	30	24	10	0	100		
Ziguinchor, Senegal	40	34	11	15	100			
Minia, Egypt	55	13	29	0	0	69	3	28
Iloilo, Philippines	46	47	6	1	0	100		
Bogor, Indonesia	23	22	33	22[a]		67	33	0
Ile-Ife, Nigeria		55	34	11	0	100		
Kingston, Jamaica	37		63					
Pune, India	64		17	19[b]				

a. 19% Java/3% outer island

b. FAO-Pune, 1986.

TABLE 8.5   Length of vendor residence in city or peri-urban village

City	Born	1 yr	1–2	2–5	5–10	10–20	>20
Manikganj, Bangladesh	37 municipality						
	45 rural		3	2	4	9	
Chonburi, Thailand	36					64	
Ziguinchor, Senegal	40	4	8.5	15.5	11	11.5	9.5
Minia, Egypt	55 city						
	28 other						
	3 rural						
Iloilo, Philippines	46						54
Bogor, Indonesia	23 city						
	22 rural	12	30			13	
Ile-Ife, Nigeria	55		3		17	25	
Kingston, Jamaica	37						
Pune, India	24	1	3	4	7	9	52

where. Another 3% of the vendors born in peri-urban villages around Minia continue to commute.

This pattern of remaining in rural natal areas was also noted in Bogor and Manikganj. Indeed, the number of vendors living in villages outside Bogor has increased by 10%, so that they account for 33% of all vendors, compared with the 67% living in town. Women represent three-fifths of these village-based vendors. In Manikganj, the 45% of vendors living in villages has remained constant, while the 18% who are migrants moved into the city limits. Among the 55% of vendors living within the municipality, only 39% live in the central area that locals call the town; the rest live in suburban villages within the municipal boundaries. A visitor could not distinguish between suburbs and village.

Vendors not born in the city or its periphery were generally long-term residents, migrating over 10 years before the study. The greatest stability of vendor population was in Iloilo where all migrant vendors had lived in the city for over 21 years, arriving at a time of unrest in the hinterland. Their ties to the area are reflected in the fact that 93% of the sellers spoke the local language of Iloilo City at home, including two vendors of Chinese ancestry. Another 6% spoke another language common on Panay. Only 1% spoke Cebuano, the primary language of Central Philippines. In contrast, many of the employees appeared to be recent migrants, and their low wages are an indication of the surplus labor situation existing in the region.

The rapid pace of industrialization hastened migration in Chonburi and Pune. Only 35% of the vendors in Chonburi were born there—that is, nearly half the men and a third of the women vendors. One-tenth of the vendors in Chonburi came from the depressed northeast provinces. All Chonburi vendors now live in town. This is also true of Pune, a city of 1.6 million people that is experiencing rapid growth. Only 24% of Pune's vendors reported the city as their birthplace, but 58% had lived there more than 10 years. A correlation was found between the type of street vending and the length of residency, with newer migrants selling from carts and representing 10% of that type of vendor, while half the kiosk operators had been born in the city and another quarter had lived there for more than 15 years.[7]

Among the EPOC studies, Bogor recorded the highest percentage of recent immigrants among vendors,[8] reflecting agricultural changes and high rates of urban migration. Of the migrants, 13% came over 15 years ago, 30% migrated during the 1970s, and 12% arrived in the first years of the 1980s. The surge of migrants coincides with the introduction of the green revolution in rice cultivation, a system that requires fewer farm laborers, many of whom were women. However, figures show that fewer women vendors (39%) than men (58%) were migrants. Rural industries offer alternative employment opportunities for women (Wolf 1992), while circular migration patterns, which continue to be strong in Java, facilitate rapid absorption into the trade, especially for men, who often leave their families in the rural areas (Bijlmer 1989, Winarno 1989). In Ziguinchor, nearly two-fifths of the migrants had lived in the city less than 10 years. Years of drought conditions, combined with political instability in Casamance and in the neighboring countries of Gambia and Guinea, also pushed many rural dwellers into town.

Housing

Although the EPOC studies did not specifically inquire about the places where vendors lived, staff visited vendor's homes to observe family roles in food preparation. These visits revealed that in Ziguinchor 60% of the vendors lived in houses they or their families owned; these homes were typical five-room single-story structures made of mud bricks covered with cement and topped with an aluminum roof. In Iloilo, 44% of permanent sellers lived at the place of sale, and for many employees, a free place to sleep was part of their payment. One enterprise near the port that I visited in 1994 consisted of a long wooden counter about six feet out from a wall and a shelter with a tin roof attached to the wall. Shelves along the wall held bottles of beer, soft drinks, and rum, as well as a radio playing loudly. Behind the counter in the center of the area was a gas stove and a refrigerator. The young woman behind the counter said she was a college student studying commerce at the local university; she said the enterprise paid 700 pesos per quarter for a vendor tax. It was clear that she, and the whole family, slept in the bunk areas at either end of the shack.

The Pune study found that over one-third of all vendors lived in shanty settlements "where shared basic services are provided on an inadequate scale and services like refuse collection are nonexistent" (Bapat 1992, 23) and where walkways are used to extend workspace (Gilbert 1992). Another 55% lived in deteriorating old subdivided houses or worker quarters; only 7% had "independent flats or houses." Obviously, such unsanitary conditions have a major impact on the safety of street foods produced in them. In contrast, a majority of vendor's houses in Nigeria were made of cement block with a cement floor and a tin roof; latrines were located outside the house in Ibadan (Akinyele 1991).

Running a Sreet Food Enterprise

By the EPOC definition, street food vendors sell ready-to-eat food along the street or from a structure that does not have four permanent walls. Because this definition encompassed all enterprises serving fast food outside the formal commercial sector, the EPOC studies distinguished among the types of operations, particularly between permanent and mobile enterprises. This section begins with an analysis of these types and their locations throughout the city. A description of vendor effort daily, weekly, and yearly shows distinct gender differences due primarily to women's parallel household responsibilities. Information about the vendors' longevity in street food vending completes this picture of a broadly differentiated trade. These variations of type and functioning exhibit many correlations with income that is discussed in the next section.

Mobility of Operation

Each census of street food vendors mapped each street food enterprise in the city and described the manner of operation as permanent or mobile. Permanent structures included stalls in market areas, shacks erected against walls, free-standing kiosks, heavy tables sheltered by canvas tents, or a veranda or room in the vendor's own house. Any other type of enterprise was considered mobile: vendors with baskets or shoulder poles, vendors pushing or pedaling carts, vendors squatting behind a table spread with goods. Elaborate carts that had to be pushed into place and remained in a fixed spot all day were considered semi-mobile. The distinction rested on whether, if threatened, the vendor could close shop and rapidly leave the area.

In reality, these distinctions are not always so clear. How do you categorize a vendor who leaves his table and cooking apparatus under a tree in Kingston, but *could* move it easily? Or the vendor couple in Minia who never move their cart for fear of entangling the electric wires? EPOC would classify both as mobile; but the Kingston study differentiates between fixed-place and moving vendors, not among modes of selling. Similarly, the follow-up Bogor "streetfoods" study under Winarno combined as stationary all vendors with fixed location, whether they sold from structures or boxes on the street. This research focused only on vendors selling "on public spaces which were originally not intended for this purpose" and emphasized location in order to encourage the formation of vendor associations that could serve as intermediaries for training in food handling (Winarno 1989, 5).

As shown in Table 8.6, in none of the cities were vendors selling from permanent structures a majority, but they predominated in Minia and would become a majority if the permanently attached carts were included. The two cities with the fewest ambu-

TABLE 8.6   Vendor enterprises reflecting mobility

City	Permanent	Nonpermanent	
		Semi-mobile	Ambulant
Manikganj, Bangladesh	47	50	3
Chonburi, Thailand	36	46	18
Ziguinchor, Senegal	8	85	7
Minia, Egypt	49	21	30
Iloilo, Philippines	46	54	
Bogor, Indonesia	12	88	
Ile-Ife, Nigeria	33	40	27
Kingston, Jamaica	88 fixed place of sale		12
Pune, India	13	73	14

lant vendors are small cities enclosing poor rural areas whose inhabitants have little discretionary income. Gender differences were particularly marked in Bogor, where 28% of women vendors sold from permanent structures, compared to only 9% of the men.

Permanent and semi-mobile vendors could be found all over the cities; ambulant vendors usually followed a set route through residential neighborhoods. But the description of where the vendors sold throughout the city is confusing. Vendors selling from stalls *in* markets were definitive. But street food vendors can seldom afford to rent permanent market stalls; rather, they set up tables or carts on the periphery or along paths leading to the markets. Most studies considered these vendors to be selling in the markets, but in Iloilo they were considered part of the general commercial area. Vendors at bus stops or train stations were usually part of an informal market but could also be considered to be in a commercial area. Street food sellers in major shopping or office areas or near factories were usually grouped together as commercial.

More confusing is the classification of nonambulant vendors in residential areas, where several shops might cluster at a crossroads. The Ife study calls this "mixed residential," but other studies consider them "neighborhoods." Schools, hospitals, and mosques are primarily found in residential areas, but not always. In Minia 19% of the vendors were near schools, but fewer than 2% were in Pune. Churches were not mentioned as a venue for street foods, perhaps because in the Philippines churches tend to border the main square in the commercial areas, while in Ife and Kingston most vendors did not work on Sundays. Parks were a favorite selling site for vendors in Pune: Is this commercial or residential? In Bogor the vendors congregated at the entrances of the Botanical Gardens, where no food can be sold inside. Many vendors could be found outside movie halls; these are located in both residential and commercial areas.

Some gender differences related to location. In Ife most men sold drinks and snacks at the gas stations that rim the city. In Iloilo men in the city were likely to be ambulant, selling ice cream or fish; those with permanent enterprises were more likely to be in outer areas.

The concern of the government authorities has focused on the market and commercial areas. Permanent operations are clearly easier for the government to control, so that owners were marginally more likely to obtain licenses and to observe health standards. Water and electricity are also easier to supply to permanent enterprises. Many governments aspire to the Singapore model of relocating vendors in shopping malls; "street foods" are readily available in upscale shopping malls in Bangkok, Manila, or Washington, D.C. The economics of this shift have yet to be studied, but indications are that these centers are alternatives to American fast food chains for the middle class. Efforts to replicate the forceful removal of vendors in downtown Jakarta were not successful (see the chapter on Bogor) because neither the vendors nor their customers could afford the higher costs. Jamaica moved hawkers selling dry goods to enclosed arcades in 1986, but has not yet implemented this relocation for street food vendors.

Vendors are found in a variety of places selling an amazing selection of foods from carts, homes, stalls, tables, baskets, or open-air cafeterias. They may vie for customers in crowded streets during the day, in parks at midnight, or in isolated neighborhoods in the evening. Standing along major highways, they may interfere more with automobile traffic than do vendors in congested market areas. Regulations, licensing, and problems vary by type of operation, type of food sold, and location. Solutions need to be adapted to the various categories; vendor associations are considered a key to improving communication with governments.

Vendors' Workday

In most countries vendors work very long hours, seven days a week, year-round. The foods each vendor sells affects both when they sell it and how long it takes to prepare. Some vendors work only in the morning, some work until late at night, and many work all day. In Minia the night markets are more crowded than those in the day; part-time vendors without licenses say it is safer to sell at that time. Ife recorded the most vendors selling at breakfast—1,107, as compared to 713 for lunch and 730 for dinner; 56% worked from 7 A.M. to 10 P.M. In contrast, two-thirds of all vendors in Pune, mostly men, only worked in the evening from 7 P.M. on, selling in parks and outside entertainment centers. Similarly, men sell late at night, catering to the uptown nightlife in Kingston or to truck drivers and fishing boat workers in Chonburi.

Overall, men worked longer hours at the trade than women did in Ziguinchor, Minia, and Kingston; in Chonburi the women spent somewhat more time preparing and selling than did male sellers, but time differential related more to the type of food than to gender. Where women dominate the trade, as in Ife or Iloilo or Manikganj or where men were the primary vendors, gender differences were not recorded. In many countries women spend more time in preparation than men, two hours a day, compared to less than one in Ziguinchor, an indication that most of the foods they sold were traditional foods that require many hours of preparation.

In Kingston only a quarter of the vendors worked on Sunday; in fact most women seemed to take the weekend off, while men might work throughout, and then take Monday off. Ife reported no vendors working on Sunday in 1984; Akinyele found this true in his first study of Ibadan in 1987, but by 1991 nearly one-quarter of vendors were working on Sunday, a sign of increasing economic stress. Men in both Minia and Bogor were more likely than women to work only six days a week: one-third of the men took a day off, compared to 11% of the women.

Despite their perception that they work all the time, most vendors take days off during the month for family or religious reasons: three to four days in Chonburi and five days in Ziguinchor, for example. As noted, extended time was often taken off to work in the fields or to visit home when demand for their products was low. Vendors also stop selling temporarily or permanently for illness or business reasons. Particularly in Manikganj, vendors enumerated in the first census disappeared, to be replaced by new ones. What little we know about failure rates is discussed later in this chapter.

Longevity

The street food trade in the cities studied exhibited extreme volatility: 40–50% of the vendors had been selling for less than five years, but between one-sixth and one-third had been in the trade for over 15 years. Over half of all vendors in Ife, Bogor, and Ziguinchor and over two-fifths in Pune and Manikganj had entered the trade five or fewer years before. In Iloilo the figure was about 30%, while in Minia 14% had been selling for less than one year. These data on recent entrants are balanced by a significant number of vendors in most of the cities who have been selling for a considerable time: 37% in Pune and 23% in Manikganj had been selling for over 10 years; 14% in Bogor, 16% in Ife, and 35% in Iloilo had been selling for over 15 years; in Minia 20% had been selling for over 20 years. Women in Chonburi and all vendors in Minia had been vendors for an average of seven years; even more stable was the vendor population of Iloilo, with an average of 12 years. In contrast, the median years in the trade in Ziguinchor was two; it was only two and one-half for men in Chonburi.

A high failure rate among small businesses characterizes this activity worldwide: about half of these ventures fail within a year in the United States. Our data on failure rates must be deduced from two facts: the large number of vendors counted in the first census who disappeared, and the high percentage of new entrants into the trade. Because EPOC studies covered only one year and used working vendors as its point of entry, the fluctuations of vendors due to seasonality were difficult to distinguish from those due to failure. In Iloilo, 8.8% of the vendors surveyed had already disappeared by the time of the customer survey. In Manikganj, where staff got to know many of the vendors and their families, Owens computed the failure rate at 8.75% per year. Given the difficulties vendors faced, perhaps the longevity is the more surprising data: in Ife over 8% had been in business for over 26 years! Length of time as vendors was the most important variable in predicting high income in Iloilo.

Economics of the Street Food Trade

Most street food enterprises are operated by a single vendor or by a vendor couple with no employees, but with considerable unpaid family assistance. How to value this labor is a problem in computing income and profits of the enterprise, particularly in the absence of written records. Information on costs and expenditures of each operation was based on repeat interviews that were tested against information gathered during the year-long observation of the street food trade. Home visits refined data both on family labor and on costs of ingredients.

Capital to start the enterprise typically came from the family or from personal savings; skills often came from apprenticing. The nature of the trade—selling foods in warm climates without refrigeration—dictates much of the business strategy. Foods are prepared daily in the amounts calculated for sale that day. Leftover food is usually consumed by the family, occasionally recycled, fed to animals, or thrown out. Expansion of such an enterprise is difficult; credit is as likely to cause overextension or failure as growth. Rather, expansion takes on an amoeba-like character, with a daughter splitting off from her mother's firm and replicating the enterprise on another corner. Or a husband, as in the Philippines, may join the firm and lower the cost of ingredients by buying them in the rural areas. The quantum leap from sole proprietor or family proprietor to a business with employees is rare; such expectations are unrealistic and not necessary, except in the eye of some economists, for a successful street food enterprise (Barth and Kuo 1984).

Business costs reflect food costs, which vary according to availability, quality, and source. Other expenses include rental and license fees, more often paid by permanent vendors than mobile ones. Lack of payment is a convenient excuse for harassment, but conversely, payment does not protect street food vendors, even in the markets. Indications of institutionalized bribery in connection with obtaining permits were reported in Manikganj and Minia, while an Iloilo mayor reorganized the whole system after uncovering corruption in the assignment of permits to party loyalists. Obtaining water was often costly; in Manikganj most of the female employees hauled water for enterprises on a part-time basis. Fuel usage and costs varied widely across the countries; the high price of fuel was often a deciding factor in motivating customers to eat out rather than cook for themselves.

Food pricing was seldom competitive; rows of vendors would sell the same food at the same price. To maintain a consistent price as ingredients fluctuated and to keep one's customers, vendors often reduced their own profit margin or altered proportions of ingredients. In Ziguinchor the rise in the cost of millet led many producers of the breakfast porridge *monie* to thin the millet with cheaper subsidized rice. Regular customers received larger helpings or choice bits of meat.

Income from the vending enterprises was either the sole or major income of the family for most vendors. When the operation was not a family enterprise, other adult members might bring in alternative income. In Bogor, husband and wife frequently operated complementary street food enterprises rather than working together in one. In Minia, low-paid government workers or teachers supplemented their income with part-time vending; such a combination of jobs provided the family with a minimum safety net from government and income from market enterprise. Illness was found to be a principal cause of temporary or permanent cessation of single-operator enterprises, as doctor and hospital bills often consumed their entire assets.

Shifting, and generally hostile, government policies toward vendors contributes to the vicissitudes of the trade. The most persistent harassment of vendors occurred in Nigeria, yet even there alternative voices proposed less draconian approaches, emphasizing training and site upgrading. These intermediary groups have encouraged vendors to form their own associations that would provide a mechanism for vendors to interact and negotiate with government and provide services for their own members, from bulk buying to crisis funds to health clinics.

Starting the Business

Becoming a successful street food vendor is not a simple matter. Capital investment may be low for vendors who sell from carts or tables, but even this small amount separates an aspiring vendor from the poorest 20%, who are unlikely to have either the savings or the self-confidence to become microentrepreneurs (Grant et al. 1989). Research in Ziguinchor provided another reason that the poorest people do not become vendors. Since rice from their own fields took less time to harvest than it would take to earn money vending in order to buy replacement rice, poor Diola women continued to engage in subsistence agriculture; only older women in polygynous households where younger wives brought in the harvest had sufficient leisure and could afford the risk of becoming a vendor (van de Laar 1989).

Equally important are skills in both production and management. Vendors learned from their parents as unpaid family help. Others worked as employees or apprentices for family or friends. In Bogor, the *jamu* seller who had attached herself to an experienced producer-vendor sold her health drink on commission for five years before starting her own business. The noodle soup vendor learned the trade through kinship connections and utilized not only the cart and utensils but also the supply chains of these relatives. In return, he paid them a portion of his proceeds. Elsewhere, successful vendors hired assistants on a daily wage at first.

Experience among the least skilled vendors, such as those selling peanuts or cut fruit, was often minimal: it was usually limited to day labor or farming. Many had tried other forms of hawking, while a high percentage of women entering their first job had previously been housewives, a useful preparation for producing appetizing food, but perhaps not for making money. Vendors began selling street foods to earn money;

few were passionate about food. None of the restaurants in Iloilo were run by former vendors (Barth and Kuo 1984), who instead aspired to businesses with less spoilage such as grocery stores or taxi driving.

Employees

Most street food enterprises were family businesses. Even though visually most vendors appear to run their enterprises alone, they all rely heavily on unpaid family, both at the place of sale and to help produce the food at home. "Family" in the Asian cities and in Minia included spouses, but in the two African cities cultural traditions segregated the family by gender. In Ife and Ziguinchor female relatives helped prepare and sell street foods while others might take over household duties for the primary vendor. Although the Kingston study did not pursue the issue of paid or unpaid help, the descriptions of vendors suggest a similar pattern, only somewhat modified by the 10% of enterprises operated by couples.

Vignettes throughout the city chapters illustrate the admixture of paid and unpaid help and show how difficult it was to define unpaid or family help. Wherever the preparation of foods was at home, the vendor almost certainly received assistance, seldom acknowledged. Other tasks frequently carried out by family members, young and old, was buying ingredients, pushing the cart or carrying the table to the place of sale, or watching the food when the primary seller was absent.

Data collected on paid employees emphasize how critical street foods are to the survival of the urban poor. As shown in Table 8.7, the enterprises employ significant numbers of assistants, even in poverty-stricken Manikganj where many women earn money fetching water several times a day. A quarter of the enterprises in Iloilo actually paid workers and some of the larger carendarias employed four or five staff; sta-

TABLE 8.7   Paid or unpaid assistants in production and/or selling (%)

City	Work alone or operate as couple	Enterprises with assistants[a]	
		Paid	Unpaid
Manikganj, Bangladesh	36	22	64
Chonburi, Thailand	56	17	31
Ziguinchor, Senegal	95	5	25
Minia, Egypt	23	8	72
Iloilo, Philippines	47	26	44
Bogor, Indonesia	54	14	38
Ile-Ife, Nigeria	87	13	55
Pune, India	28	16	72

a. Many enterprises used both paid and unpaid help. In working couples, both are considered owners and so are not counted as unpaid family help.

tistically, the average enterprise in Iloilo employed 1.1 persons and utilized 1.8 unpaid family members plus the owners.

Although a majority of the vendors are self-employed, successful vendors also used kin or young apprentices to sell their food at another location. In Ife, 13% of the vendors were such apprentices; in Pune, 12% of the operators of kiosks or carts owned more than two, while another 2% owned three or four such outlets. In Iloilo, over 19% of vendors sold at more than one location, usually with help from relatives. Franchises were noted in Bogor, where one chicken farmer supplied 15 outlets. Producers of the local soybean cakes supplied vendors with their product, along with a cart containing a deep vessel in which the vendor deep-fried the food. Vendors of ice cream and bakery goods sometimes made the products they sold, but many more sold on commission. Vendors in Bogor pedaled bicycle carts selling bread at prices they set themselves, and returned unsold bread to the bakery. Migrants often sought out these jobs and even slept at the bakery. Most ice cream vendors also sold on commission. Together, these vendors were part of the 14% who did not own their own equipment.

Such apprentice arrangements help account for the low pay most employees received. Kin labor may only be rewarded with meals or a place to sleep. In Iloilo, employees were younger than their employers, with an average age of 24 years; they were also somewhat better educated; 30% worked part-time and were primarily students who also received free food and a bed. Across the cities, most paid employees received very low wages, especially women, but others did quite well. In Pune, where females constituted 70% of employed adult laborers, they were consistently paid between a quarter and a third less than males; male children received more than adult females. Such discrimination mirrors the general society, where unequal pay is legal. Full time male employees average monthly earnings were 513 rupees; this amount is only somewhat less than income earned by 30% of the self-employed vendors, who made under 850 rupees per month, and who utilized unpaid family assistance.

Investment Costs

An overwhelming number of vendors used their own savings to start their businesses, according to statistical data and narrative accounts. But saving strategies and alternative sources of support vary by country. In many countries, vendors used traditional rotating savings associations such as the *esusu* in Ife, *tontines* in Ziguinchor, or *arisan* in Bogor. Women used their own savings to start a venture in Ziguinchor, but they often obtained help from family members to keep the enterprise going; apparently it was more acceptable to borrow once you had proved your acumen. Although spousal income is generally included as self-investment, in Ife, where women are expected to earn a separate income, the contribution of the husbands was tabulated separately and was the source for nearly a third of the vendors. Family and friends supplied even more starting capital, a fact consistent with the system of apprenticing: eventually the young women strike out on their own, often with the help of their mentor. In Minia, many of the vendors inherited their equipment (carts, presses for sugarcane juice, mixers for ice cream) from their fathers or in-laws; one woman sold her inheritance to set her husband up in business.

Most loans for capital were interest-free, with two notable exceptions. In Iloilo, nearly one-quarter of the vendors obtained high-interest loans ranging from 5 to 40% *per month*; these vendors usually borrowed only a portion of the money needed. In Pune, by contrast, the government offers low-interest small enterprise loans up to 5,000 rupees; only 15% of the vendors spent that much on start-up costs and some 40% of vendors spent less than 1,000 rupees, which is an amount equal to monthly income for some 75% of the vendors. In other countries, vendors without access to capital started as employees; others took credit from a supplier wanting a new outlet.

Fees for Permits and Rent

The image of the independent street food seller crowding the sidewalks or filling alleys with eating shacks conjures up thoughts of spontaneous, not to say illegal, enterprises. In fact, the more permanent the place of sale, the more likely the vendors are to pay rent and to secure the various business and/or health permits required. Vendors in commercial areas necessarily have an arrangement with the nearby formal shopkeepers. Semi-mobile and ambulant vendors also paid assessments: in Bogor, with only 12% of vendors having permanent structures, 58% paid some sort of fee. Vendors who rent market stalls not only pay rent but also are assessed fees for marketplace maintenance and garbage removal. Market stalls at particularly good locations are either controlled by families or sold to new tenants through informal arrangements. Thus the occupier of a given stall may not be the person under whose name the stall is registered, a fact that inhibits a vendors' ability to obtain credit. Vendors without stalls also sell in and around markets; and in most of the cities, they are assessed a daily fee based on space occupied.

In Ziguinchor, on a day when the numbers of male and female vendors selling in the major market was about equal, Posner found that two-thirds of the vendors paying the minimum location fee of 25 francs were women, while men constituted 80% of vendors paying the higher fee of 50 francs; fees correlated directly with income. Vendors at bus stops or crossroads were similarly assessed the fee; there was no other license required. In Manikganj, government markets were similarly controlled; in addition, vendors sold from verandas in the commercial area, paying rent to the owner. Vendors were legally supposed to have business permits, but only 20% did. Since in fact the regulations were enforced only for vendors with permanent structures, about half the vendors in that category were licensed. Fees were low, but apparently both obtaining and renewing the permit might cost 10 times the official fee.

Both Minia and Iloilo clearly overregulated the trade, and this may have been a reason both cities reported bribes. In Iloilo, besides various regulations for type of business, permits were required for certain food items and from the departments of internal revenue and the health department. Market stall owners might pay the market business fee but not the others, often because their stall fee was not in their name.

Squatters on government or private land who tried to register were often refused for fear that such permits would legitimize their claim to stay in that spot. Daily cash tickets were issued to nonpermanent vendors in the markets. Not surprisingly, only 36% of the vendors had even the business license: 42% of those with permanent structures had a license, but only 7% of those without.

Minia forbade many of the foods that in fact were sold on the street: cooked meat, fish, or vegetables; and rice, macaroni, salads, cut fruits, fresh fruit juice, or milk. Candy and baked goods had to be well packaged or, if fresh, kept covered in a glass case. Many vendors obtained permits for other legal foods, then sold illegal foods that were in higher demand. A birth certificate was required for application, plus a clearance from security for anyone who had been in jail for criminal or political offenses. Finally, vendors needed a health certificate showing them to be free of communicable diseases. Vendors who wished to obtain permission to sell on a specific place could apply for a special permit; permanent structures were never approved, but many nearly unmoveable carts were allowed. A total of 72% of the vendors claimed to have a permit for vending, a figure less surprising in light of the fact that at the time of the study, many basic foodstuffs were subsidized, and vendors with licenses could obtain their own quotas for sugar, oil, or tea.

Health examinations were theoretically required in Nigeria as well. Laws on the books were practically unenforceable, and during the 1960s and 1970s the authorities did not even try. In 1983 a new military government began countrywide road clearance of vendor structures to reduce congestion, invoking not health concerns but transport efficiency. Health examinations given to vendors in Ife in a follow-up study showed that two-thirds of the women harbored some sort of parasite (Pearce 1992). In Ibadan, 83% of women tested in 1986 had various types of worms; most had never had a health examination before (Akinyele 1987).

In Pune, the Municipal Corporation voted in 1975 to stop issuing hawking licenses through its appropriately named Encroachment (Prevention) Department in an effort to reduce congestion. After the Health Department issued licenses to a dozen food vendors in 1983, all licensing was suspended. The Hawkers Union challenged the municipality in 1985 and referred to a recent Indian Supreme Court ruling that hawking could not be banned. As a result, special areas were established for street vending, while other parts of town were declared no-hawking zones. The Pune study actually inspected licenses of the vendors in its survey and found that 61% held one from the Encroachment Department, but only 14% had a license from the Health Department.

Vendors selling outside the markets often rented carts or stalls because they lacked the start-up capital to buy building materials; in Minia, vendors used neighbor's refrigerators in exchange for a small fee or some food. In Manikganj, 32% of the vendors paid rent for stalls outside the markets. In Ife, a question about rental fees was not included in the study, but appeared as an item when vendors were asked to list their fixed costs. In Ibadan, 61% of all vendors conducted their business from a permanent structure, locally called a *buka*, or semi-mobile cart, and of these two-thirds were rented. The predominance of rental space challenges conventional wisdom about the casual character of the trade, but it may indicate the trend toward more extensive grouping of vendors, as in many Nigerian cities, into a *bukateria*.

The emphasis on rental payments and licenses applies almost everywhere only to vendors who sell at a permanent place from a permanent structure or a semi-mobile cart. The poorest vendors, who sit on the ground or sell food from a basket, were looked upon with compassion by authorities everywhere. Sometimes a market official would overlook a poor woman in the Ziguinchor market and forego a fee if she did not seem to be selling much that day. If the vendors kept their selling areas clean and did not block traffic, they were tolerated in Iloilo. Officials in Manikganj interpreted the rules so that they did not apply to the poorest. This benign attitude was applied to all vendors in Bogor and also appeared in both Ife and Ibadan, despite the national campaign against the vendors. As discussed in Part I of this volume, local officials did support efforts to upgrade the markets and train the vendors in safer food handling techniques.

From this discussion, however, it is easy to understand the frustration of vendors at what they considered inappropriate regulations, and the exasperation of officials at vendors who did not comply with all the requirements necessary to obtain a permit. The need for bribes, or the fact that the vendor was a squatter, prevented many from applying for the necessary permits. Many vendors did not apply for permits because they could not afford to pay the inevitable bribes, because they were squatters, or because they simply did not have the time to go through the bureaucratic process. One vendor in Minia who sold deep-fried sweets near the railroad stations complained about the time spent obtaining the physical check-ups for his permit. Every day his wife sits next to him selling a wheat cereal. She does not have a permit because her husband does not want to subject her to such an ordeal. The fact that many vendors did not operate legally opened up the entire trade to government harassment and confiscation of their utensils and carts.

Costs of Doing Business

Besides rent and fees, fuel was a major cost for street vendors. When they prepared foods at home, this cost was often absorbed by the household; in Bangladesh, where females collect agricultural refuse and leaves for cooking, the cost is in women's time. Where foods are cooked at the point of sale, the costs are clear. In Iloilo, an analysis of expenditures by permanent vendors in 1983 found that fuel and rental costs were about equal, some 2.9% of total expenditures. Wages were higher, at 3.6%. Costs of spoilage were estimated at slightly more than 1%. Food purchases accounted for 90% of regular costs. By 1995, with greater emphasis on the use of water for washing utensils and hands, the purchase of water was double that of rental payments in the Terminal Market.

Prices for ingredients increased regularly due to inflation, fluctuating supplies, and changes in government subsidies that favored one food over another. Shortages resulting from government pricing regulations plagued vendors in Egypt and Senegal, leading them to buy on the black market at higher prices. Vendors often tried to keep food costs constant by substituting ingredients or reducing sizes.[9] In most countries vendors did not compete against each other in pricing, but rather rewarded regular customers with choice servings.[10] This supportive atmosphere had begun to erode in more modernized cities. In Iloilo, some 58% of the vendors charged the same price as their competitors, while 21% attempted to sell below their competitors. One mobile vendor in Minia, when asked about forming an organization during the study, thought that the severe competition among vendors would make it impossible. Vendors were asked in Bogor about their response to fluctuating prices of ingredients: 17% said they took a loss, 38% reduced portions, and 39% raised the price.

Credit to customers reflected this more traditional marketing style of a special relationship between regular customers and the vendor. In the Philippines, 71% of the vendors granted regular customers credit, or *suki*. About half the vendors extended credit in Bogor. A vendor selling grilled chicken and stewed beef under a tree in a Kingston park went out of business because he could not get his friends to pay for the food they ate:

> The openness of the place and the fact that there was a constant flow of pedestrian traffic in the park gave "Bird" the feeling that he had to depend on others to watch his shop for him. That sense of siege no doubt forced him to see the extension of credit as a form of security and defeated his purpose of making a living from vending (Powell et al. 1990, 74).

Gender differences in costs were identified in Minia, where women spend a third less than men; but of course women's enterprises also tended to be smaller. Returns in profit of daily costs ranged between 37% and 39% for both females and males. In Ziguinchor, women actually had higher return to their costs, but the level of costs and profits by men was six times greater than by women. This gender differential in the market was linked in Nigeria to women's chronic lack of capital, because most profits are spent on family livelihood needs (Afonja 1990).

Transportation was listed as a major expense in Minia, where so many vendors live in other towns, and in Manikganj, where fruit sellers buy their produce in distant markets. Rapid escalation of fuel prices in Nigeria deeply affected vendors in Ife, where bus fares had tripled during the previous three years (Pearce 1992). In congested Lagos, time was an equally important issue: a third of the vendors surveyed walk to work, often over a considerable distance, because they could walk in 20 minutes the distance it might take a bus one hour to cover (Adalemo et al. 1994).

Income and Profits

Street food vendors do not usually keep written records, but most have very clear memories of outlays and income. Their answers to the interviewers were more often meant to conceal their income than to exaggerate it; if anything, our figures are probably lower than actual income. Barth concluded that figures reported for Iloilo on the questionnaires were only slightly more than 60% of actual sales. After balancing vendor's answers against observed cash flow, all the studies concluded that, as a group, street food sellers make a reasonable income, especially compared to other available alternatives. Important is the wide variation reported not only between countries and within the occupation, but between women and men. Actual profits in most cities were lower for women, although return on their investment might equal or surpass that of men. Women tend to sell traditional foods that require little investment in new equipment or processors; they also work shorter hours than men.

In Iloilo, average profits were well above the official minimum daily wage which, there as elsewhere, was in fact seldom paid. The average income among vendors in Minia was 37% above the local minimum wage. Income in Bogor was higher than the wage for construction workers. When a successful vendor in Jakarta reported her profits as 10,000 rupees per day in 1983, an Indonesian official commented that if this vendor worked 25 days a month, her salary would be equal to that of a director general, a prestigious position in the bureaucracy (*Jakarta Post* 17 November 1983). In Manikganj, average incomes were more than twice the wage of an unskilled agricultural worker, more than that of a mason, and about equivalent to that of a carpenter; lowest incomes were about the same as unskilled manual labor. The six women averaged only one-third of the average male income, but that amount was nearly twice what a woman could earn in the rice mills and about the same as the wages for the seasonal food-for-work road-building projects open to women. The Chonburi study showed a daily income range that placed 58% of the vendors earning up to 4,000 baht per month, an income comparable to the wages paid to captains in the military or police, to middle school teachers, and to nurses; of course, these employees do have additional fringe benefits not available to vendors. The top 12% of vendors earned double that amount. In Pune, 75% of the vendors earned an income above the official poverty line for a family of four; another 15% achieved this level by combining vending income with other sources, but 10% of the vendors earned income below poverty level.

Nonetheless, averages mask poverty. The wide range of incomes is illustrated by figures from Iloilo, where the average daily sales were 236 pesos, but the median was 120. The Ife data, collected in 1983, reflected the economic recession and inflation and concluded that the majority of vendors made meager profits: 64% made about 96 naira per month. Compared to formal sector jobs, the income is low: custodial workers at the university were then being paid 100 naira per month, and a low-level government clerk would make 125 naira at the time. But the situation of the street food traders appears favorable in comparison to rural workers and other vendors (Kujore et al. 1988). In contrast, the Ibadan study reported vendors in 1991 making three times the minimum wage. These widely divergent results in neighboring towns apparently reflect the more rapid changes in the local economy and vendor characteristics in Ibadan than in Ife.

Ife reported that 1.4% of the vendors *did not break even*. They continued to sell so they would not lose customers; but they also fed their families from the food they made. Since vendors in Ife, perhaps more than in other cities, did not separate their business and other financial accounts and often engaged in other microenterprises or trading, they continued to sell as long as they could afford to produce the food. In Ziguinchor, many vendors of millet porridge took a 40% decrease in profits, while others switched products or went out of business after a poor millet harvest forced vendors to buy the scarce grain at high black-market prices. If unpaid labor was calculated as a cost to vending enterprises, many would report negative earnings. The Manikganj study, which showed great dependency on unpaid labor, calculated an overall drop in income by 62% that would have made most of the enterprises unprofitable. Yet more than half the enterprises fed their families from their food, a return not included in these calculations.

For most families, vending was the sole or major income. Data from most countries show that the more successful the enterprise, the more the family concentrated on vending; thus the poorer families were likely to have more alternative sources of income. For example, in Manikganj, vending was the sole income for only 47% of families, but it was the primary income for 67% of families. In Pune, over half the vendors in the lowest income categories supplied less than 40% of family income, while 21% of the most profitable vendors supplied 100% of family income. The relationship between headship and breadwinning was explored in Kingston because of the unusual family structure in Jamaica; researchers found that 53% of the females and 82% of the males defined themselves as household heads, while 63% of the women and 88% of the men said they were the principal support for their families.

In some countries, vendors combined trade with farming. In Bangladesh, 53% of the vendors derive their sole income from street food; for 29% it is the main source of income but is supplemented by agricultural produce, and for 18% vending income is less than that from farming. In Ife, 7% of the vendors also farmed. In Ziguinchor, the poorer women returned seasonally to rice farming, as they could not earn enough to pay for their families' total rice requirements. In Bogor, some vendors rented out their village land and reinvested the profits in their enterprises.

Income derived is essential to household survival. In Ziguinchor, 59% of the women vendors were the sole support of their families, which had an average size of 9.5 people, usually including three adults. In Minia, 55% of the women vendors provided the main source of income for their families; men did so 70% of the time. In Chonburi, 20% of the women were the primary support for their families, while another 21% of the women vendors, who were unmarried, contribute to their families' income. The women of Ile-Ife said they never shared their incomes with husbands, a fact partially explained by that fact that over half of the marriages were polygynous. Further, most women supported a large number of children, her own and those of kin: the modal family size was five to seven children.

In all countries the woman's income is used for household expenditures and for school fees. Typically, in Thailand, men supply the house, women the food. Men in Senegal are expected to provide the basic staple; in Ziguinchor, 84% of the men bought a large bag of rice each month for family consumption. Women's daily expenditures on food over the month equaled that of the cost of the staple, but in their own minds, and their husbands', they were merely supplying sauce for the rice. They reported clothes and school fees as their major expenditures. Many Iloilo women vendors cited school fees as the main reason for returning to work. In Ife, women said that as the economy worsened, they often had to assume responsibility for school fees in addition to feeding and clothing their children; the husband still provided the house. These livelihood expenditures took precedence over investment in the business and inhibited savings

Street Food Vending as a Microenterprise

The street food trade is characterized by owner-operated enterprises assisted primarily by unpaid family assistance; income and food from the enterprise provides a livelihood for the vendor and family equal to or better than low-entry formal sector jobs. A sexual division of labor predominates, influencing both the labor and capital input of women and men, resulting in a generally lower income for female enterprises, although return on capital may be as high as or higher than male enterprises. The implications of these findings for economic theory and women's studies, as well as for development practice, are presented and discussed in the chapter 10.

CHAPTER NINE

Foods on the Street and the People Who Eat Them

The fact that people *eat* what street food vendors sell distinguishes this trade from most other microenterprises. All cultures attach powerful meanings to individual foods, as well as to cooking and mealtime practices; thus patterns of street food consumption are shaped not just by what foods are locally available, but also by local norms about what kinds of food are appropriate to consume, where, when, and by whom. That people eat the vendors' products, usually without any further processing, obviously also raises a number of health and safety issues.

This chapter first presents an overview of the types of foods generally sold on the street, and then discusses who makes them and where. Definitions of appropriate textures and attributes of street foods vary by culture and custom, as do the attitudes of the customers concerning whether the food represents a snack or a meal. When considering who made the food, the EPOC studies distinguished between home- and industrially processed foods, and between sellers who produced their wares and those who bought them preprocessed. In the latter case, the vendors are defined as traders, not producers.

The second section focuses on the customers of street foods: who eats them, when, and how they define the food they buy. Data are drawn both from interviews at the point of sale and from household surveys. These findings illustrate the dietary importance of street foods to urban dwellers, particularly for the poor.

The third section examines nutritional concerns. The EPOC study was most interested in the nutritional content of those street foods eaten on daily basis, especially by children. In Bogor, the staff experimented with nutritional enrichments for children's favorite snacks. In Nigeria, training programs featured discussions on balanced diet. Often street foods reflect changing food habits due to international food aid and "modernizing" tastes; the nutritional implications of such shifts are briefly discussed.

The chapter's fourth section explores the health and safety aspects of street foods, an issue of critical concern to governments. A number of studies show that food consumed immediately after cooking and eaten directly from a stick or banana leaf is generally safe. Contamination comes primarily from utensils and plates via the water used to "clean" them, as well as from airborne pollution. Standards of food handling during processing and cooking mirror local habits, which often prove hard to change. Local groups, frequently with support from the FAO, have initiated various training programs designed to teach both vendor and customer about food contaminants and safe food handling practices.

Varieties and Attributes of Foods Sold on the Street

Vendors in the streets of the cities studied sell a stunning array of foods. The varieties of foods and their popularity reflect culture and custom, as well as economic circumstances. Even the categorization of foods varied by country. In Manikganj, as throughout South Asia, foods are considered "hot" or "cold" not in terms of serving temperature or spicing, but rather in terms of their effect on the body. This influences which foods are sold in which seasons. Elsewhere the seasonality of foods is less structured but still apparent: in the hot seasons, Indonesians quench their thirst with hot noodle soups, but there as in the other cities they also cool the palate with ice cream and shaved ice with syrup. Certain foods are considered appropriate for specific holidays such as Ramadan or Christmas. Food textures also vary. Nigerians like their foods in heavy sauces, almost like soup or stews; most Asian curries top rice with liquid sauces, but many foods eaten with rice or noodles in Iloilo are fairly dry. Wet and dry tended to parallel the distinction between a meal and a snack.

All studies sought to distinguish between street food meals and snacks, but the definition of these categories varied by country. In many countries a *meal* requires rice at home, so food on the street becomes a "light meal," a snack, or a meal substitute. Snacks also mean "munchies" or sweets, hardly an alternative to a meal unless it is part of the pattern of "grazing," as in Iloilo or Bogor, where many poor eat frequently to keep up their strength. The term "meal constituents" is used to describe foods normally eaten with other foods, whether at the vending site or at home.

In larger and more congested cities, more people tend to eat meals at the point of sale rather than at home; many stationary vendors erect stalls in or move their semi-mobile carts out to the neighborhoods where their clients live. Also, in cities where eating out is socially acceptable and commuting home for lunch is impractical, customers are also more likely to eat full meals, rather than simply snacks, on the streets. In such cities many street food enterprises resemble small cafeterias, complete with tables and chairs. Although the EPOC definition of street foods—those sold from structures with three or fewer permanent walls—seemed clear when the study began, establishing the distinction on the spot was less obvious. Most studies mapped all food establishments in their cities before determining which would be considered a street food. In Minia, the census mapped 29 establishments that offered cooked meals and shish kebab: of these, 19 were formal sector restaurants; the rest were street foods, seven three-walled structures, and three semi-mobile carts. A subsequent study in Iloilo detailed the 122 restaurants, canteens, and bakeries of the central city and found no street food entrepreneurs had crossed over to this formal sector. However, canteens resembled street food *carendarias*, which emphasizes the next step for urban prepared food (Barth and Kuo 1984). The *carendarias* of Iloilo, the *bukas* in Nigeria, the parking lot street foods in Bogor, the "hotels" in Manikganj, the *tanganas* in Ziguin-chor—all are forms of "street cafeterias," at the top end of the street food trade. These establishments prepared and processed the food at the site, served a variety of foods and beverages, usually had employees, and totaled the highest profits of all vendors.

In Pune, where caste considerations limit the food that practicing Hindus will eat from vendors of a different or lower caste, the number of vendors is increasing, but it is still tiny in comparison with the city's 1.5 million inhabitants. Even including paid and unpaid assistants, the number of people in street vending accounts for less than 1% of the total labor force. Snacks are the predominant street food and are sold by 86% of the vendors. These foods are often fried in clarified butter (*ghee*), a cooking method that relaxes some caste restrictions which apply to food cooked in water.[1] Inexpensive street meals, cooked with water and so subject to food restrictions, are a new phenomenon in Pune; the study staff decided to include all 21 such vendors among their survey sample of 236 vendors. Of these, 13 were women, a figure that accounted for 40% of all female street food vendors. These street meals consisted of traditional foods, curry made either with lentils or animal intestines and served with millet flatbread. Three-quarters of the customers interviewed were caste Hindus, but all were homeless or in familial disgrace. Street meals provide critical food for these marginalized men and women.

This limited demand for street foods is opposite the situation in Southeast Asia. Over 200 foods were identified on the street of Bogor and Iloilo; in Chonburi, general categories encompassed choices too numerous to detail. In all three countries the most common meal consists of a selection of dishes served over rice or noodles. Purchasing meal constituents in small quantities, to eat at a table on the premises, or taken home to serve over rice from the electric cooker, allows for variety with an ease that home cooking cannot.

The Yoruba have a long history of eating meals on the street. Vendors in Ife offered 335 different foods and 74 usual combinations from which customers could choose. Most were traditional foods based on yam, cassava, beans, and corn and were the favorite foods of the less affluent living in the Yoruba city center. University area vendors found a higher demand by students and faculty, about 25% non-Yoruba, for more recently introduced foods such as tea, bread, and biscuits.

Vendors who produced at home, typically with unpaid family help, often sold this single food from a cart or table. Most women in Ziguinchor fit this pattern; they said if they had more money they would add a less labor-intensive food to their offerings: production time was their major constraint in making more food, but spoilage was always a concern in a one-person enterprise with no refrigeration. Two popular but very time-consuming foods, morning porridge (*monie*) and millet couscous, are more often taken home than eaten on site, although the market vendors do breakfast on *monie*.

The Kingston study recorded 44% of the vendors selling only one type of food. In Manikganj, 29% sold only a single item, primarily snacks; almost half of all vendors sold three or fewer items. But the other vendors ran cafeteria-type establishments or grocery shops that also sold ready-to-eat food. This division between sit-down cafeteria and take-out snacks was clear in the customer survey; large majorities said they never buy ready-to-eat meals of any kind.

Food-related gender differences were identified in many cities. Women were not observed selling ice cream in any city, although they may have produced it; ice cream vendors had to push heavy carts and usually sold on commission. The four adult male vendors selling at bus and taxi stands in Ife all sold food made by someone else, primarily bottled sodas and packaged snacks. In Ziguinchor, only men sold brochettes, bon-bons, and coffee, all French-influenced foods. Young men move up into the coffee stalls serving *tangana*, a local version of the continental breakfast, consisting of Nescafe or herb tea, sweetened with condensed milk, and served with French bread and butter. Bon-bons are wheat cookies baked in large ovens; most bakers had worked in French establishments, where they acquired both the skills and savings for the business.

Perhaps surprising in a country with such conservative sex roles, the six female vendors in Manikganj were each in a different activity. But they were all destitute, and apparently so marginalized that it did not matter what they sold. In most other cities there was a considerable overlap in the types of food sold by men and women, but some specialities exist. Nonindigenous foods from China or India were mostly sold by men in Chonburi. In Bogor, women made *gado-gado*, the boiled salad with peanut sauce, while only men sold fruit salads. Men also predominated in selling noodle soup or salty snacks, both sold from mobile carts, and only men sold bread on commission, peddling the carts through the neighborhoods. The study in Minia did not record any women selling *kushary*, the local specialty of macaroni, rice, and lentils with sauce; but personal observation showed that many operators were couples. Special tonics for the health were sold almost exclusively by women in Bogor but by men in Kingston, "concoctions . . . believed capable of enhancing their masculinity" (Powell et al. 1990, 22). Men also dominated the selling of traditional meals in Jamaica, in contrast to the situation in Ife; as street foods are recognized as a profitable trade, more men are joining in both Jamaica and Nigeria.

Processing Street Foods

The overwhelming majority of vendors made what they sold, from over three-quarters to a high of 96% in Ziguinchor, with the notable exceptions being Manikganj and Kingston (see Table 9.1). Manikganj is characterized by an intricate marketing system, whereby village women produce traditional favorites such as spiced munchies (*canacur*) or chutney at home and sell them either to itinerant middlemen or directly to grocery stores or street vendors. A seventh woman vendor in the Manikganj market was actually a wholesaler of *canacur* that she and her family produce. Most of the dry snack

TABLE 9.1   Vendors as food processors and/or sellers (%)

City	Process and sell food	Sell already processed foods
Manikganj, Bangladesh	43	57
Chonburi, Thailand	88	12
Ziguinchor, Senegal	96	4
Minia, Egypt	85[a]	15
Iloilo, Philippines	75[b]	25
Bogor, Indonesia	86	14
Ile-Ife, Nigeria	74	26
Kingston, Jamaica	19	81

a. Of food; 75% of beverages were industrially made.
b. 56% of total food processed on site; 16% processed at home.

sellers, who constitute 37% of all vendors, buy these snacks from local women for resale and are thus defined as middlemen. Sugar candy, made from date or sugarcane juice, is another food commonly resold to vendors. As a result, well over half the vendors are middlemen, though many also sell foods they process themselves.

These backward linkages to home-based food producers are typical throughout Southeast Asia. Women produce traditional sweets, such as sweetened and spiced shredded coconut enclosed in sticky rice and steamed in a banana leaf. Selling such delicacies is so pervasive that the Indonesians call this custom *titipan*. In Iloilo some vendors of these sweets sold directly, while others sold to other vendors or stores. Selling meals on contract directly to customers is also widespread. This custom is referred to by the name of the *tiffin* boxes (stacked aluminum containers secured by a handle from the bottom) used to transport the food, *rantangan* in Indonesian, *pin-to* in Thai. The household survey in Iloilo found that 13% of food eaten but not produced at home was actually home delivered. We termed this "invisible street foods" as it is sold *through* the streets but not *on* the streets; this important part of urban feeding patterns needs further study. Because the EPOC studies used the vendor as the entry point to ready-to-eat foods, we only observed these practices incidentally.

The data from Kingston shows the opposite trend, away from home-produced foods in favor of industrially packaged snacks and bottled drinks. In contrast to other EPOC studies where the foods selected for closer observation were those produced by the vendor, in Kingston, where food industries' products saturate the street foods market, two of the five categories were specifically selected to include "pre-prepared, nontraditional" liquids or solids.

Most, but not all, of the foods in these categories were industrially processed foods, such as chips or carbonated beverages. But classifying milk, tea, and shaved-ice drinks as "nontraditional" in Jamaica shows how differently local inhabitants perceive the same foods. In Bogor, for example, shaved-ice drinks have a long tradition. Vendors in Manikganj have long run tea shops, but tea is considered a new food in Ife. Milk is seldom sold because of lack of refrigeration; presumably, milk in Kingston was irradiated. Buns and cheese were listed in the pre-prepared solids list: most yeast breads are in fact relatively new products in the cities studied, but they have become so pervasive elsewhere that they were accepted as part of fast foods on the street. Increasingly all these items, from tea to ice, are industrially produced.

Except in Kingston, most products on the street were thus homemade. The percentages are much higher for solid foods than for liquids. Almost everywhere carbonated beverages and beer have replaced local drinks, much to the delight of municipal health officers, who know these industrially produced beverages are much safer. So pervasive are beer and cola that in Iloilo, wholesalers actually delivered crates of beverages to permanent street food stalls. One reason that Ziguinchor has the highest percentage of self-processed foods is that the vendors there do not usually sell bottled drinks, because they cannot afford to buy a cold storage container. Beer is sold in bars which, having four walls, were not included in the study; in the market, small grocery stores sell soft drinks. Alcoholic drinks were not openly available either in Minia or Manikganj, although in the latter town an alcohol-based medicine could be purchased at ayurvedic medicine shops and was drunk when eating a local specialty of curried chickpeas and potatoes (*chatpotti*).[2] Three-quarters of the drinks in Minia were industrially made. As noted, in Ife all four adult male street vendors surveyed sold drinks and packaged snacks; women made the food they sold.

As men and women often sell different foods, so do they also spend different amounts of time producing and selling their wares. In Ziguinchor, women vendors sell traditional foods that require many hours of preparation, which their customers can thus avoid; out of the six-hour day they devote to the street food trade, the women spent about two hours at home preparing the food and four hours in the market selling. The men, on the other hand, sold foods demanding much less advanced preparation; that and the absence of household responsibilities allowed the men to devote at least eight hours a day to vending, only one hour of which was spent in preparation. In Minia, a majority of both men and women prepared their foods at home (51% of the males and 62% of the females), but more men did their preparation on-site (30% of the males and only 19% of the females); women were twice as likely as men (12% to 6%) to buy pastries from a tradesman for resale.

Processing does not always take place at home. Vendors selling meals in Ife prepared the foods on site. In Iloilo, 56% of the foods were prepared on site, 16% at home. Other foods are partly prepared at home; for example, meat balls and other ingredients for noodle soup are ready for combining with noodles cooked to order in Chonburi or Bogor. Time invested in preparation still varies tremendously by food item; less complex vending operations such as the ubiquitous roast corn require little preparation at site and none at home. The type of food prepared rather than gender explained time differentials in Chonburi.

Street vendors play many economic roles, making their trade difficult to classify: at all levels they produce, trade, and serve food. But distinctions exist within the trade by the type of food served, amount and place of processing, and place of sale. This broad spectrum of foods and services shows the depth of the urban food system outside formal restaurants, and underscores the necessity of distinguishing among them in legislation, interventions, and training.

Demand for Street Foods

According to a 1990 survey of the world's 100 largest metropolitan areas, food costs exceeded 50% of household incomes in 23 cities, the highest being Ho Chi Minh City (80%), Lima (70%), and Lagos (58%). The survey emphasized that the poorer the family, the higher the percentage of their income that goes toward food (Population Crisis Committee 1990). Our studies of food expenditures found similar rates, with figures ranging from 51% of household income in Iloilo to 74% in Ziguinchor (see Table 9.2). In Chonburi the lowest income quartile spent 65% of income on food, versus 44% among the highest; the contrast was even sharper in Iloilo, where the poorest quartile spent 77%, while the wealthiest spent only 40% of their income on food.

Street foods are frequently cheaper than home-prepared foods, especially when time spent shopping and cooking is factored in. The preparation of traditional dishes, such as millet porridge in Ziguinchor, is often extremely time-consuming; for this reason many people prefer to buy these foods on the street. In Ife, as the economic recession worsened and the cost of imported food increased, the middle class reported eating more traditional foods, bought on the street to save time. A food consumption survey in Dakar found that while 32% of families eat couscous daily, only 12% of the urban women prepared it themselves (CILSS 1980). Both food and fuel costs are higher per capita when cooking for only a few people. Small families in Chonburi spent 58% of their food budget on street foods, compared to the 36% spent in families having eight or more members.

TABLE 9.2   Household expenditure on food/street foods (%)

City	Food	Street foods
Manikganj, Bangladesh	64	16[a]
Chonburi, Thailand	55	47[b]
Ziguinchor, Senegal	74	NA
Iloilo, Philippines	51	23[a,b]
Bogor, Indonesia	60 urban	25
Ile-Ife, Nigeria	NA	50

NA = not applicable.

a. Expenditure on street foods is higher for the poorest quartile: 23% in Manikganj and 28% in Iloilo.

b. Expenditure on food is much higher for the poorest families, with those in Chonburi spending 65% and in Iloilo 77%.

Other factors also influence the consumption of street foods. In Iloilo, travel costs to go home from downtown, when added to the cost of a home-prepared meal, came to as much as or more than the cost of eating street foods near the workplace, without considering the costs of time lost. In addition, eating street foods avoids wastage from leftover home-cooked meals, which do not keep well in the many poor homes without refrigerators. The rising cost of firewood also affects food costs for many traditional foods grilled over coals to enhance their taste; such costs are promoting a switch from firewood to kerosene or natural gas for most cooking purposes, a shift that also reduces pollution that was identified as a growing problem in the FAO study on Kampala, Uganda (FAO 1992c).

As shown in Table 9.2, our data on the percentage of the household food budget spent on street foods goes from nearly half in Ife and Chonburi to 16% in Manikganj. Yet even in this Bangladeshi town, members of the lower-income group spent 23% of their food budget on street foods. Such customers are primarily men who lack the time to go home for a meal and who find street foods economical. In Chonburi, busy working women spent nearly 50% of their household food budgets on prepared food, but even nonworking housewives, who presumably have more time to cook, reported spending 40%. In the Southeast Asian cities, as well as in Ibadan, street food expenditures increased with income. In both Manikganj and Lagos, however, they declined dramatically at higher income levels.

Much of the food purchased on the street is taken home to eat. In Chonburi, three-quarters of all households bought prepared food for lunch, and 13% of the households surveyed never cooked at home. In Ife, 83% of all households surveyed bought breakfast between four and seven days a week. Snacks, which can be eaten any time for any meal, were the favorite purchase in Iloilo.

These data are based on one-time household surveys and lack the robustness of the economic data on the street food enterprises,[3] but they do demonstrate the crucial contribution to the urban diet of foods eaten *outside* the home. This finding is especially important given that food and nutrition studies conducted by the FAO and other organizations used to count only those foods consumed within the household. Morever, there is every indication that cities in developing countries become larger and more congested, and as citizens spend more time working farther away from their homes, they are eating out more often, as are people in the United States. In the United States, the Restaurant Industry Report for 1993 stated that the average family spent 36% of its food budget on meals and snacks outside the home, an increase from 25% in 1950; the typical person eats 3.5 meals per week away from home (National Restaurant Association 1993).

Customers

An estimated 47,000 customers a day, or 60 customers per enterprise, ate street foods in Minia in 1984; that figure equals one-quarter of its total population. Customers in Minia and around the world represent all occupations and all income levels; but their

TABLE 9.3   Occupations of customers (%)

City	White-collar	Market trader/ laborer	Students	Housewives/[a]	Other	Male
Manikganj, Bangladesh	43	43[b]	12	0	2	98
Chonburi, Thailand	20	48	15	10	7	38
Ziguinchor, Senegal	34	7	35	17	7	55
Iloilo, Philippines	21	47	16	12	4	51
Bogor, Indonesia	14	37	33	12	4	56
Ile-Ife, Nigeria	29	31	37	0	3	58

a. Housewives means unemployed women.
b. Includes 22% farmers.

demographic mix varies by country (as shown in Table 9.3).[4] As expected, the largest group of customers in most cities came from the informal sector of non-waged workers: market traders, taxi drivers, domestic servants, construction workers, and other street food vendors. In no city were they an overall majority, though in Iloilo this group accounted for 47% of the customers. Manikganj was the only city where large numbers of farmers were recorded; adding them to the list of the self-employed brings that total to 43%. At the other extreme, only about 7% of customers came from these informal and blue collar jobs in Ziguinchor. Of course some traders ate their own product, but most adult customers (and 34% of all customers) were men with regular income, namely government employees, merchants, and salaried workers. In Ife, the customer base was considerably more diverse.

The studies expected students to be well-represented, but found both the totals and the ages of student customers surprisingly variable. About a third of all customers in Bogor, Ziguinchor, and Ife were students. In Iloilo and Chonburi, schools provide canteens for students so that theoretically they eat street foods only as snacks. However, as detailed in the chapter on Iloilo, the canteens often purchase their foods from street vendors; in Manikganj also, schools make direct arrangements with street food sellers to supply a light midday meal. Because these foods were not sold directly to the children, the transactions were not recorded in the EPOC statistics, thus reducing the number of student customers recorded in the two cities.[5] In Chonburi, schools often hire former street food vendors as cooks, who then provide meals at schools using school equipment. Other vendors must wait outside the school or university enclosure. Our figures do not include on-campus sales. Data from Chonburi, Ziguinchor, and Manikganj all show that young children consume more street foods than older students, perhaps because the parents give young children money for a treat.

White-collar workers included government officers and clerks, teachers, and lawyers; businessmen and shop owners were also classified as such, but the customers specified their occupations and there was an ambiguous line between market vendor and business owner. In Manikganj, 24% of the customers were listed as business/

selling, for example, even though some of the sellers might elsewhere be considered from the informal sector; they are combined with the 19% of customers who were government servants, police, army, or salaried employees in private firms. The non-waged group includes rickshaw pullers, construction workers, and domestic servants (male in Bangladesh), as well as shop employees. Clearly, local status perceptions affected how people classified their occupations in different cities.

"Housewife" was a residual category for women who did not state an occupation. In many cultures, working, especially in agriculture, confers a lower status on women than unemployment; certainly some of the "housewives" in Ziguinchor worked in the fields. In contrast, none of the female customers identified herself in this manner in Ife.

About half of all customers were male in Ziguinchor, Ife, Iloilo, and Bogor. In Chonburi, because so many people carry food home, men account for only two-fifths of the customers. Data from Manikganj reflect the restrictions of purdah; 98% of the 436 customers interviewed were male. Among the 10 women interviewed, only one identified herself as a housewife, which is not surprising given that women who stay at home in Manikganj are expected to cook there as well. The other nine female customers included four students, three wage laborers, one schoolteacher, and one beggar.

Gender differences among customers appeared in most of the other cities as well.[6] Late-night customers, who often washed down their street foods with alcohol, were overwhelmingly male, whether they were munching snacks in Iloilo, enjoying the high life in Kingston, drinking "medicine" with *chotpotti* in Manikganj, eating noodles after the cinema in Chonburi, or relaxing in the parks in Pune. In Ziguinchor, men frequented the bars at night, but since these are four-walled structures they were not counted as street food enterprises. Men in Ziguinchor bought the French-style *tangana* for breakfast, while women bought *monie* to eat or take home. The sole exception among the cities studied is Chonburi where women indulge in public eating.

Breakfast was the most popular street food meal in Ife and Ibadan, as well as in Ziguinchor. Yet numbers of customers observed in the morning and at noon did not correspond with the data on meals eaten. This apparent contradiction is due to the fact that Nigerians take the word "break-fast" literally: the first meal of the day, at whatever hour, is breakfast. Nearly three-quarters of all consumers in Chonburi eat a street food lunch of light meals and snacks. The line between a light snack and a heavy meal is a definitional one; in Iloilo, because of the *merienda* custom of eating throughout the day, snacks were the food most consumed.

Cultural definitions of meals versus snacks vary, but because most street foods are served or packaged for fast take-out, the trade as a whole plays a similiar role in the urban eating patterns of developing countries as do fast food chains in the West. The increasing number of Kentucky Fried Chicken, Pizza Hut, and McDonald's outlets opening in poorer countries, however, tend to cater to expatriates and the local elite. Entrepreneurs in both Indonesia and the Philippines are challenging these chains with local versions. The Manila-based Jollibee's now serves hamburgers throughout the

Philippine archipelago, while two Central Javanese fried chicken chains, Sri Candi and Ayam Goreng Kalasan, are standard fare in Bandung, Jakarta, and Bogor. Street vendors claim that these chains compete against each other but pose no threat to their own businesses, which not only charge far lower prices but also offer familiar indigenous dishes, spiced and sauced in accordance with local tastes.

But Is It Nutritious?

The wide popularity of street foods in the urban diet of developing countries raises concerns of their nutritional value, particularly in the face of dire statistics showing that one in five people in the developing world are chronically undernourished (FAO and WHO 1992a) and that the caloric deficit is greatest among the urban poor (Berg 1987). Malnutrition is particularly severe among poor urban children; nutritional deprivation at young ages often impairs both mental and physical development. Improving the nutrient value of street foods, especially snack foods favored by children, is considered an effective way to address these low nutritional levels (FAO 1989).

Snack foods in the United States are indelibly linked in most people's minds with the idea of junk food or "empty calories" because of their high fat and/or sugar content. Yet all calories, from whatever source, do contribute to the body's energy needs; bottled soft drinks in developing countries are expensive, but safe to drink, and fried foods add nutrients to otherwise spartan rice-based diets. Household food consumption studies completed in the Philippines by the Food and Nutrition Research Institute during the 1970s reported chronic undernutrition and an intake of fats and oils less than half the recommended daily allowance (see Barth 1983, 8–9). But today such a study would combine household and street food consumption and show a more balanced and adequate nutritional status.

Many particularly nutritious street foods contain complementary vegetable protein. In Minia, for example, the protein in bean-based *foul* and *tamia* is enhanced when it is served in a wheat bread sandwich. One plate of *kushary*, which combines cereals and legumes, provides one-fifth of the daily requirements of calories and proteins for a laborer, or one-quarter for a sedentary adult.

In Bogor, representative meals costing 300 and 500 rupiah (Rp.) were purchased, weighed, and analyzed. (Recall that the average daily income earned by a vendor in the lowest quartile was Rp. 790 per day, an amount considered barely adequate for subsistence.) Tests showed that the cheaper meal was the best bargain, as it supplied almost half the total nutritional needs for calories and protein and more than half the iron and vitamins A and C. The more expensive meal was not proportionately more nutritional. Chapman called the Rp. 300 meal "an unsung bargain that the urban poor must make use of and the better-off can use to occasionally economize," and she emphasized that two well-chosen meals at this price "can supply virtually all the nutrients needed for a day" (Chapman 1984, 53). Based on the household survey data about consumption levels of street foods, the staff concluded that each household member received 14% of calories, 20% of protein, and 4% of vitamin A from prepared food purchases.

The importance of selecting nutritious foods among the plethora of dishes available in the Philippine cities studied is underscored by a similar analysis of the nutritional values of four commonly purchased foods: meat, fish, vegetable *viands*, and rice. Meats provide the most calories and proteins, while vegetable dishes are important for their minerals and vitamins. But when these advantages are weighed against cost, rice provides the most calories per peso and helps explain its dominant role in the local diet. Snack foods provide an important protein source: a single serving contributes 10% of protein and 11% of calories of the recommended daily allowance. Well-chosen *viands* snacks add necessary nutrients to the local rice diet. But customers do not tend to consider nutritional content when making their selections; rather they "merely depend on the matter of taste and satiety values" (FAO-Pune 1986, 65).

Such considerations have motivated nutritionists in both countries to encourage street food vendors to introduce new nutrient-enriched foods. A soybean "cheese" was sold first through vendors in Manila.[7] Attempts in Bogor to add protein value to the puffed cassava or rice chip *krupuk*, however, were undermined by rising soybean prices. Since bottled weaning foods are expensive in these countries, mothers often buy fruit or porridge on the street. In Ziguinchor, the staff tried introducing a special cowpea purée for babies. A government-supported Infant Cereal Project in Benin distributed dry infant cereal through street and marketplace vendors in the capital city Cotonou (Cohen 1987).

Schoolchildren are major consumers of street foods: in Indonesia alone some 30 million elementary school children buy snacks and small meals from vendors every day, spending several hundred rupiahs each en route to and from school and during recess. To enhance the nutritional value of some favorite snacks, faculty at the Bogor Agricultural Institute added beans to cassava cookies and thus provided complementary protein. Street foods play a similiarly important role in the diet of Filipino schoolchildren; there the Food and Nutrition Research Institute has developed a nutritionally enhanced recipe for fish balls. As early as 1978, the Catholic Relief Services introduced a high-protein version of cheese curls fortified with soy, vitamins, and minerals; puppets were used to introduce both the new snack food and nutrition messages to the schools (CRS 1978). Children devour the improved fish balls and cheese curls; a baked "nuti-bun" that used fortified flour donated through American food aid was less well received because the flour was so old it smelled and was full of bugs (interview with a school nutritionist in Iloilo, 15 June 1994).

European and American food aid has altered food habits and street foods in many countries. Bread is now a major breakfast food in Indonesia and Senegal; neither country produces wheat, but both received considerable amounts of subsidized wheat. Women yogurt makers in Ziguinchor saw their fresh-milk yogurt business undercut by the arrival on the market of large bags of donated dried milk; men with more capital began to make bulk purchases of the milk powder in order to produce and market larger quantities of yogurt themselves. Many sellers used the subsidized rice to extend the usually cheaper millet in this breakfast porridge. When the Egyptian government reduced longstanding wheat subsidies, street food vendors in Minia saw the price of flatbread for their sandwiches rise dramatically.

Consumption of meals and meal constituents by street vendors and their families proved to be an important source of food in most of the cities. Eating from the pot was common in Ife; relatives came to fetch free meals in Bogor and Iloilo. Single-item vendors in Ziguinchor and Manikganj seemed better able to estimate the daily demand and so were less likely to have leftovers for their families. In Minia, leftovers not eaten by the family were fed to the livestock.[8] Food was seldom thrown away. Some foods, such as yogurt or dried snacks and chips, could safely be held over for later sale. But reheating or mixing certain leftovers into soups poses a health threat; such practices were not widespread, probably because the family was happy to eat up all the remaining food.

Is It Safe?

Food safety is of great concern to municipal authorities, usually more so than nutrition, but few customers of street food vendors seem overly concerned, with good reason, as food handling practices of vendors generally reflect prevailing local standards and food sold on the street is not significantly more contaminated than that sold in restaurants.

Contamination comes primarily from either dirty plates, utensils, and hands, or from dust or flies that land on the food while they are held for sale. Foods just cooked and eaten off a stick or served on bread or a banana leaf are generally safe. Sometimes regular customers bring their own bowls and spoons for soups or sauce dishes. Efforts to persuade vendors to use paper plates failed because of the cost. Both the EPOC and FAO studies conclude that until customers demand more sanitary food handling, and are willing to pay for it, local practices are not likely to change substantially (FAO 1988, 1992a). Regulations that required expensive equipment or new carts or stalls would drive up product prices, and thus would be resisted by customer and vendor alike. Food held longer than six hours is at much greater risk of contamination; but in Indonesia it is customary to cook early in the morning, then allow the food to cool to room temperature before eating it at midday or evening, or even the following morning. Even when guests are present, food brought hot from the kitchen is left to cool while conversation continues. As long as customers, raised in this tradition, assume that cold cooked food is safe, no demand exists for reheating food or keeping it warm.

That said, these studies did point to two important ways that street food safety can be improved. The first calls on the municipality to improve water and garbage removal services and to provide public latrines near popular vending sites. The second focuses on training the vendors in simple practices to make their products safer and often more nutritious. Both measures have proven more effective than punitive laws and regulations.

Food Handling

Food may be contaminated at any step of the process, from origin to consumption. With the exception of polluted oysters sold in Ziguinchor, which had been harvested from the river just below the city's major sewage outlet, the samples of street foods tested in the EPOC cities were safe to eat. Pesticides did not seem to be a problem, although reports of illness from the use of vegetables treated with illegal pesticides was reported at an FAO workshop in Accra (FAO 1992a). Meat was served in all countries studied, but nowhere was insufficient cooking linked to illness from street foods. Because most vendors shop daily, food does not spoil in storage. But in Senegal, Indonesia, the Philippines, and Thailand, where peanuts and peanut butter are widely used for snacks and sauces, aflatoxin is a danger. Produced by a mold that flourishes on damaged peanuts, as well as other grains, stored in warm, moist conditions, aflatoxin is a carcinogen that can cause serious liver damage.

The sanitary conditions of the neighborhoods where vendors live and often produce their goods are hardly conducive to safe food preparation. In Iloilo, for example, women cook a popular midday snack, sweet rice wrapped in banana leaves, every evening in their homes in the squatter areas. Due to the lack of any type of sewer or drainage system, the area floods every time it rains. Because houses are packed very close together and only a few alleys lead into the area, most people have to reach their homes along narrow foot paths that may contain human excrement. The water used to soak the rice comes from a well that is often inundated by flood water. Once the cakes are made, they are allowed to dry in the open, where they are exposed to flies and rodents.

Vendors' workspaces in their carts and stalls are open to customers' view. Research staff in Manikganj rated the street food enterprises on a five-point scale: very clean, clean, OK, somewhat dirty, and very dirty. Even though the research staff were all college graduates from urban areas, they judged two-thirds of the enterprises as clean and one-fifth as very clean. No vendors were graded very dirty. As I visited the area, my own mental grading would not have been so generous, a reaction that underscores the cultural basis of cleanliness standards.

The faculty directors of the Ife project found much to criticize about the food handling practices of *buka* operators:

> The standard of hygiene and sanitation within and around these structures leaves much to be desired. . . . Refuse is left uncleared and open drains uncleaned. . . . Clothing of sellers was dirty, so were the utensils for cooking. . . . open latrines were round the corners from where cooking was being done. Crockery and cutlery were left in a filthy state, not having been washed immediately after use. When eventually washed, it was done with dirty water" (Kujore and Pearce 1989, 75–76).

Besides the risks posed by poor sanitation, some of the vendors' methods of "embellishing" products or cutting costs may themselves be dangerous. Among the riskiest practices in some countries is the use of general-purpose dyes to color certain foods a bright but potentially poisonous red. Others, of more or less concern in various countries, include the use of rancid oil in deep frying, the dilution of milk or fruit juices with unboiled water, and the use of unauthorized sweetening compounds or excessive quanitities of monosodium glutamate. Finally, inappropriate packaging of take-out foods poses a commonly overlooked threat. Old newspapers are frequently used to serve or wrap street foods as 41% of vendors did in Pune, a practice assumed reasonably safe. There are, however, important exceptions. In May 1984, the Indonesian news media reported a child's death caused from eating food packaged with cardboard from a DDT canister. Plastic bags may be clean and convenient but can accelerate microbial activity.

In addition to observing food preparation and sanitary conditions at the vendors' worksites and in their homes, the EPOC studies tested for the presence of coliform bacteria or fecal matter, as well as for contamination by the more common enteric pathogens such as salmonella, shigella, and cholera organisms. Food selected for sampling had often been cooked some hours before, so that the actual time of cooking, as well as the time of purchase for testing, was recorded. As in Ife, the tests indicated that recently cooked food had no pathogens present. An exception in Iloilo were donuts, which may have become contaminated when they were brushed with margarine and dipped into an open container of sugar. Fried peanuts remained free of coliform organisms even after they had been allowed to stand almost 24 hours. All other foods that stood for six hours, including food cooked six hours earlier and reheated, showed intermediate bacterial contamination. Uncooked foods, such as yogurt, were also frequently contaminated.

In Pune, a more extensive analysis included 252 samples of cooked and uncooked food and of water, collected not only from 85 street food vendors, but also from 27 restaurants and from 37 nonprofit "eating houses" for the poor. All samples were allowed to incubate for 48 hours, allowing for contaminants to bloom. Not unexpectedly, the results were that 80% of the street vendors' samples contained bacteria and 49% contained fecal matter. However, only two samples, both of uncooked food, showed pathogens.

Further examination of the results produced three significant and unexpected conclusions: First, a comparison of contamination with the level of sanitation where the vendors had their stalls showed that "the bacteriological quality of street food is not related to the environmental conditions around vending sites" (Bapat 1990, 44). The survey had found 37% of vending sites near a municipal refuse dump, 25% near uncleared garbage, 19% near stagnant water, and 13% near open drains; some vendors were selling near all these hazards. The Pune report emphasized these findings to show that Pune Municipality policy of assigning vending sites away from degraded environments will not alone ensure food safety. Other factors, such as vendors' food handling practices and the quality of sanitary services, are equally critical.

Second, foods served in the restaurants and eating houses were bacteriologically no better than street foods. Samples from both restaurants and eating houses contained more fecal coliforms than did those from street vendors, but marginally fewer bacteriological contaminants. The conclusion concerning public restaurants is consistent with similar findings elsewhere (Jayasuriya 1994). In Pune, the findings regarding eating houses is particularly important in light of these nonprofit services' efforts to implement safety and sanitary practices "at all levels such as mode of preparation distribution, storage and serving" (FAO-Pune 1986, 84). Such groups as the Indira Community Kitchen Society and Hamal Panchayat cook inexpensive meals in a centralized kitchen and then sell them at outlets near the railroad and places where laborers are concentrated. Although their operations appear clean, the high rates of fecal contamination suggest inadequate handwashing.

Finally, and most surprising, the data show that the cheapest street meals, cooked by the poorest vendors under the worst conditions (mostly women living in squatter areas) then sold and eaten on the pavement, were actually slightly less contaminated with bacteria and much less likely to contain fecal matter than other samples. "It is creditable on the part of women street food vendors who sell food in such degraded environment . . . that the quality of the food they sell is less unsatisfactory than that served in restaurants" (Bapat 1992, 48).

Water samples from vendors' storage tanks were collected by both Pune street food studies and found to be a major source of contamination. Some 84% of the vendors used potable city water, so contamination came from unsanitary storage. About 5% used questionable sources such as the canal or wells; the other vendors, mostly selling packaged snacks, did not provide water for drinking, nor did they use it on-site. Disposal of waste water is a related problem, since lack of such facilities encourages continued use of dirty water for washing: 60% of vendors made no arrangement for disposal and 26% used buckets or tins; only 4% were judged to have adequate arrangements.

Water availability and safety varied dramatically across the countries studied. In Ife, only 35% of the vendors used running tap water; almost half used wells, many of which are shallow and undoubtedly contaminated. Since customers eat with their fingers, most vendors provide water for handwashing, but this may only expose them to more germs. In Bogor, only 8% had water on-site (Chapman 1984); for preparation or selling, less than one-third of the enterprises had access to tap water and used water from wells and springs instead, storing the water in open containers (Winarno 1990). The safety of tap water is not assumed in many countries. In Iloilo, rows of 5-gallon "jerry cans" are lined up near most *carendarias*. Each day the vendors filled these cans from the city water taps at a cost in 1994 that ranged from 1 to 2.5 pesos; because of the high mineral content, vendors reported that city water had to be boiled. Some vendors paid 3 pesos per can for clean Guimares spring water from a nearby island. Manikganj water was drawn from deep tubewells and was safe for drinking; taps were spaced throughout the town. Street food vendors hired women to come periodically throughout the day to fetch their water supplies. FAO studies found the water supply reasonably safe in Calcutta (FAO 1992a) but deplored its misuse in Africa (FAO 1992a).

Although street foods are by no means uniformly hazardous, the EPOC studies did document unsafe food preparation practices and additives, inadequate access to water and sanitary services, and cases of potentially dangerous food contamination. Together, these findings point toward two distinct courses of action: improving municipal services and training vendors.

Improving Food Safety

Efforts made in EPOC cities to improve food safety have focused on training vendors; details may be found in the city case studies. In all cases, pressure on the government to offer training to vendors came from researchers who were studying the trade; in Ife, Ibadan, and Bogor, the motivators were faculty members of the local university; in the latter two cases, FAO was a major funder. In Minia and Pune, research groups stimulated training efforts but used different routes to accomplish their goals. In Manila, efforts were prompted by a government official in the Food and Nutrition Research Institute.

Reaching the vendors implies some intermediary mechanism. Organizing street food vendors into some sort of association seemed an obvious approach; efforts by EPOC and FAO researchers to set up vendor groups in several cities are described in chapter 10. Utilizing existing low-level governmental offices located in neighborhoods was tried in Bogor by the IPB team; local health officials worked with research teams in Ife and Ibadan in Nigeria and also in Minia, Egypt, to set up training programs for street food vendors. A major problem facing those initiating training courses is how to persuade the vendors to attend. Time is a major factor in the lives of women vendors, especially, since they usually must combine work and household duties. But if incentives are sufficient, vendors will arrange to attend the training programs.

Current training no longer aspires to unrealistic goals, but enforcement should go hand-in-hand with attainable standards. Self-policing by vendors' associations may be the most effective; such an approach has worked for short periods in the Philippines and is a part of the SFVO activities. Overall, programs emphasize safe food preparation and serving practices, along with maintaining a clean workplace. Defining "safe" in basic terms is still contentious, but the focus is increasingly on the hazards of such additives as non-food dyes. Instead of blaming the vendors for using these dyes to enhance the appeal of their foods, governments are urged to intervene in the production or importation of such unauthorized colorants or to tax the product so that vendors are less likely to find or use them (Jayasuriya 1994). Besides sanitation practices, training programs should also help vendors avoid cooking stove fires and other threats to their own safety.

Because street food vendors practice locally acceptable standards of food handling, public attitudes toward cleanliness and sanitation are considered the best way to encourage vendors to use the information they receive in training courses. At the global level, both FAO and the World Health Organization (WHO) urge the creation of consumer organizations to promote dialogue on food issues (FAO and WHO

1992a). An FAO Expert Consultation recommends that consumer organizations should be invited to participate in discussions about food safety; that mass media, particularly the radio, should be utilized to popularize "catchy food safety messages"; and that consumer education should start in schools (FAO 1988:21).

Local government officials, especially government health officers who had frequently been taught to apply rigorous health standards to vendors, also became the focus for training programs on the realities of the street food trade. Familiarity with vendors and their problems prompted local government officials in all the EPOC city studies to alter their application of health regulations; exemplary vendor training programs in Ife, Nigeria, and Minia, Egypt, were run by local health officials. FAO provided graduation certificates to the 39 participants of the first training program in Africa for local government official who represented 17 state health ministries and health officials from Lagos and Ibadan (Akinyele 1989). A major component of the IPB "Streetfoods" project was to organize a municipal task force at city and neighborhood levels who would help vendors organize themselves and so promote ways for continued consultation and cooperation (Winarno 1990, Bijlmer 1992).

Policy Shifts

Research on street foods, initiated by EPOC and expanded extensively by FAO has compelled government authorities and development planners to recognize the trade as an essential and useful part of urban food provisioning. This attitudinal shift has moved the debate from confrontation and harassment toward cooperation and education in most countries. Problems of regulating and monitoring the diversity of enterprises and activities encompassed by the term "street foods" are by no means solved. Producer vendors share some but certainly not all of the same problems and priorities with trader vendors. In fact, the customary division of economic activities into these categories only compounds the difficulties of monitoring the trade. Similarly, the variety of outlets for street foods and the distinct forms of enterprises makes both classifying and organizing the sector extremely difficult. Nonetheless, the transformation in attitudes should make a solution to these problems possible.

Of particular importance are the key policy shifts by both FAO and WHO toward the regulation of street food vendors. The importance of "good quality and safe foods at affordable prices" (FAO and WHO 1992b, 4) has caused these institutions to seek ways to improve health safety without stringent government regulations and licensing. Further, FAO experts warned that if vendors are banned only for the sake of traffic requirements or modernization plans, such actions will drive the street foods "underground and thus make safety controls or upgrading even more impossible than currently existing" (FAO 1990, 21). Rather, governments should recognize the street food sector as an "intrinsic aspect of their responsibility for urban planning and administration" (FAO 1992d, 8). The Bellagio International Declaration of Street Vendors that emanated from SEWA's 1995 conference of hawkers and vendors echoes these charges to governments and further requests that representatives of vendors be invited to participate in plans for urban development.

At a recent global conference on the epidemioogy of street foods in Beijing, a representative of WHO commented that attempts to set up a global code of practice for street-vended foods as inappropriate, and he recommended that "detailed codes should be left to local authorities." His statement summarizes the policy shift of WHO in words that equally apply to FAO:

> The World Health Organization has long recognized the need to regulate street-vended food in the interest of public health and safety. However, WHO has also recognized that street-vended food in many countries played an important role in the food supply system, offering conveniently able food at affordable prices. Therefore, WHO has stressed that care should be taken in regulation of such foods so that their availability and accessibility are not diminished (ISLI 1993, 7).

CHAPTER TEN

Implications for Research, Planning, and Policy

The ultimate goals of the Street Food Project were from the beginning focused on both the micro and macro levels. At the city level, our objective was to utilize the findings of the studies to identify interventions that would improve the economics of the trade and the safety of the food the vendors sold. These interventions were to recognize and support the critical role women, as well as men, play in each city's trade. At the international level, our objective was to influence the organizations and debates that shape food policies. Chapter 9 illustrates how these twin goals played out in the food arena. At the local level, training programs in food handling replaced sporadic enforcement of unrealistic health standards in many cities. At the macro policy level, the EPOC studies helped reorient public health experts, particularly at the Food and Agricultural Organization, away from the support of stringent laws restricting the sale of food on the streets, toward a recognition of the value of the trade.

This chapter focuses on the institutions and policies that shape the business climate of street food vending. At the conclusion of each study, participants in final briefing seminars proposed a range of interventions to help vendors as microentrepreneurs. These included measures specific to the street food trade, such as ideas for improved vending carts, or for providing better-serviced locations, or for setting up mini food centers. Most other suggestions for local initiatives reflected the development community's contemporary approach to helping microenterprise more generally: creating organizations of vendors in order to better provide services, particularly credit, as well as to facilitate communication between vendors, their middle-class advocates, and government.

At the time of the street food studies, two broad debates were shaping both research and aid policies for microenterprise. Both originated from the fact that neither neoclassical nor Marxist economic theory could satisfactorily explain why apparently premodern artisanal and trade activities were not disappearing with the advent of urbanization and industrialization, but in fact appeared to be proliferating. Within the development community, debate revolved around the definition of economic activity. Many economists argued that enterprises that did not accumulate capital and grow were "pre-entrepreneurial" (Farbman 1981). Street food enterprises seldom expand and so were assigned to this category. As part of the "community of the poor" (House 1984), it was assumed they were simply surviving—certainly not contributing to economic development.

The second debate, which began as a policy concern but later developed into a heated and at times obscure academic argument, centered on the definition of the "informal sector." This term became popular in the 1970s, when a series of International Labor Organization studies on alternatives to formal sector employment in developing countries highlighted a vast and diverse range of small-scale enterprises. But because most street food vendors work alone or with family assistance, most often unpaid, they were typically overlooked as not offering employment opportunities. Subsequent scholarly analyses drew on fairly orthodox Marxist models, which focused on the perceived exploitation of informal sector enterprises and their dependence on the formal sector for resources and markets. Since neither the scholars nor ILO was really interested in microenterprise, we did not see how either debate would contribute much to EPOC's efforts to understand and assist street food vendors. Our findings, however, would challenge their assumptions about some of the smallest-scale entrepreneurs of the informal sector.

Although gender issues were relevant to both debates, of the two the development community initially took more notice of women's economic activities. But since women in the informal sector are more often engaged in microenterprise than in small enterprise, they were assigned to the "community of the poor" or the "pre-entrepreneurial" category that allowed economists to dismiss their work and leave any assistance efforts to NGOs. EPOC's Street Food Project, by contrast, specifically intended to document women's entrepreneurial activities.

Gender became more central to informal sector theory as industries around the world began to increasingly "informalize" their workforce in the 1980s (Portes et al. 1989). In order to cut labor costs, they contracted abroad with larger factories, which in turn subcontracted assembly and sewing to home-based workers. Women were predominantly hired at both levels. The increasing use of industrial home workers in everything from electronics to toys rekindled trade union concerns over regulating this form of employment.

In this manner, the debate over whether the informal sector exploits workers or provides opportunity centered on the household: Is home-based work, whether industrial homework or microenterprise, a form of oppression or of opportunity? Are women microentrepreneurs such as street food vendors really independent, or are they tied into an exploitative capitalist system? And because they are women, are they further exploited within a patriarchal household that controls women's labor, or are they partners with their husbands in managing family survival? In this respect, is there any real distinction between women as microentrepreneurs and as home-based workers? (Prügl and Tinker, forthcoming).

The Street Food Project speaks to all three discourses by providing detailed data on informal-sector microentrepreneurs through its case studies. The reality presented challenges the theories at many points. As background for the policy discussion, this chapter begins with a review of the recommended interventions of the advisory committees in each city that were meant to improve the health of the street food enterprises. The interventions reflect the perspectives of the development community, along with their own internal inconsistencies, which revolve around participation versus government planning, or "bottom-up" versus "top-down" strategies. The difficulties encountered when trying to implement the interventions often had their roots in common assumptions made by the theorists in the distinct policy debates about microenterprise and about the informal sector. The current controversy over home-based work is more pertinent than the earlier discourses to street food microentrepreneurs; these feminist debates speak to the economists, some of whom are reexamining household economic theory.

Improving Microenterprises

For much of the postwar era, both international development agencies and centrally planned governments attempted to impose social change and economic development through top-down programs and policies. As passive resistance and noncompliance undermined these efforts, an alternative school arose, advocating participation of the affected populace.[1] EPOC's efforts to work with street food vendors marked an intermediate position between conventional development planners and proponents of "bottom-up" development, who too often saw each others' methods and priorities as completely incompatible: one side argued that sidewalks were for pedestrians, the other for selling space for vendors; one side was more concerned about safe food, the other about cheap food. But the ideas and impetus for interventions and change came from outside the vendor community. To affect changes in the behavior and practice of the vendors, they had to be involved. The current wisdom recommends both organizing vendors (to make them more effective participants in planning, assistance, and advocacy processes) and giving them incentives to comply with regulations and safety standards. Training programs that supply vendors with health certificates, as well as access to well-serviced vending sites, are one example of the latter method.

Carts, Kiosks, and Vending Centers

The aesthetics of vending intrigued many vendor advocates. If the carts looked cleaner and more attractive, advocates argued they would enhance the tourist trade, as in Minia, or mitigate objections in crowded Makati in Manila. Indeed, in Makati, the vendors had to wear aprons and hair coverings as food safety measures. To encourage the vendors to use the new carts, they were sold to vendors in both cities on long leases at subsidized cost. Using a new cart also signified completion of the training courses. Confusion arises over what types of foods are sold from carts. In fact, no city seemed concerned over truly mobile vendors, with or without a cart. Most ambulant vendors sell pre-prepared food such as ice cream, bread, or peanuts; exceptions are noodle soup and *sate* vendors in Indonesia. Focus was on the "permanent" semi-mobile carts: vendors who use them do some food preparation at site, usually behind or at the side of the cart, which in fact serves more as a counter than a kitchen. Often their food is served on plates. Water for washing is obviously necessary, but the sites are temporary. In Minia, the carts were first designed with two water tanks—one for clean and one for dirty water. These tanks made even the aluminum cart too heavy to move even twice a day; the current design requires only a clean water tank. In Makati, the municipality delivers water to the carts. Most of these theoretically mobile carts were in reality permanent in both cities. The fiction is maintained for legal reasons—permanent establishments fall under different, more critical regulatory statutes; permanency implies the right to be where they are, yet they are intruding on public spaces.

Erecting permanent stalls replete with water, electricity, and sewage control and renting them to vendors would seem a more logical solution than allowing permanent "mobile" carts, especially for vendors selling food outside congested market areas. Location is a major problem; vendors resist being moved away from customers, as the Jakarta attempts underscored (see chapter 1). Efforts to acquire land for kiosks in Minia have to date been unsuccessful. The *bukaterias* in Ife and Ibadan add covered seating space to street food sites and assemble many establishments together, providing a cafeteria selection. The stalls face inward to a common green, and entry to the area is restricted for security purposes. Place this concept within a modern shopping center, and you have the upscale street foods now sold in Manila or Bangkok or Jakarta.[2]

As vending structures improve, the rents often increase, pricing many vendors out of the market. A low-cost alternative is to provide scattered vending sites near customers throughout the city. In Iloilo, vendors relocated from commercial streets to a nearby cul-de-sac found that the added seating space encouraged customers to walk the extra block. The Pune municipality allocated vending sites, but since it did not extend infrastructure facilities, they are not well utilized. Several cities have set up successful but inexpensive selling sites and water points around bus stops.

Organizing Vendors

By setting up an advisory committee in each city studied, the EPOC project hoped to create a group of local scholars, activists, and government officials aware of the vendors' problems and willing to address them. During the study, the EPOC staff became the conduit for information flows between vendors and the committee; representative vendors were often invited to participate in the final seminars. But an ongoing mechanism was needed. Organizing the vendors seemed a logical next step, but this is a time-consuming activity, and vendors may not have either the time or interest to become active.

Typically, social change organizations in developing countries, such as NGOs, trade unions, or some political parties, have been run by educated middle class members for the benefit of the less well-off. The extent to which the beneficiaries, or so-called grass-roots activists, can influence the actions of the organization is extremely variable and hotly debated, and is the subject of a growing literature which is certainly applicable to organizing vendors.[3] At the heart of the debate is the issue of contrasting motivations and incentives between leaders and members. In developing countries today, most organizations working with street food vendors, like those concerned with poverty alleviate in general, operate as nongovernmental organizations (NGOs) playing an intermediary role between government and the poor. These intermediary NGOs grew out of a tradition of groups devoted to charity.[4] Because they are presumed to have no stake in the activities for the poor, their members are able to play a judicious role among the beneficiaries, preventing powerful economic, kin, or ethnic groups from excluding others. The Manikganj Social Service (MASS) organization offered to administer a credit program started with funds EPOC secured. The Pune report entreats the Rotary and Lions Clubs to work with the vendors.

In contrast to these charitable groups, market organizations exist in many cities to promote the interests of all vendors in a particular location; a primary concern was keeping the market clean and orderly. Health officials in Nigeria used these groups to convey information about training programs for street food vendors. In Bogor, the IPB project planned to organize all vendors by location on the street, much as market vendors are organized by their position in the market. The street vendor–only association that existed in Iloilo in 1983 appeared to be a self-organized group; subsequently taken over by politicians, the association became a vehicle for corruption and was later disbanded. The FAO research team in Penang, Malaysia, reported that "the existence of a Hawker's Association is beneficial to its members, to local government and customers." The association provided a good mechanism for the exchange of grievances: both by vendors against the health authorities, who were enforcing food safety standards, and by customers against the vendors, who demanded safe street food (FAO 1990:14).

Associations of vendors appear fairly powerless against the government, but middle-class advocacy groups lack the perspective of the vendors. In Ibadan, Akinyele was instrumental in setting up two distinct organizations, one for vendors and one for advocacy. In 1985 he encouraged graduates of his training classes to organize as the Ibadan Women Food Vendors Association; a few years later he established his own intermediary NGO, Food Basket Foundation International, to further his advocacy efforts.[5]

A unique solution to this problem of bridging the advocates and the beneficiaries is being pursued in Minia. The Street Food Vendors' Organization (SFVO) of Minia, described in detail in chapter 5, presents a unique solution to the problem of coordinating the efforts of advocates and beneficiaries. It challenges the prevailing models, straddling the gap between altruistic organizations and self-interested groups. Although the Board of the SFVO is comprised of vendors and local elite, the organization is dominated by its strong-willed chair. As a government employee, she works a 36-hour week and attends to the affairs of the SFVO most afternoons. In contrast, many vendors work eight to ten hours a day, seven days a week, producing and selling their foods, which limits their participation in the organization. Because the SFVO is not yet financially self-sufficient, the chair's ability to obtain grants is central to its success. Donors push for self-sufficiency as if the organization were a trade union, yet the numbers of street food vendors in Minia are insufficient to support the level of services currently available, even with a greatly increased dues structure. These services are exemplary, but the question of whether they are too ambitious and expensive for such a small organization persists. Long-term efforts at financial sustainability include increasing categories of members to include other types of vendors and a nationwide network of street food vendor organizations (Tinker 1993d).

The Self Employed Women's Association (SEWA) in Ahmedabad, India, offers a modified trade union model for organizing vendors. Founded in 1971 by Ela Bhatt, SEWA includes both street sellers and home-based workers among its members, organizing each into separate units. SEWA trains and employs natural leaders from each unit to work as organizers and liaison with the unit membership; informal discussions about women's rights are an important activity of these outreach workers. Educated women serve as paid employees of the organization, avoiding the potential "charity trap" conflict between worker and educated middle-class. Its large membership base has allowed it to initiate and sustain membership services, including bank and health clinics, both of which charge small user fees. Bhatt has used the prestige and experience of her organization to give worldwide visibility to self-employed women, both those who work at home and those who sell on the street. SEWA has been prominent in ILO meetings on the Convention for Home-Based Workers, and in 1995 it convened a global meeting that produced the Bellagio International Declaration of Street Vendors.

Services to Vendors

Once an organization is set up, the organizer must persuade vendors to become active participants; the types of incentives and services offered are critical to the continued existence of the organization. Vendors work long hours preparing and selling their products, although in many countries women reduced their time spent on the street food vending because of their household duties. In Ziguinchor and Ife, female vendors often utilized female kin to carry out these household chores. In Minia, the vendors who are active in the SFVO are all male, but the percentage of members who are women has steadily risen as the benefits of membership become clear. In Manikganj, once the credit program was disbanded, vendors ceased their participation in MASS.

Vendors in both the EPOC and FAO studies identified their insecure legal states as their most pressing concern, not credit as had been assumed by the wider development community that works with other microentrepreneurs. Most vendors did not borrow money either to start or to run their enterprise. When vendors got into debt, it was often because of a family crisis, usually related to the health of family members or the vendors themselves. In Iloilo, a successful barbecue vendor nearly went bankrupt when her son contracted hepatitis; to pay the hospital bill of 2,000 pesos, an amount that was more than her monthly earnings, she had to borrow from moneylenders at the usurious rate of 40% per month. Aware of the pitfalls of borrowing at high interest rates, most vendors were scrupulous about the obligations, personal or financial, that they incurred.

As an outcome of the EPOC studies, programs in Manikganj and Minia began offering credit to vendors. The Manikganj scheme emulated credit programs run by BRAC or the Grameen Bank throughout Bangladesh, which utilize affinity groups in lieu of material collateral to guarantee repayment of production loans (Tinker 1989). In Minia, the SFVO made credit available to members in a program similar to the loan service offered through SEWA. The payback rates in both instances were much higher than those at local banks. Both programs charged a commercial interest rate (Tinker 1993c). When vendors had difficulty repaying loans, it was usually for reasons unrelated to their enterprises. In Manikganj, the only vendor who defaulted did so after a divorce. In Minia, one vendor was late with his repayments because he was in the hospital for a week after his cart fell over and broke his leg. More troubling was the vendor who borrowed money to build a house, then was unable to repay the loan from business proceeds.

These problems demonstrate the importance of providing distinct types of credit for different purposes. Vendors and other microentrepreneurs typically have no access to loans for social, that is, nonproductive, purposes. The vendor who misused the limited loan capacity of the SFVO for a housing loan might well have been willing to pay a higher interest rate and accept more stringent collateral requirements had such loans been available. Crises that cause borrowers to stop repayments need to be met by separate arrangements. People living on the margin lack savings that they might use for unexpected bills; indeed, the hospitalized vendor was assisted by the crisis fund started by a group of SFVO members, though not by the organization itself. The Grameen Bank provides a useful model for these needs: it links two subsidiary funds to all regular loans—one to provide for loan repayment in an emergency, the other to accumulate funds available to members for nonproductive or social loans. A separate housing loan program is also available to long-term members. Such alternative loans avoid both the misuse of productive loan funds and the necessity for members to borrow from moneylenders.

Health problems of members and their families cause many vendors to go out of business; working capital is used up, and the business cannot be restarted. Even though both the Philippines and Egypt have national health programs, vendors in those countries, as elsewhere, have to pay for prompt and decent care. In Ife, Kujore obtained funds from the local branch of Soroptomists International to support a health clinic in the market for a short time. Research on vendors' health awareness showed the need for general health education. SEWA provides just such a service through its Community Health Program, which also runs clinics in the squatter settlements where members live; local women were trained as health workers. The clinics are open to all comers for a small users' fee; in the long run, SEWA hopes the clinics will become self-sufficient. At the same time, SEWA is lobbying the central government to create a national fund, open to self-employed workers, that would include health insurance (Rose 1992). The SFVO is also lobbying for the existing social pension schemes available to self-employed businessmen to be opened to vendors (Tinker 1993c). In Bangladesh, the Grameen Bank is investigating what type of health coverage its membership prefers.

Alternative Mechanisms

Experiences gained from these various attempts to reach and/or organize vendors show the difficulties of privileging only one model. Street food vendors are a subset of vendors, a subset of home producers, and a subset of food handlers. Joining with larger groups would minimize effort and maximize the vendors' influence. The problems of market vendors focus on keeping physical space attractive, clean, and safe; street vendors are necessarily more worried about harassment and legitimacy. Home producers often stop their own street selling activities and become contractors or traders. Opportunities for organizing self-interest associations with similar microentrepreneurs depends on local circumstance. The legal and political climate affect how both self-interested and charitable organizations champion the cause of the vendors. Governmental structure can encourage local officials to circumvent national policies less advantageous to street food vendors, or they can promote stricter enforcement.

Despite plans in five of the seven EPOC cities, only one street vendors' organization, the SFVO of Minia, is functioning today. The combination of charitable and self-interested perspectives in one organization is unique; it is a work in progress and deserves long-term observation. Continued viability of the organization will likely require an expansion of the membership base so that the organization can move toward greater, but hardly total, self-sufficiency. The many services offered its vendor members show how difficult it is for a single-purpose organization not to enlarge its scope, and thus often its expenses, under pressure from membership.

Macro-Discourses and Policy

During the 1970s, two bodies of literature emerged from the escalating criticism of the prevalent development policy. Investment in infrastructure and large industry in developing countries, promoted by the U.N. First Development Decade, had exacerbated the disparities of income between rich and poor; plans for the Second Development Decade shifted the focus to basic human needs of the poor. On the other hand, industrial growth in these countries of the South was not keeping pace with population growth, raising the specter of wide-scale unemployment. To mobilize resources to address this issue, the International Labour Organizations (ILO) held a conference to plan for full employment by the year 2000, then mounted a major research effort to look beyond industry for job opportunities. Both the U.N. and ILO initiatives spurred studies at the micro level to find out how the poor really lived and survived. But because of the preoccupation with growth and employment, such studies rarely reached down to the micro level of street food vending. Data from the Street Food Project thus both supplements and challenges assumptions and policies flowing from these distinct discourses.

Reaching the Poor

Large development agencies had few channels to people outside government and industry, so with increasing frequency, bilateral assistance channeled funds for basic needs programming through NGOs. Most international NGOs at the time had experience primarily providing services, such as maternal and child health, or charity, such as food distribution or cash transfers. Programmatically they tended to work with or through local NGOs. Their approach to helping the poor was multifaceted, lengthy, and labor-intensive; success was hard to demonstrate. Critics complained that these all-encompassing programs actually created dependency, not self-sufficiency, while proponents lauded the NGOs staying power, which was needed to address the causes of poverty. The alternative, many economists argued, was to provide the poor with jobs or self-employment so they could help themselves, particularly if the registration procedures in the host countries were simplified and the regulatory requirements relaxed (de Soto 1987; House et al. 1993). In the late 1970s USAID funded a multi-country study of 20 existing urban poverty programs to determine which approaches were most effective and replicable (Farbman 1981).

Among the many groups helping the poor earn income, the USAID study revealed a clear distinction between the charitable NGOs, working with poor "pre-entrepreneurial" women whose needs reached well beyond business skills, and the business NGOs, whose clients were existing entrepreneurs, predominantly men, who needed access to technology and credit to expand their enterprises.[6] As the concern with poverty faded in the 1980s and private enterprise became the focus of U.S. development assistance, the funds for programs that worked with "pre-entrepreneurs" were cut, on the grounds that these microentrepreneurs were not acting in a properly economic manner and so money spent on them was essentially welfare, not development funding.

It was against this backdrop that the Street Food Project was framed. The project findings undermine many assumptions about the street food trade. Vendors are clearly entrepreneurial; the income of most male and female vendors places them well above the poverty line. Vendors would benefit from improved registration requirements and procedures; an array of credit programs could help them both survive and improve their enterprises. New technologies could help producer vendors both improve their foods and increase their volume. But with all these prescriptions for small entrepreneurs fulfilled, most street food vendors' operations would probably still not satisfy the economists' standards of growth.

The EPOC findings show that few vendors invest in their enterprises to the extent that economists anticipate. Their enterprises do not grow into large restaurants, although some replicate their stands in amoeba-like fashion. Where and from what kinds of facilities (permanent or mobile) they sell relates to what foods they sell, and most vendors do not change their products over the life of their enterprise. Vendor families manage the activity as they might a farm; the many tasks involved provide livelihoods for extended family members; profits are invested in the next generation. Improved production is desirable, but the family does not seek to expand. Yet planners and economists have persisted in calling such behavior, whether by microentrepreneurs or peasants, "traditional," "pre-capitalist," and "pre-entrepreneurial." It could also be based on fundamentally different values: family over individual, cooperation over competition, altruism over selfishness (Tinker 1995). Both men and women vendors exhibit these perspectives, which surely cannot be dismissed simply by calling them traditional.

But these values also make economic sense in survival terms. First, in countries without social security or pensions, the family is a fallback position. Yet family disfunction and disintegration is a familiar phenomena as modernization proceeds. Many vendors commented on the importance of helping out their children and younger kin so that they would in turn be taken care of in old age. In Chonburi and Ziguinchor, vendors spent income on family rituals and obligations; in Ife, women supported children of kin. In Bogor, some vendors felt familial obligations kept them from accumulating savings that they could invest in housing, and avoided kin pressure; but most studies of Indonesia report the continued rural-urban connection as part of long-range survival strategy (Evers 1980).

Second, the quantitative leap from self or kin employment to an enterprise with paid, non-kin employees cannot be exaggerated.[7] Such a move is as likely to cause bankruptcy as growth; over half of all new enterprises in the United States fail in the first year. Third, the issue of unpaid or underpaid labor looks different from this family perspective. Spouses and children received support in return for work; when demand for their labor diminished, they had more time for education, starting new employment, or retiring. Most family assistants to street food enterprises were apprentices; many were also students who received room and board, as well as minimal pay. For all these assistants, low or unpaid jobs in street food enterprises are probably cost-effective, given time constraints and alternative job opportunities.[8] Such reasoning is similar to the situation of welfare recipients in the United States, who find that entry-level jobs cost them too much in lost governmental support.

In the last decade, the success of microcredit schemes in a variety of countries around the world has muted the economists' criticism, although the debate continues with regard to assistance funding (McKean 1994). Both the affinity model of the Grameen Bank and the individual banking model of SEWA have been replicated, adapted, even combined (Otero 1990; Rhyne and Otero 1992; Timberg 1993), and extended to the United States (Sirola 1991). In the United States, pressure from international NGOs on Congress maintained line-item funding, despite administration policy; a study of 11 successful microenterprise finance programs in nine countries found that the programs reached the very poor, while the financial institutions themselves grew and are approaching self-sufficiency (Fox 1995). The fact that the more successful lending programs include many additional services besides micro-credit tends to be downplayed in the current political climate.[9] As was shown in the Street Foods Project, vendors making different levels of income and producing or selling different products in different countries require different types of programs. For many vendors, credit might be a useful service; for others, legitimation, training, new technology,[10] or vending sites may be a higher priority.

Providing Employment

The impetus and much of the funding for studying the informal sector came from the ILO's search for employment opportunities (Sethuraman 1981). As the agency responsible for developing employment statistics in the 1930s, ILO began to expand its definitions in the 1970s.[11] In looking beyond the formal sector, ILO legitimized research into a variety of economic activities not previously thought worthy of study. But debate over the precise definition of the informal sector clouded much of the empirical findings and made comparisons across sectors or countries difficult.[12] As field studies proliferated in the 1970s, academics debated theoretical models of relations between the formal and informal. One particular question centered on whether the sector was subordinate to and exploited by capitalism, or whether the sector was comprised of independent entrepreneurs. Subordination implied that low wages in the informal sector subsidized higher earnings in the formal sector. Unpaid family labor compounded the exploitative nature of informality, keeping costs low and preventing accumulation that might allow the enterprise to grow. Disaggregating owners from workers in informal sector enterprises also showed that employees received very low compensation (Portes et al. 1986). Such conclusions were not the good news about the employment potential of the sector that ILO had anticipated (Moser 1994).

Despite these bleak conclusions, members of the development community saw the potential to alleviate poverty by promoting microenterprise. They portrayed the informal sector in a more positive light. Proponents estimated the informal sector's share of total employment at anywhere from 40% to 75%, depending upon what activities are included (Gilbert and Gugler 1992; Otero 1994). Although they called for more attention toward ways the government could support the sector, ILO's Sethuraman continued to believe "that informal units are not run by entrepreneurs in the true sense of the term" and applauded the ability of NGOs to provide tailor-made technical advice to these units (Sethuraman 1985, 734).

The next round of studies examined how small enterprises within the informal sector could reduce costs for large formal industries in both advanced and less developed countries (Portes et al. 1989). This research focused on various industrial strategies to increase flexibility and avoid high labor costs, such as subcontracting, downsizing enterprises, or offshore sourcing. The authors emphasized the high level of integration among firms, with smaller enterprises dependent on the larger formal firms for input, technology, and markets. Beneria's study of subcontracting in Mexico City shows how the more marginal workers, especially women, are clustered in the lower-paying illegal enterprises at the bottom of the pyramid (Beneria 1989). Despite the exploitative nature of this work, Beneria and Roldan write, "we do not conclude that, from the perspective of women themselves, their engagement in homework is totally negative"; their income may improve their position within their households (1987, 169). Also, homework allows women to move in and out of employment at different points in their life cycle (Prügl and Tinker, forthcoming).

This evolving discussion about the position of informal sector enterprises in the local and global economy helps place the street food trade in the macro policy debate. EPOC data contested many of the early ILO characterizations of the informal sector: most vendors were not recent migrants; they possessed skills that included both an understanding of the local economy and of food preparation; and for the more successful, street food vending was a lifetime occupation. Key findings document the profitability of full-time vending enterprises, and the contribution of the street food trade to the urban economy. Such findings have helped change perceptions that the informal sector was a refuge for the poor. Still, the income data showed wide variation among street food vendors, indicating that many poor women and men do use vending as part of a survival strategy, usually combined with seasonal agricultural work, as in Manikganj and Ziguinchor, or with other forms of petty trade, as in Ife.

Informal-sector enterprises were also presumed to be illegal. Regarding street food vendors, this issue of legality is complicated. In Bogor and Minia, vendors had paid the fee required for selling (58% and 72%, respectively); but many in Minia sold foods other than those on the permit. In Pune, where two licenses were needed, 61% had the license from the Encroachment Department but only 14% had the one from Health. Virtually all vendors paid a daily selling fee in Ziguinchor and a majority did so in Manikganj; in the latter town, however, only 20% had the required business document. Market vendors in Iloilo and Chonburi also paid the daily or monthly fees; sidewalk vendors in those cities and in Manikganj made some arrangement with the store owners for the privilege.[13] Yet in most countries the trade remains officially illegal, so paying a fee reduces but does not eliminate the risk of harassment. Overregulation and erratic enforcement clearly inhibit investment and accumulation, for the street food vendors, as well as for many other informal sector microenterprises.

Street vendors, like many other workers outside the formal sector, often produce, retail, wholesale, and even consume their own merchandise. This multiplicity of functions questions and confuses prevailing categories of economic activity. Many cities required all vendors, whatever functions they carry out, to have permits for all of them. In contrast, census enumerators, finding that vendors do fit not their classifications, miscount or ignore these enterprises, rendering them invisible in national statistics. Until vendors are correctly enumerated, policies to improve their conditions will be difficult to implement.

Gender Aspects

The above discussion shows some divergence of women's roles from men's in the debates surrounding microenterprise and informal sector. Overall, women vendors made less money because of the time they devoted to household responsibilities.[14] In large or polygynous families found in Ife and Ziguinchor, vendors were sometimes able to turn over these domestic responsibilities to other female family members and work longer hours. But most female vendors maintained the double day, juggling work and home. Vending is a attractive occupation to women because of its flexibility. Women, even more than men, spend earnings on their families and therefore do not accumulate capital for investment in their enterprises; lack of investment capital in turn keeps them at the low-technology, low-earning end of the spectrum. Nevertheless, women's return on investment, at least in Ziguinchor, was as high as that for men.

I have argued here that the case studies show many vendors, male and female, view their enterprises as part of family survival strategies. But the authors of the Jamaica Street Food Study see a the diversity of motivations of the vendors:

> Women and men appear to have different approaches to vending. Women, though they might have been vending all of their lives and might be part of a family of vendors, seem to see this activity as a temporary thing to make two ends meet rather than as a career. Men see it as a business: they have dreams of moving from a foodstand to a restaurant. (Powell et al. 1990, 81).

The production functions undertaken by many vendors place them within the debate over home-based work even though few engage in subcontracting (Tinker 1993b, 1994). Most vendors and their families produce or prepare the foods they sell, and much of this activity is done in the home. In some countries, families even grow the foods they process and sell (Evers 1980; Drakakis-Smith 1991). Other food producers sell directly to middlemen or to customers without selling on the streets. Strassmann argues that home-based family-operated enterprises enjoy a comparative advantage typical of the informal sector: flexible labor supply and free working space (1987). Such cost savings allow the informal-sector entrepreneurs to find niches in which they are more efficient than formal-sector industry. In other words, these enterprises can only survive with free family labor.

Many feminists see this system as inimicable to women because the male household head controls both women's labor and the use of the house. In fact, many microenterprise projects were subverted by men precisely because they felt they were losing control of their wives. Because the bulk of unpaid family labor in the street food trade is female, these women would seem to be particularly exploited by patriarchal control. According to Kandiyoti (1988), however, even unpaid economic activity can improve the household bargaining position of women. This observation was echoed in the case studies of women producers in Manikganj.

In many of the countries studied, whether spouses' incomes were pooled, as in Thailand and the Philippines, or kept separate, as in Nigeria, Jamaica, and Senegal, women are expected to help meet regular household expenses.[15] Elsewhere, women participate in family survival strategies as necessary. Overall the studies corroborate the growing evidence that a woman's income, no matter how small, improves not only her bargaining position within her family but also the nutritional level of her children (Engle 1995, Beneria and Roldan 1987, Kennedy and Peters 1992, A. Sen 1990, Senauer 1990). It even "alters established patterns of social/spatial interaction"— that is, the way different spaces in and around the house are used and by whom— according to research in Guadalajara (Miraftab 1994, 468).

At the micro level, then, working at home for income is perceived by both researchers of the informal economy and by proponents of microenterprise as a useful strategy for women. Besides allowing a woman to better meet her and her family's expenses within marriage, she also needs her own money in case her husband divorces or abandons her. Income may allow women to leave abusive unions (Miraftab 1995). Beneria and Roldan (1987, 165) identified "the two fundamental mechanisms of husbands' control over their wives: husbands' predominance . . . was found to be based, not on ideological mechanisms alone, but significantly on privileged access to income and coercive means of control." Many European and American feminists wonder why women remain in marital unions, and indeed the rise in households headed by women has been widely documented (Varley, 1996). However, women in other cultures, particularly in Asia, argue that too much emphasis on individual rights undermines the greater values of family and community (G. Sen 1988, IURD 1994). There is a cautious move on the part of some feminists in the United States, concerned with the conservative appropriation of the term, to reimage the family and demonstrate its relevance to development (Jaquette 1993).

At the macro level, trade unions in Europe and the United States fought for years against the existence of home-based work. The global expansion of subcontracting has begun to undermine regulations regarding homework that currently exist in industrialized countries as corporations in those countries attempt to cut production costs in order to compete with industry in developing countries. In response, the ILO conducted research into the issue and reiterated that "homeworkers constitute a particularly vulnerable category of workers due to their inadequate legal protection, their isolation, and their weak bargaining position" (ILO 1995, 1). Many in the labor movement consider home-based work exploitative and would prefer to ban it; failing that they would organize homeworkers to demand living wages and benefits, although in the past, organizing homeworkers has been unsuccessful. They have proposed that the ILO adopt a Convention on Home Work recognizing homeworkers as dependent workers and promoting "equality of treatment between homeworkers and other wage earners" (ILO 1995, 161).

In contrast, NGOs working in developing countries celebrate the major successes of their microenterprise projects, most of which are home-based. They consider income from these enterprises as essential for both survival and empowerment. This dichotomy of exploitation versus opportunity mirrors the overall positions taken during the informal sector between those who thought small-scale entrepreneurs were independent versus those who saw them as dependent workers within the capitalist economy. The difference is that the former debate did not usually reach into the family or the home. Only with the growing research on women were the gendered aspects of the informal sector clarified. In contrast, the microenterprise programs from the beginning were focused on women and their familial roles.

In the home, as illustrated in the Street Food Project, it is difficult to distinguish between industrial homeworkers and microentrepreneurs. Even when women work within a subcontracting pyramid, the distinction is one of degree. A woman seamstress may bring in family workers in times of high demand, or she may hire a neighbor and thus become a jobber herself (Miraftab 1994). In this way, home-based workers often are both employer and employee, but they continue to be constrained by their socially constructed roles as mothers and housewives. At the 82nd International Labour Conference in June 1995, when the proposed convention on homework was discussed, homework advocates from industrialized countries and development groups such a SEWA cooperated in support of the convention, against opposition from those concerned with employer rights. They see the categories as fungible and perceive the need to extend protection to the increasing number of workers outside the formal workplace, whatever they are called (Prügl and Tinker, forthcoming).

Influencing Theory and Practice

The Street Food Project provides a wealth of information that expands, deepens, and challenges the two major debates of the 1970s and 1980s over the role of poor, small-scale entrepreneurs in developing countries. Neither free-market liberals of the development community nor Marxist-influenced informal-sector scholars initially paid much attention to family and individual enterprise. Over the past decade, both these discourses have themselves evolved. The success of microcredit schemes proved to the development community that microenterprise merited investment and assistance. The expansion of subcontracting accompanying the restructuring of the global economy increased labor movement concern over work outside the factory, bringing the debate over oppression versus opportunity into the home and family.

Street food vendors are generally independent microentrepreneurs, but some are dependent workers or subcontractors; the dichotomy is hard to maintain because it rarely fits reality. Microentrepreneurs move between the categories or may be both at once. Considering that most homeworkers are women, one cannot discuss their labor, whether as independent microentrepreneurs or as subcontracted employees, without reference to their other socially constructed roles as wives and mothers.

Early literature in both the women-in-development field and in women's studies tended to focus on the woman *apart* from these social roles. This limited vision resulted in development projects, meant to make women's lives easier, that instead added to their workload. The feminists' narrow conceptualization of family has alienated many who believe that individual rights should not always take precedence over the needs of family and community. Most women street food vendors appeared to subscribe to family welfare. Research on men's responses to rapid social and economic change is in its infancy. The opinions recorded in the street food vendor case studies often show similar concern with the family, but perceptions of what their own roles should be certainly differed from women's perceptions. Clearly more research is needed to understand better how household and family dynamics shape the economic strategies of the urban poor.

Putting It All Together

Weaving together the individual reports of these seven diverse cities, each using the basic design of the Street Foods Project to produce distinct patterns, has been a daunting task. Each study expanded into new areas propelled by the demands of the local situation and the curiosity of its staff. The focus and success of interventions to improve the trade in both its economic and food service aspects varied even more, dependent on the local political as well as cultural climate.

Returning to the field five to ten years after each study was completed was both a humbling and exhilarating experience. In Iloilo, the present and former mayors welcomed me at the airport with a banner and flower garlands, and the former regional director of the national planning authority produced data about economic change over the last decade. In comparison, all the members of the research team in Ife had scattered abroad—to Zimbabwe, Saudi Arabia, and the United States—but the local public health coordinator continues to train vendors. In nearby Ibadan, as in Bogor and Minia, local leaders have expanded their concerns for street food vendors far beyond the EPOC project and are engaged in impressive programs that combine research, training, and organizing. In Manikganj, the local nongovernmental organization shifted its focus from credit for vendors to technical assistance for producers and producer/sellers of street foods. Rapid economic development in Thailand has altered the patterns of the trade as more foods are produced industrially, mostly by indigenous firms; meanwhile, the popularity of taking quick meals on the street has, if anything, increased as congestion magnifies transit time between home and work. In contrast, the economy of Ziguinchor, constrained by civil unrest, has sent many vendors to Dakar to survive.

These stories have all been chronicled in the individual city chapters. EPOC city data have been amplified in many countries with materials from subsequent studies completed by local researchers; the analytical chapters include results from case studies in Kingston and Pune that utilized the EPOC methodology and often include information drawn from FAO studies. Taken together, these data conclusively estab-

212

lish the street food trade as a significant economic activity and an essential part of the urban food system.

The first four EPOC studies—in Iloilo, Bogor, Manikganj, and Ziguinchor—were perhaps the most influential. For the first time, estimates were available on the aggregate annual sales of street food vendors in each city (see Table 11.1). When the mayors of each city heard these figures that documented the importance of street foods to municipal revenues, we caught their attention. Reacting to the estimates, Alex Umadhay, regional executive direction of the National Economic and Development Authority and member of the Iloilo advisory committee for the project, compared his previous attitude toward street food vendors to flies: they are so pervasive that you tend to ignore them and just brush them off! Like most people involved in the project, he became a champion of street food vendors.

The sheer size of the total labor force involved in the trade is striking. The average number of owner-operators and paid assistants in each enterprise was between 1.5 and 2 in Bogor and Manikganj and over 2.9 in Iloilo; only in Ziguinchor were most vendors sole operators. Unpaid family labor, shown in Table 8.7, was unevenly documented, but adds at least another person to each enterprise. Conservative estimates of the percentage of labor force in each city is indicated in Table 11.1. These figures could be greatly increased if, in addition to the number of paid and unpaid persons directly involved in processing and selling street foods, all the people making or growing ingredients, selling water of fuel to the vendors, or delivering beer and soft drinks to the enterprises are included.

These figures on aggregate annual income and on the percentage of labor force involved in the enterprises are estimates and should be interpreted only as a general indication of magnitude. The estimates were determined after taking into account many variables: the fluctuations of foreign exchange, the seasonal variations in the numbers of vendors, the accuracy of translations in the survey instruments and the

TABLE 11.1   Economic importance of the street food trade

City	Population	Aggregate annual sales 1983/84 (U.S. $million)	Labor force[a] (%)	Avg. income of street food vendors	Comparison
Manikganj, Bangladesh	37,996	2	4	77 taka	3× agricultural labor
Ziguinchor, Senegal	98,295	4	3	379 francs	250 francs minimum wage
Iloilo, Philippines	244,827	28	8	54 pesos/day	33 pesos minimum wage
Bogor, Indonesia	248,000	67	17	1700–3100	2× minimum wage

a. Assuming labor force equals 40% of the population.

validity of vendors responses, and care of transcriptions and analysis. Results for each city were much debated by the advisory committees before they were agreed upon. We publicized these figures because, even if the total income and labor force were extremely inflated, the figures still establish the street food trade as a serious economic activity.

Data on vendor income, also shown in Table 11.1, are based on observation of the vendors' economic activities at the site as much as on vendor responses. These figures provide a solid base for comparisons with minimum wage or with other types of low-skilled labor and clearly document the income opportunities that street food vending offers to the poor, especially poor women.

Demand for street foods is equally impressive. The percentage of total household food budget that was spent on prepared food was nearly half in Chonburi and Ife, a quarter in Iloilo and Bogor. The smaller and poorer the family, the higher the percentage of their food budgets they spent on street food.[1] In Minia, one vendor served 60 customers a day or about 50,000 a year; if each person ate only one time, that number would that about one-third of the citizens who ate street foods in a year, considerably less than the 82% of all Americans who eat at least once a year at a fast food establishment (NRA 1993). Nonetheless, the income and food that this represents in a low-income country is significant.

The EPOC definition of street food enterprises encompassed ready-to-eat food sold in the informal sector. Like that term, our definition was residual and generally included all nonformal restaurants. In the cities studied, a restaurant was a place frequented by the middle or upper classes and by foreigners. As a result, our data reveal a hierarchy of enterprises that ranged from the local equivalent of restaurants and bars to the seasonal ambulant seller of agricultural surplus. By focusing on working vendors, we selected the successful entrepreneurs; what happened to the vendors who dropped out of our enumeration we do not know. Our observations suggest that many poor try a variety of jobs in order to survive. Those who are not skilled entrepreneurs probably take up another activity.

By using the street food sellers as an entry point, our studies left out three important types of activities essential to investigate in order to document urban food habits in developing countries. First, our data do not include the multitude of food producers and processors who made street foods but sold their product to others to sell, such as the *canacur* producers in Manikganj. Second, we did not include the many food sellers who did not offer their goods on the street but rather delivered it directly to offices and homes, those preparing *rantangan* in Bogor or *pin-to* in Thai cities. Finally, we collected only anecdotal evidence about urban food production: the cows inside homes in Minia, the rabbits and chickens in Ife. This extensive study of urban food and income in developing countries documents convincingly the importance of street foods; it also suggests other critical research themes. Only with information about these aspects of the urban food system will planners and scholars begin to understand how cities in developing countries *really* feed themselves. Without this basic understanding, how can we avoid crisis and starvation in the mega-cities of the twenty-first century?

The Future of the Street Food Trade

Singapore's "solution" to street food vending is widely admired among government planners in Asia (FAO 1990). In the course of its rapid modernization from Malay houses on stilts in the 1950s to a world-class metropolis today, Singapore pressured its street food vendors to get off the street by building food stalls over parking garages or in market malls and prohibiting street selling; a few night markets on parking spaces were also permitted. As a result, the number of registered vendors dropped by one-half (Drakakis-Smith 1991). EPOC was not successful in its efforts to secure funding for a small survey of mall vendors in order to find out how many formerly sold on the street, but our Iloilo study showed that no street vendor moved up to run a formal food establishment. Most observers believe that these new outlets require substantially more capital and a different style of doing business than is typical of street food vendors, and so they draw on a more wealthy sector of the business community.

Emulating Singapore and the United States, new shopping malls are opening in Thailand, Indonesia, and the Philippines that include an indoor "street food" bazaar along with fast-food franchises such as Kentucky Fried Chicken and Pizza Hut. Clientele at these malls seem to come from the middle and upper classes. But in the large cities in all these Asian countries, vendors still sell their more affordable food to a broad range of customers. Even in Singapore, street food vendors may be found near construction sites where they sell to immigrant labor that arrives daily from Malaysia. The challenge for planners is to arrange serviced mini malls or bus stops with rental spaces that street food vendors can afford. Expensive relocation on the Sinagpore model does not serve the majority of people in developing countries.

Regulations for street vending need to be appropriate and easily understood. The benign administrator is preferable to the unpredictable and malevolent enforcer, but reasonable rules that are applied fairly will help stabilize the trade and encourage vendors to invest in improved technologies that increase income and food safety. Once the importance of street food vendors is accepted, then finding accommodation for their enterprises that does not infringe on rights of pedestrians or store owners should be possible. Some sort of organization that mediates between the vendors and the government is clearly desirable; further research into the functioning of such organizations is needed.

If local sweets and munchies are to survive the onslaught of industrial snacks, NGOs and/or government need to work with the producers of these foods to help them package and market their goods. In Chonburi, local *bon-bons* were already produced centrally and sold by mobile vendors throughout the town, much as bread was sold in Bogor and ice cream sold in almost every city. Larger *bon-bon* manufacturers in Bangkok are expanding. Because fresh food is preferred and storage is a problem, support for local food industries of all sizes makes economic and employment sense for local governments.

As the street food trade becomes more institutionalized at the top end of the hierarchy, more educated vendors and more men will be attracted by its profitability. Such acceptability marks a shift in the attitude of the educated toward business and commerce from the earlier belief that a college degree meant government employment. Where the economy is depressed and alternatives are scarce, this transition will be faster, as is already apparent from Nigeria to Jamaica to the Philippines. Whether women, with their double day, will be able to compete is questionable. Interventions at all levels of the trade are needed to maintain gender equity and to provide credit and services.

Street vendors, at least the successful ones, are not the very poor. Programs to help them improve and expand are very different from those required by smaller and ambulant vendors. Further, alternative employment for the casual seasonal, and often very poor, vendors will still be needed. Recognizing the diversity of vendors within the street food trade is the first step toward meeting their needs. Finding incentives for vendors to improve their food handling, and providing facilities that make such upgrading possible, is a challenging prospect. The realization that vendors reflect community health standards means that long term change requires customer as well as vendor education.

Bon Appetit

The case studies provided a gastronomic travelogue and an insight into the lives of the street food vendors. Comparative data documented the similarities and differences across the countries and showed demographic and gender variations among the vendors. Cultural attitudes affected what foods were eaten, by whom, and when. Details about the income to individuals, families, and the city underscored the importance of the trade economically; figures about household expenditures on street foods showed the central place prepared food has in the diets of people in most, but not all, of the cities studied.

The goals of the EPOC project were to assist the vendors at the micro level and to influence macro policies affecting the vendors and the trade. These impacts in both theory and practice focused on the dual nature of the trade as a microenterprise and as a provider of food. What remains is to stimulate further research into the many unexplored areas of urban feeding and food production, to encourage new organizations and support mechanisms for the urban poor, and to explore the different roles and expectations of the women and men who engage in the street food trade.

Notes

Introduction

1. Washington women leaders recall their individual efforts from 1960 to 1980 to change the shape of U.S. society through legislation in a book I edited in 1983, aptly titled *Women in Washington: Advocates for Public Policy*. Many of us set up organizations to our purpose; among others, in 1972 I was elected first president of the Federation of Organizations for Professional Women, and in 1974, I was co-founder of the Wellesley Center for Research on Women. A temporary collaboration between these two organizations led to the founding of the International Center for Research on Women (ICRW) as a federation project in 1976; ICRW became independent the following year.

2. Boserup (1970) utilized much early literature on Africa; for pioneering studies in the early seventies see Hafkin and Bay 1976.

3. This issue is of even more critical concern in my current research on urban food production. County-wide boundaries typical in China mask the variations of food density in urban core, peri-urban areas, and rural farms.

Chapter One

1. A major demand of the Darul Islam was for a federal system of government that would allow the Sundanese to have their own Islamic state (see, for example, Feith 1962).

2. For this reason, both male and female college students were hired as staff and were paired whenever they conducted surveys or interviews.

3. Much of the funding for these groups came from external sources: international and bilateral aid agencies, foundations, and international NGOs.

4. Such parking lot restaurants are very popular in Malaysia and Singapore, where restrictions on daytime street foods are increasing.

5. The most widely distributed commercial brand of *jamu* is "Jago," the term used for fighting cocks in Indonesia.

6. UNICEF subsequently funded a similar training program in Manila; see its analysis in chapter 2.

7. S. V. Sethuraman, a major theoretician of ILO's informal sector work, visited Jakarta as a consultant to the government of Indonesia in 1985 to recommend measures the government might take to support the informal sector activities. He noted that available data still excluded very small enterprises, which for planning purposes need to be counted. Concerned that a substantial proportion of informal-sector participants have a very low level of income, he lists the constraints, such as usurious interest rates or misguided administrative policies, that keep even profitable activities from prospering. His observations on the street-cleaning exercise of the Jakarta city officials were widely publicized.

8. A high school graduate from rural West Java, Lubis had sold a variety of dry goods on Jakarta streets from 1962 until the removals in 1980. In 1969 he had established a school to teach Arabic and the Koran to dropouts in his *kampung*. After the removal of vendors, and in recognition of his earlier activism, he was offered a fellowship to study cooperatives and Islamic Studies for a year. Subsequently, he worked with LSP to set up cooperatives in Jogjakarta and Bandung before doing the same in Jakarta.

9. In July 1990 the organization had 1,000 members, 90% of them men, and primarily selling clothes, but also shoes, bags, books, medicine, fruits, and food. Organizations were also being formed in other sections of Jakarta. In 1987 the government had instructed all vendors to join cooperatives, but Lubis said many vendors still were afraid. (Interview in Jakarta 18 July 1990).

10. The city administration took over relationships with the vendors on 1 August 1990.

11. Barbara Chapman ran the two words together in her reports on the EPOC project in Indonesia; this project continues that version.

12. The three groups are: the Food Technology Development Centre, Institut Pertanian Bogor (IPB); TNO Division of Nutrition and Food Research in Zeist, The Netherlands; and the Centre for Development Cooperations Services, Free University (VU), Amsterdam. In the following section, the project is identified as IPB; authors of the reports are identified by those responsible rather than by the project name alone. Suprihatin Guhardja, who had done consumer studies for EPOC, continued in a similar role in this follow-up project. Joep Bijlmer, a development sociologist from the Free University in Amsterdam, served as the Dutch consultant.

13. Of the sample of 40, 23 indicated a strong attachment to their home village, a higher percentage than typical of the vendor population as a whole.

Chapter Two

1. Interviews in Iloilo, 15 June 1994. The culture of corruption that pervades the country makes efforts to help the poor, undertaken by such conscientious men as these, extremely difficult.

2. Information on Iloilo and its street foods is based on the 1983 project report by Gerald Barth.

3. The 10% sample for the survey was based on type of site (permanent or not) and type of food sold (meal or snack). Location was implicit in the selection between markets, streets, and the interior.

4. Two exceptions were easily identified: the manager of the cooperative was interviewed, as was the manager of an enterprise in which the owner did not work.

5. The customer survey was based on two persons per vendor, except for the 12 vendors who could not be located. This means two customers each at 123 vendors = 246 people.

6. Barth estimated in 1983 that a *carendaria* meal cost 4.1 pesos, at a time when fuel to cook the equivalent food cost 1 peso and transport home cost 1.6 pesos. Costs for raw materials would certainly be 1.5 pesos. Eating street foods thus costs the same or less than cooking at home, and it is a much more efficient use of time. All these costs have increased dramatically over the last decade, but in 1994 the mathematics remained the same: eating out is still more efficient than returning some distance home for a meal.

7. For a representative sample, the household survey consisted of 30 households chosen to reflect different income levels, drawn from six different *barangay* (the smallest political unit of local government) throughout the expanded city. Thirty were added to these from the customer survey, along with another 15 street vendor households, adding up to a total sample of 195.

8. Vendors sold for an average of 11.93 months per year; 97% reported selling year-round.

9. Estimates given in an interview with Jovita "Pee Wee" Culaton. Manila, 8 April 1983.

10. Interview with staff at Ilolilo City Department of Social Welfare, 15 June 1994.

11. Based on interviews in Iloilo with Mayors Malabor and Herrera and with the former executive director of NEDA Region VI, Attorney Alex Umadhay, 15 June 1994.

12. Information on the FNRI/FAO project comes primarily from interviews in Manila, 10–16 June 1994, but also from de Guzman et al. 1994. Besides individuals cited in the text, I visited the offices of UNICEF and FAO, as well as several foundations and NGOs. Adoración "Babes" Mondala escorted me during the visits to schools on June 10 and translated my questions to the vendors. Principal Angelita L. Santana arranged for the project team of teachers and municipal health officials to meet with me. Vendors in the program were not supposed to sell foods not approved by FNRI. At San Juan, some vendors were discouraged from selling cheese curls because they were not nutritious; so they stopped selling at the school until a new menu, consisting of hot dogs, and cheese or egg sandwiches, was introduced. The municipal nutritionists showed me the food vendors outside the high school and compared the practices of participating and nonparticipating vendors: carts of the trained vendors were in a row and near a seating area; up the hill untrained vendors were selling *lugaw*, a stew of rice and pig intestines, and *bananacue*, both favorites of the students.

13. Schools of under 2,000 students were not allocated a teacher to cook, so use of vendors was high in small urban schools. In rural areas, students brought lunches. Profits were apportioned, with 30% going to the administration and 70% for school use. (Interview in Iloilo with Dr. E. de Guzman, deputy director of the Regional Department of Education, Culture, and Sports, 15 June 1994.) Teachers liked the assignment, as it broke the monotony and often provided a bit of additional income to the poorly paid women. Most teachers have to earn income on the side by sewing or selling clothes.

14. The second pilot school was located in a rural area of Los Baños.

15. Students in grades 1 and 2 arrive at school by 7 A.M., break between 9 and 9:30 A.M., and finish school at 11:30 A.M.; their classwork lasts for four hours. Students in grades 3 and 4 arrive at 11:45 A.M., break about 2:45 P.M. for half an hour, then finish at 4:30, for

a class day of four and one-half hours. Grades 4 and 5 have eight hours of instruction and three meals. Enrollment in each class is about 400 students, but there is attrition in top classes.

16. When setting up the vendor market at San Juan, the school first tried to reclaim the use of land previously rented as a market for fresh fruit and produce. The buy-in costs of 100,000 pesos and the monthly rent of 5,000 pesos made that market too expensive for the street food vendors. The municipality had built stalls for the school and received the buy-in funds. Rent is divided, with the school receiving 60%. These figures suggest that vendor markets would have to receive subsidies.

Chapter Three

1. No data exist to show whether this food was purchased from street vendors, supplied by the "invisible street food" *pin-to* system (see Part I), or at restaurants. In 1990 the Ministry of Labor enumerated 16,895 eating places throughout the country, nearly two-fifths in Bangkok itself (Yasmeen 1992).

Chapter Four

1. The Manikganj Street Foods Study was carried out by Naomi Owens and Naseem Hussain; they lived in Manikganj from January 1983 until April 1984. Data in this section are drawn from their reports.

2. Recent data find a significant drop in the total fertility rate, from 7 children per woman in 1970 to 4.7 in 1992 (See WRI 1994, 30).

3. Urban increase in Bangladesh is greatest in the largest cities; Dhaka, which had only 3.3 million inhabitants in 1980, is expected to exceed 10 million inhabitants by the end of the century (WRI 1994, 288).

4. Widows have few income choices. A comparison of two rural areas in Bangladesh found that in the traditional village women might work in the homes of wealthier neighbors or beg; where new agricultural technology had been adopted, giving rise to an increased demand for agricultural labor, some women were hired to work in the fields (Rahman 1982).

5. For a critical analysis of the impact of industrialization on Bangladeshi women, see Feldman 1992.

6. The burning chamber of these typical stoves is dug into the ground when the mud is soft; the mouth of the hole is shaped to fit the frying pan. Each time the cookstove is used, the women must renew both the inner and outer surfaces with a mixture of clay and water before lighting a fire of bamboo sticks or twigs in the hole.

7. See the section on site selection in the Introduction; see also the sections on the Philippines and Thailand.

8. Western alcoholic beverages could at the time only be legally sold and consumed in four stores in Dhaka. Of course, diplomatic missions had their own supplies.

9. The Chief Martial Law Administrator of the country at the time of the study was from Rangpur; he passed through Manikganj en route to the capital. In June 1983 he also had all vendors cleared out of his home town.

10. Owens and Hussain separate the *mudidokan* sales of packaged dry snacks at 19% from other dry snack and sweet sellers at 37%.

11. Fruit was counted as a street food when sliced, dried, cooked, pickled, or sold one at a time for immediate consumption; fruit sold by the pound for home consumption was not counted. Only bananas were grown locally; mangoes, apples, papayas, grapes, dates, lichi, jackfruit, tamarind, and several varieties of citrus and olives were available in season.

12. The traditional Bengali calendar, reflecting the importance of climate in an agricultural community, records six seasons: spring, summer, rainy, Indian summer, fall, and winter. Variability in the numbers of vendors clearly relates to planting seasons; local poverty and the need for multiple income sources reflect extensive flooding, which prevents the double or triple cropping typical in other parts of the country.

13. In Bangladesh, 89% of the rural (though only 30% of the urban) population has access to clean water (WRI 1994, 274).

14. More recently, several new indigenous NGOs have extended credit programs modeled on the Grameen Bank and BRAC to urban slum dwellers, and Proshika has expanded its program to urban areas.

Chapter Five

1. Sarah Loza, head of the research organization that conducted the study, is herself a Protestant whose family comes from Upper Egypt and were formerly Copts. Names proclaim the distinction between Copt and Muslim to anyone in Egypt.

2. Ministry of Housing and Utilities Decree 635/1968 regulates standards for carts and utensils used in street food vending; Decree 707/1968 lists foods "street peddlers" are forbidden to sell. Decree 97/1967 of the Ministry of Health relates to the health of the vendors themselves.

3. Development NGOs as intermediary organizations frequently help set up or work with existing community-based organization/associations that have broader goals than a single occupation. The SFVO organization is trying a new hybrid in which clients and patrons, or beneficiaries and providers, serve together on the decision-making body. For a discussion of development NGOs, see Tinker 1996.

4. Reviewers of my evaluation of the SFVO objected to my use of "middle class" to describe the members of the steering committee. Certainly, the low income and modest lifestyle of these dedicated men and women are distinct from the growing materialistic culture of the middle class in Cairo. Calling this group in Minia the "influentials" captures their political, as opposed to economic, position.

5. The youth and university representatives have both subsequently resigned from the board and have not been replaced. The board can designate additional ex-officio members if it wishes.

6. *Haga* is an honorary term indicating that the individual has completed the *haj* to Mecca. The category of volunteer was added to the steering committee to ensure some women members. A woman medical doctor was the other volunteer representative.

7. Egypt has a variety of specialized police forces; those concerned with public order on streets are called *Shorta el Marafig,* usually translated as "utilities police."

8. SPAAC was retained to provide technical assistance to SFVO for two years, from October 1987. Ford also supported SFVO directly, providing a grant to cover the costs of staff, office facilities, and advocacy meetings. In addition, Ford contracted with the Institute for Cultural Affairs (ICA) to provide 12 training workshops to SFVO board and staff over a two-year period.

9. Securing good-quality beans for *foul* and *tamia* continues to be difficult. Before, vendors had insufficient funds to buy in quantity and were often forced to buy remnants at the end of the week; not surprisingly, many early loans went to the purchase of beans. The warehouse may eventually guarantee a constant supply of good beans; but market instability made this difficult in 1993.

10. Large landholders and Jewish merchants offered credit before the revolution, but Islamic prohibitions against cash moneylenders seems to have prevented the existence of usurious moneylenders found in much of Asia.

11. One of the most successful banking schemes for the poor, the Grameen Bank in Bangladesh, specifically builds social and emergency loans into their borrowing regulations. A percentage of each loan goes into an account controlled by the borrowers circle. They can decide to whom and at what rate to grant a loan for illness, marriage, and so on. In addition, a fund is created to repay defaulted debts.

12. Until 1990 the Egyptian government guaranteed employment of educated young women and men. With overloaded bureaucracies and workers returning from the Gulf, the government had to seek alternatives. A social fund to assist young graduates to become entrepreneurs has been established. Some members fear that middle-class graduates might try to take over the kiosk idea and compete with present vendors. Offering places to children of vendors, who undoubtedly helped their parents while young, is popular among the members.

13. Today there are three types of social insurance or pension programs in Egypt. The original program covered salaried employees. Self-employed businessmen were then covered under Law 108 if they worked at an address and could produce a card showing they had paid taxes. In both cases, the employee contributes to the fund; the payout is reasonable because it includes government contributions as well. Later, a small pension designed for widows, but open to anyone contributing, was established under Law 112. Vendors can use this program, which is inexpensive but has very low payments.

14. The turnover among staff directors has been high and is at least partially related to clashes with Haga Fatma. Pay is another. Once staff are trained by working at such indigenous groups as the SFVO with fair salaries by local standards, they are often hired away by international NGOs at much higher pay.

Chapter Six

1. Jill Posner's *Street Foods in Senegal* is the primary source for data in this section.

2. Van Oostrom suggests that because the bride price was so high, young urban men put off marriage; they would rather spend their bride wealth on a radio or television; "just as they are willing to pay for their food and laundry, so they are prepared to pay for companionship and sex" (1989, 87).

3. Mariama Ba records the responses of two educated women to the second marriages of their husbands in her evocative novel *So Long a Letter*, published in French in 1980; available in English through Heinemann.

4. Posner assumes a 5–10% undercount of those not taxed either for benevolent reasons or because they sell away from crowded areas.

5. In Ziguinchor, the typical group consists of 16 members and the average sum was 200 francs per day. Each member puts in a fixed amount each period, and each member

receives the entire sum in turn. Sometimes a lottery is used to determine the order of payout, but everyone receives the sum before the cycle begins again.

6. Occasionally a roving vendor might hawk cold drinks in the market; these vendors were not included in the census because the soft drinks were industrially made.

7. A Dakar survey found 32% of the families eating couscous, but only 12% preparing it at home. In rural areas in the north, millet is the usual evening meal. The switch away from millet products is due not only to the time-consuming preparation of millet but also to the low cost of subsidized imported rice available in town.

8. Couples can declare they will remain monogamous at the time of marriage, but such declaration is not frequent. Even professional women find themselves accepting a second wife: society frowns on complaining. The contradictions of French contemporary culture and polygyny, described by Mariama Ba, continue to affect contemporary Senegalese women.

Chapter Seven

1. The name is a bone of contention among local ethnic groups; for the remainder of this chapter I will simply use the term "Ife."

2. Between the 1963 census and that of 1991, population figures for Nigeria were based on local government area estimates rather than on canvassing the populus. Because representation in legislatures is based on population totals, the politics of the census precluded publication of interim censuses and undermines the accuracy of the 1991 figures.

3. Fapohunda (1988) found that 76% of women in Lagos did not pool income with their husbands. Male-specific expenditures were rent and furniture for the household and medical expenses and school fees for their children. In Ife, market women assumed much of the responsibility for school fees, as noted in the second-phase Street Food Project in Ife reported later in this section.

4. Data on street foods in Ife in 1983, when not otherwise attributed, is based on the series of project reports and on articles and papers written by Olufemi O. Kujore and Tola O. Pearce with other members of the Street Food Project in Ife and cited in the bibliography. Information and descriptions of the area are based on visits by the author to Ife, Lagos, and Ibadan in January 1994.

5. The team was eventually able to carry out these tests; they are reported in Kujore 1991.

6. Other campaigns introduced as part of the War Against Indiscipline required citizens to stand in line at bus stops, learn the Nigerian anthem, and keep streets and empty lots clear of trash and garbage.

7. The First Seminar on Street Foods was held at the Faculty of Health Sciences of Awolowo University in February 1985.

8. The study site was the Odo-Ogbe market in the center of Ife. Within the market the women engaged 67% in foodstuffs, 26% in dry goods, and 7% in services.

9. Details of the health findings are not included here, but of interest for the training program was the fact that local women knew more about Western medications than about indigenous practices. The Women's Health and Action Research Unit at the Medical School of Awolowo University is promoting community health and has found that mis-

information about over-the-counter medicines often inhibits treatment, according to Dr. Andrew Okoruwa in an interview with the author on 11 January 1994.

10. Family rituals and obligations remain the responsibility of women and are essential to the maintenance of kinship network support systems.

11. Nigeria has experienced the rise of development NGOs only since the 1980s; throughout the oil boom citizens looked to the government for social and economic development (Trager and Osinulu 1991).

Chapter Eight

1. While Bapat found 13% of the vendors were women in Pune in 1991, a 1986 survey jointly sponsored by FAO and the government of Maharashtra found only 4.2% in a study that underrepresented vendors without stalls. This study also stresses the family nature of the business.

2. Data for assistants to vendors were not keyed to individual vendors, so that the number of women assistants to men, as opposed to women, is an estimate based on other materials in each country study.

3. The relationship of food to caste and social transations inhibits the expansion of street foods in many parts of India. See Thakur 1994 for information on street food vending in Gauhati, India.

4. Census figures on ethnicity are not available. Concern for the impact of such data actually resulted in the suppression of earlier censuses. Ethnicity data were collected in the 1987 study as they were in Ife; both found non-Yoruba street traders negligible. Hausa vendors in Ibadan were under 2% of the sample; the figure was even lower in Ife because many Hausa women sold kola nuts, which had been ruled out as a food. Igbo traders were 4% of street vendors in Ife, only 1.4% in Ibadan.

5. In the Caribbean, legal marriage "does not necessarily denote the initiation of child-bearing" and may take place when couples are older. Common-law and visiting unions are other culturally accepted arrangments. The fluidity of these unions encourages women to seek their own income. (Massiah 1990, 234)

6. Husbands of the Ife vendors had a similar educational history: 56% had not attended school.

7. The FAO-Maharastra study of Pune in 1986 reported that 64% of the vendors interviewed were born in the city. This sample was less representative and favored stall owners, so the data are not contradictory. According to this study, 17% of the migrant vendors came from the state and 19% from the rest of India.

8. Only 37% of vendors were born in Kingston; the influx from rural parishes accounted for 63% of the vendors, but when they migrated was not recorded.

9. Since measurements in the market use an old Nescafe or cigarette can, a handful, or a banana leaf packet, sizes of servings may be easily varied.

10. Sellers would not rush new customers but wait until they had selected among the vendors. However, there was less civility among vegetable sellers in the Ziguinchor market when trying to sell to foreigners: women still sold at the same prices, but they were aggressive in trying to attract a new customer's attention.

Chapter Nine

1. Mina Thakur is studying street foods in Gauhati, India, with "special attention to the connotation of food—its significance in the traditional normative pattern of food transaction." She explained in a letter that *kacca* food is cooked with water, and only eaten from vendors of one's own caste, but in practice most castes will eat from Brahmin vendors; *pakka* food cooked in ghee is more readily consumed on the street. (24 November 1993) Preliminary data from her dissertation are recorded in a 1994 article.

2. Selling Western-style liquor required a license, which none of the vendors possessed, but covert sellers were observed in Manikganj. The town had one licensed dealer in hashish and opium who was counted in the initial census as he sold on the streets of the market area. Not included among street vendors were *pan* sellers (betel nut with lime and spice wrapped in a digestible leaf), even though the juice is swallowed. Most vendors of *pan* also sold cigarettes; the Bengali word for using either *pan* or cigarettes is the same as for eating, so they may regard them as food.

3. Most consumption studies utilize the recall method; to avoid pitfalls of inaccurate memory, the Bogor research team requested households to record actual purchases of prepared food over a two-day period. Their findings of 25% may still be low, but they are two-thirds higher than the Indonesian national consumption surveys.

4. Data based on interviews at the point of sale; for size of sample, see Table 8.1.

5. In Bangladesh, fewer than half of the school-aged children under 15 years old are in school; in the Manikganj customer survey, only 8 of the 38 children in the sample were in school.

6. The FAO study in Calcutta, India, where all vendors in the studies were male, reported that 16% of the customers were women who were predominantly university students (FAO 1992b). In Kampala, Uganda, 73% of the vendors were women but 76% of the customers were men, a majority of whom lived alone (FAO 1992c).

7. Barth notes that none of the customers in the Iloilo survey had ever purchased the packaged fortified processed foods developed by the Food and Nutrition Research Institute and distributed through grocery stores. Direct fortification of street foods is a more effective way to reach the poor, as illustrated by the improved fishballs in schools in Manila; see Chapter 2.

8. Many rural and semi-urban families continue to keep one or two cows in their homes as a source of milk for butter and cheese, important elements in the local diet.

Chapter Ten

1. Participation is a slippery concept that is too complicated to discuss here. When planning village development, for example, is consulting the patriarchal male head, even though he might be "elected," sufficient? Of course, I would say, women must be consulted (Which women? Organized for what purpose?). What about ethnic groups, the elderly, children? Where is the line? Affected groups? The need to have representation from many viewpoints has sparked the formation of a range of nongovernmental organizations throughout the world. This plethora of local groups reflecting community and single-topic interests are perceived by some as clogging the machinery of government.

2. It is unclear whether the vendors in these malls have moved up from the street.

Casual interviewing in Singapore suggest that while a few vendors make the transitions, many retreated from downtown after street food selling was abolished there.

3. These issues were explored in a recent study of NGOs and summarized in Tinker 1996. Country cases were completed on Mexico by Faranak Miraftab 1996, on India by Neema Kudva 1996, and on Indonesia by Millidge Walker 1996. All are available through the Institute for Urban and Regional Development, University of California, Berkeley, CA 94720-1870.

4. Leaders of many outstanding contemporary development organizations for the poor are middle-class charismatic leaders who provide a bridge between the power elites and the poor, often protecting their members from retribution. Mohammed Yunus, who started the Grameen Bank, was a college professor; Ela Bhatt, founder of SEWA, the Self-Employed Women's Organization of India, was an organizer for a union.

5. In Nigeria, the government set up many GONGOs, government dominated NGOs, to help cushion the effects of structural adjustment; many activists wished to distance themselves from these efforts by setting up their own organizations (Trager and Osinulu 1991). Politics in Thailand discouraged the formation of NGOs as student leaders in particular left Bangkok after the government crackdown on opposition in the mid-1970s.

6. For a presentation of the PISCES studies and subsequent literature critiquing this dichotomy, as well as a review of development programs subsequently introduced, see Tinker 1987. My comments of competing values of the two approaches are expanded in my "The Human Economy of Microentrepreneurs," 1995.

7. Management is an entirely different skill. Many a consultant in Washington, D.C., deciding to set up a small firm, has been overwhelmed by booking and overhead requirements.

8. Strassmann (1987) argues that this fungibility of family labor, along with free use of dwelling space, contributes to the comparative advantage of successful microenterprises.

9. In an interview in Dhaka in 1991, a top Grameen Bank official insisted that they operated as a "bank" and not an NGO, despite continued emphasis on social messages that range from family planning to reduced spending on weddings and funerals.

10. At some point with microlending schemes, recipients need to acquire some training in business and learn about new technologies if they are to move beyond survival existence to create a viable microenterprise. Intermediate Technology (IT) of England has devoted itself to providing this type of training for several decades because "NGOs often have no more knowledge of business and entrepreneur development than the groups they are trying to assist" (*Food Chain*, 1992/6:11). Many of its small technologies are for food processing; one program assisted in packaging *canacur* in Bangladesh.

11. The under-counting of women's work is a major theme of women in development; a majority of women globally work in occupations that do not fall into the traditional statistical definitions. The U.N. Statistical Commission has held periodic hearings on how to count more of the informal-sector jobs. See Beneria 1982, Dixon-Mueller 1985, Tinker 1990.

12. Two edited volumes review the progress of the debate: Bromley 1978, and Mathur and Moser 1984. A commentary on the fuzziness of the concept and a call to focus research on the real world was written by Peattie in 1987. Two recent commentaries by Moser and by Rakowski place the debate in historical context; they are part of Rakowski's

significant collection on the informal-sector debate in Latin America, *Contrapunto* (1994), which includes Bromley's interpretation of de Soto. The specific urban aspects of the informal sector is succinctly presented in Gilbert and Gugler 1992.

13. Vendors might pay a fee, act as a guard, or steer customers inside. Similar arrangements were identified in New York City, where mobile carts needed licenses but "stoop-line" vendors, those in front of shops, had a symbiotic relationship to merchants (Gaber 1994).

14. Similar observations about differential incomes and reasons were made among Nairobi traders by Robertson, 1995.

15. Articles tracing women's contributions to family budgets are collected in Dwyer and Bruce 1988.

Afterword

1. The National Restaurant Association in the United States reports that 82% of all U.S. families have eaten in a fast food restaurant in the past year, and that the larger the family, the more likely they are to eat fast food (1993).

2. These linkages with market women have been detailed by Trager (1981) for Nigeria. Dasgupta (1992) looks at linkages in Calcutta and concludes that ethnic contacts form the base for trading allegiances.

Glossary

acar   varieties of chutney or pickles (Manikganj)

acara/akara   cowpea fritters (West Africa)

agar-agar   gelatin-like thickener used in sweets (Bogor)

amala   doughy porridge (Ife)

arisan   rotating savings association (Bogor)

balut   fertilized duck eggs (Iloilo)

barangay   smallest unit of local government (Iloilo)

batchoy   noodle soup (Iloilo)

becak   pedicab (Bogor)

beignets   donut-like sweets (Ziguinchor)

bellila   wheat porridge (Minia)

bhaji   fried spiced vegetables (Manikganj)

biris   indigenous cigarettes (Manikganj)

bisap   drink made from an herbal infusion (Ziguinchor)

boli   roasted plantain (Ife)

bon-bons   hard cookies (Ziguinchor); small cakes (Chonburi)

brochettes   grilled meat and onions on bread (Ziguinchor)

buka   a covered stall with tables and chairs (Ife)

canacur   crunchy fried snack (Manikganj)

carendaria   stores selling pre-cooked food (Iloilo)

chatpotti   potato/pulse/egg snack (Manikganj)

chira   heated and pounded rice (Manikganj)

couscous   millet-based pasta (Ziguinchor)

dal   cooked pulses (Manikganj)

dim sum   Chinese steamed snacks using wheat dough

dodo   ripe plantain (Ife)

dokar   horse-drawn vehicle (Bogor)

douaniers   custom officials (Ziguinchor)

eba   cassava dough (Ife)

eko   cornmeal loaf (Ife)

emping   nut chips (Bogor)

esusu   rotating savings assocation (Ife)

foul   Egyptian snack (Minia)

fuchka   fried circles of bread (Manikganj)

gado gado   blanched vegetables served with peanut sauce (Bogor)

ghee   clarified butter

gur   date sugar (Manikganj)

haap rae   pole vendors (Chonburi)

Haga   honorific for a woman who has completed the *haj*

haj   the Muslim pilgrimage to Mecca

hat   rural market (Manikganj)

hong thaew   shop-house vendors (Chonburi)

iftari   foods eaten to break Ramadan (Manikganj)

ipkere   green (unripe) plantain (Ife)

iyan   mashed yams (Ife)

jamu   medicinal herbal drink (Bogor)

kaki lima   "five-legged" cart (Bogor)

kampung   village (Bogor)

kariwallah   "food server" in India; used to refer to those who feed textile workers on contract in Bombay

krapah pla   fish soup (Chonburi)

kretek   clove-laced cigarettes (Bogor)

krupuk   rice or cassava chips (Bogor)

kushary   rice-, lentil- and macaroni-based meal (Minia)

lot kaen   push-cart vendors (Chonburi)

lumpia   egg rolls (Iloilo)

mae ban tung plastic   "plastic bag housewives" (Chonburi)

matha   milk curd drink (Manikganj)

merienda   all-day snacking (Iloilo)

mohila mela   women's market (Manikganj)

monie   traditional millet porridge (Ziguinchor)

moyin-moyin   cowpeas steamed in banana-leaf (Ife)

mudidokan   small grocery store (Manikganj)

muri   puffed rice (Manikganj)

naths   Wolof term for rotating savings groups (Ziguinchor)

oba   King of the Yoruba (Ife)

ogi   cornmeal porridge (Ife)

pan   betel leaf/nut preparation widely chewed in Asia (Manikganj)

panas   hot in temperature (Bogor)

pasars   market place (Bogor)

pedes   hot in flavor (Bogor)

petits poissons   tiny fried and salted fish snacks (Ziguinchor)

phaeng looy   vendors selling from tables (Chonburi)

pikulan   carrying pole (Bogor)

pin-to   tiffin container for carrying food (Thailand)

pondok   enterprise providing residence as well as equipment (Bogor)

puto maya/puto bumbong   rice/milk sweet (Iloilo)

Ramadan   Muslim ritual month of fasting

rantangan   tiffin container for carrying food (Bogor)

roti/ruti   flat bread in India and Bangladesh

ruti   dry-cooked dough balls (Manikganj)

Sandoug el Zamalah   SFVO's crisis fund (Minia)

sari-sari   grocery stores (Iloilo)

sate   small pieces of skewered meat grilled over charcoal

sate ayam   chicken kebabs (Bogor)

Shorta el Marafig   "utilities police" (Minia)

sukhapiban   sanitary districts (Chonburi)

suki   personalized vendor-client relationship (Iloilo)

sunduof   Wolof steamed and sweetened rice snack (Ziguinchor)

tahu   hot ginger drink (Iloilo)

tamia   chickpea balls (Minia)

tangana   French-style breakfast (Ziguinchor)

tempe/tahu   soybean curd fermented with or without beans (Bogor)

tiffin   English word for light meal, usually midday

tiffin boxes   stacked containers used in Asia to carry meals

titipan   steamed sweet rice and other snacks sold on commission (Indonesia)

tong   protection racketeer (Iloilo)

tontines   French term for rotating savings groups (Ziguinchor)

tuba   coconut-sap alcoholic drink (Iloilo)

viands   meal constituents over rice (Iloilo)

warung   fixed stall (Bogor)

zalabia   deep fried sweet dough (Minia)

Bibliography

Acharya, Meena and Lynn Bennett. 1981. *The Rural Women of Nepal: An Aggregate Analysis and Summary of Eight Village Studies.* Kathmandu: Center for Economic Development and Administration, Tribhuvan University.

Achleitner, W., and E. Ndione. 1981. "La consommation en milieu infra-urbain." Working paper. Dakar: ENDA.

Adalemo, Ayinde, et al., 1994. "Government policy toward vending." Draft Report of the Working Group on Urban Regulatory Policy Towards Informal Sector Employment to the American African Institute, Lagos.

Afonja, Simi. 1981. "Changing modes of production and the sexual division of labor among the Yoruba." *Signs* 7/3:299–313.

———. 1990. "Changing patterns of gender stratification in West Africa," in Tinker, *Persistent Inequalities*, p. 198–209.

Agarwal, Bina. 1985. "Women and technological change in agriculture," in I Ahmed, ed., *Technology and Rural Women: Conceptual and Empirical Issues.* London: Allen and Unwin.

Akinyele, Isaac Olaolu. 1987. *Study on Street Foods in Ibadan, Nigeria: Characteristics of Food Vendors and Consumers—Implications for Quality and Safety.* Ibadan: FAO.

———. 1989. *Women and Street Foods in Nigeria: Training programme for women on the Safe Production and Sale of Street Foods.* Ibadan and Rome: FAO.

———. 1991. *Study on Street Foods in Nigeria: Comparative Study of the Socioeconomic Characteristics of the Food Vendors and Consumers in Ibadan, Lagos, and Kaduna.* Ibadan: FAO.

Ashe, Jeffrey, ed. 1985. *The PISCES II Experience.* 2 vols. Washington, D.C.: U.S. Agency for International Development.

Ba, Mariama. 1981. *So Long a Letter.* Oxford: Heinemann.

Babb, F. 1989. *Between Field and Cooking Pot: The Political Economy of Marketwomen in Peru.* Austin: University of Texas Press.

Banerjee, Nirmala, ed. 1991. *Indian Women in a Changing Industrial Scenario.* New Delhi: Sage.

Bapat, Meera. 1992. *Street Food Vending in Pune.* Pune, India: Center of Studies in Social Sciences

Barth, Gerald. 1983. *Street Foods: Informal Sector Food Presentation and Marketing.* Washington, D.C.: EPOC.

———. 1986. "Street food vendors in selected Asian cities," in F. G. Winarno, ed., *Street Foods in Asia: A Proceeding of the Regional Workshop.* Jogjakarta: FAO and Food Technology Development Center, Bogor Agricultural University.

Barth, Gerald, and Mei-Jean Kuo. 1984. *Crossing the Gap between Microeconomic Activities and Small-scale Food-catering Enterprises.* Washington, D.C.: EPOC.

Bascom, W. M. 1951. "Yoruba food." *Africa* 2:41–53.

Beneria, L. 1982. "Accounting for women's work," in L. Beneria, ed., *Women and Development: The Sexual Division of Labor in Rural Societies.* New York: Praeger.

———. 1989. "Subcontracting and employment dynamics in Mexico City," in Portes et al., *Informal Economy,* pp. 173–188.

Beneria, Lourdes, and Martha Roldan. 1987. *The Crossroads of Class and Gender: Industrial Homework, Subcontracting and Household Dynamics in Mexico City.* Chicago: University of Chicago Press.

Berg, Alan. 1987. *Malnutrition: What Can Be Done? Lessons from the World Bank Experience.* Baltimore: Johns Hopkins University Press.

Berger, Margaret, and Marya Buvinic, eds. 1990. *Women's Ventures: Assistance to the Informal Sector in Latin America.* West Hartford, Conn.: Kumarian Press.

Bijlmer, Joep. 1986. "Employment and accomodation in the ambulatory street economy: The case of Surabaya, Indonesia." Urban Research Working Paper No. 10. Amsterdam: Institute of Cultural Anthropology, Free University.

———. 1989. "The informal sector as a "lucky dip": Concepts and research strategies," in van Gelder and Bijlmer *About Fringes, Margins, and Lucky Dips,* pp. 141–159.

———. 1991. "The wholesomeness of common people's food in Indonesia. The Bogor streetfood project: a bird's-eye view." Working paper. Institut Pertanian Bogor (IPB).

———. 1992. "The wholesomeness of common people's food in Indonesia. The Bogor streetfood project: final report 1988–1992." Bogor: Institut Pertanian Bogor (IPB).

Blanc-Szanton, Christina. 1990. "Gender and inter-generational resource allocation among Thai and Wino-Thai households," in Leela Dube and Pajni Palriwala, eds., *Structures and Strategies: Women, Work, and Family.* New Delhia: Sage. pp. 79–102.

Blumberg, Rae, Cathy Rakowski, Irene Tinker, and Michael Monteon, eds. 1995. *Engendering Wealth and Well-Being.* Boulder, Colo: Westview.

Boserup, Ester. 1970. *Woman's Role in Economic Development.* London: Allen and Unwin.

———. 1990. "Economic change and the roles of women," in Tinker, *Persistent Inequalities,* pp. 14–24.

Boserup, Ester, and Christina Liljencrantz. 1975. *Integration of Women into Development: Why, When, How?* New York: United Nations Development Programme.

Boris, Eileen, and Elizabeth Prügl. 1995. *Homeworkers in Global Perspective: Invisible No More.* New York: Routledge.

Bromley, Ray, ed. 1978. *The Urban Informal Sector: Critical Perspectives.* Special double issue of *World Development* 6/9 & 10.

———. 1994. "Informality, de Soto style: From concept to policy," in Rakowski, *Contrapunto,* pp. 13–15.

Bryan, Frank, P. Teufel, S. Riaz, S. Roohi, F. Qadar, and Z. Malik. 1992. "Hazards and critical control points of street-vended *chat,* a regionally popular food in Pakistan." *Journal of Food Protection* 55/9:708–13.

Bunster, Ximena, and Elsa Chaney. 1985. *Sellers and Servants: Working Women in Lima, Peru.* New York: Praeger.

Catholic Relief Services. 1978. *Nutrinews.* 6/3 (May–June).

Chapman, Barbara Anne. 1984. *Streetfoods in Indonesia: Vendors in the Urban Food Supply.* Washington, D.C.: EPOC.

Chen, Marty. 1989. "Developing no-craft employment for women in Bangladesh," in Ann Leonard, ed., *Seeds: Supporting Women's Work in the Third World.* New York: Feminist Press.

Chr. Michelsen Institute. 1986. *Bangladesh: Country Sudy and Norwegian Aid Review.* Bergen, Norway: Chr. Michelsen Institute.

CILSS. 1980. *Etude sur marché urbaine Sahelien (Senegal et Haute Volta) des cereales locales et de leurs derives susceptibles de se substituter aux importations.* Paris: Marcomer.

Cohen, Monique, 1984. *Informal Sector Activity in Regional Urban Areas: The Street Food Trade.* Washington, D.C.: EPOC.

———. 1986. "The influence of the street food trade on women and children," in Derrick Jelliffe and E. F. Patrice, eds., *Advances in International Maternal and Child Health.* New York: Oxford University Press.

———. 1986. "Women and the urban street food trade: Some implications for policy." Gender and Planning Working Paper No. 12. London: Development Planning Unit, Bartlett School of Architecture and Planning, University College.

———. 1987. "Street food trade" issue of *Urban Examples* 14. New York: UNICEF.

———. 1988. "Third World Rice Krispies." *Intercom* 47.

———. 1990. "Microenterprises as vehicles for nutritional assistance: lessons from the street food trade," paper presented at roundtable entitled "Nutribusiness: A Strategy for the 1990s."

———. 1993. "Commerce urbain d'aliments de rue," in M. Chauliac, P. Gerbouin-Rerolle and A.-M. Masse-Raimbault, eds., *Villes et alimentation: La consommation dans les rues.* Paris: Centre International de l'Enfance.

Coquery-Vidrovitch, Catherine. 1990. "A history of African urbanization: Labor, women and the informal sector—a survey of recent studies," in Satya Datta, ed. *Third World Urbanization.* Stockholm: Swedish Council for Research in Humanities and Social Sciences.

Daly, Herman. 1990. "Sustainable growth: An impossibility theorem." *Development* 3/4: 39–41.

Dasgupta, Nandini. 1992. "Linkage, heterogeneity and income determinants in petty trading: the case of Calcutta." *World Development* 20/10: 1443–61.

De Guzman, Patrocinio et al. 1974. "Dietary patterns and eating habits of public high school students: the relation to socio-economic status." *Philippine Journal of Nutrition* Jan–March:1–10.

de Soto, Hernando. 1987. *El otro sendoro.* Buenos Aires: Sudamericana. [English trans. 1989. *The other path.* New York: Harper and Row.]

de Treville, D. 1987. *Small-Scale Enterprise Assessment: An Analysis of Renewable Energy Users and the Informal Sector.* Chevy Chase, Md.: Equity Policy Center.

Dignard, Louise, and Jose Havet, eds. 1987. *Women in Micro- and Small-scale Enterprise Development.* Boulder, Colo: Westview.

Dioup, Fatima, 1992. "Actual practice of the sale of street food in the Dakar region," Ph.D. diss., Ecole Inter-état des Sciences et Medicine Vetenaire, Dakar.

Dixon, Ruth. 1983. "Land, labor and sex composition of the agricultural labor force: An international comparison." *Development and Change* 14/3: 347–72.

Dixon-Mueller, Ruth. 1985. *Women's Work in Third World Agriculture*. Geneva: International Labour Organization.

Drakakis-Smith, David. 1991. "Urban food distribution in Asia and Africa." *Royal Geographic Society* 157/1: 51–61.

Dwyer, Daisy, and Judith Bruce, eds. 1988. *A Home Divided: Women and Income in the Third World*. Palo Alto, Calif.: Stanford University Press.

East-West Center. 1983. "Problems of rapid urbanization: Provision of food and basic services." Report of a conference in Manila, September. Honolulu, Hawaii: Resources Systems Institution, East-West Center.

El-Sherbeeny, M., M. Sadik, E.-S. Aly, and F. Bryan. 1985. "Microbiological profiles of foods sold by street vendors in Egypt." *International Journal of Food Microbiology* 2:355–64.

Engle, Patrice. 1995. "Father's money, mother's money and parental commitment: Guatemala and Nicaragua," in Blumberg et al., *Engendering Wealth*, pp. 155–179.

Everett, Jana, and Mira Savara. 1991. "Institutional credit as a strategy towards self-reliance for petty commodity producers in India: A critical evaluation," in Heleh Afshar, ed., *Women: Development and Survival in the Third World*. New York: Longman.

Evers, Hans-Dieter. 1980. "Subsistence production and the Jakarta floating mass." *Prisma* 17:27–35.

Fapohunda, Eleanor. 1988. "The nonpooling household," in Dwyer and Bruce, *Home Divided*, pp. 143–154.

Farbman, Michael. 1981. *The PISCES Studies: Assisting the Smallest Economic Activities of the Urban Poor*. Washington, D.C.: U.S. Agency for International Development.

Feith, Herbert. 1962. *The Decline of Constitutional Democracy in Indonesia*. Ithaca, N.Y.: Cornell University Press.

Feldman, Shelley. 1992. "Crisis, Islam and gender in Bangladesh: The social construction of a female labor force," in Lourdes Beneria and Shelley Feldman, eds., *Unequal Burden: Economic Crises, Persistent Poverty, and Women's Work*. Boulder, Colo.: Westview.

Findlay, Allen, Ronan Paddison, and John Dawson. 1990. *Retailing Environments in Developing Countries*. London: Routledge.

Folbre, Nancy. 1986. "Cleaning house: New perspectives on households and economic development." *Journal of Development Economics* 22:5–40.

Food and Agricultural Organization (FAO). 1986. *Study on Street Foods in Pune*. Pune, India: Government of Maharashtra.

———. 1988. "Street foods; *Les aliments vendus sur la voie publique; La venta de alimentos en las calles*." Yogjakarta, Indonesia: FAO Expert Consultation on Street Foods. Reprinted 1990.

———. 1989. "Urbanization, food consumption pattners, and nutrition," COAG/89/5. Committee on Agriculture, Tenth Session, 26 April–5 May. Rome: FAO.

———. 1990. *Assessment of the Economic Impact of Street Foods in Penang, Malaysia*. Rome: FAO. Author listed inside as Grace P. Pendigon, FAO Consultant.

———. 1992a. "Intercountry workshop on street foods in Africa." Accra, Ghana: FAO Regional Office for Africa.

———. 1992b. *Street Food in Calcutta: Socio-Economic and Related Factors*. Calcutta: Department of Biochemistry and Nutrition, All-India Institute of Hygiene and Public Health. Author listed inside cover as Dr. Indira Chakravarty.

————. 1992c. *Study on Street Foods in Kampala, Uganda.* Kampala, Uganda: Makerere University. Author listed inside cover as Dr. G. W. Nasinyama.

————. 1992d. "Street foods in Asia: Second regional workshop." Report of workshop in Kuala Lumpur. Rome: FAO.

FAO and the World Health Organization (WHO). 1992a. *Nutrition and Development: A Global Assessment.* Background paper for the international Conference on Nutrition. Rome: FAO and WHO.

FAO and the World Health Organization (WHO). 1992b. *Final Report of the International Conference on Nutrition.* Includes Proceedings, World Declaration on Nutrition, and the Plan of Action for Nutrition. Rome: FAO and WHO.

Food Chain. 1992/6 and 1995/14. *Food Chain* Rugby, England: Intermediate Technology Group.

Food and Nutrition Research Institute (FNRI). 1994. *Improvement of Street Foods: January 1992–March 1994.* Report to FAO. Manila: FNRI, Government of the Philippines.

Fowler, D. A. 1981. "The informal sector in Freetown: Opportunities for self-employment," in Sethuraman, *Informal Sector in Developing Countries.*

Fox, James. 1995. *Maximizing the Outreach of Microenterprise Finance: The Emerging Lessons of Successful Programs.* Washington, D.C.: U.S. Agency for International Development.

Freeman, Donald. 1993. "Survival strategy or business training ground? The significance of urban agriculture for the advancement of women in African cities." *African Studies Review* 36/3:1.

Gaber, John. 1994. "Manhattan's fourth street vendors' markets: Informal street peddlers' complementary relationship with New York City's economy." *Urban Anthropology* 23/4:373–408.

Gilbert, Alan, and Josef Gugler. 1992. *Cities, Poverty and Development: Urbanization in the Third World.* 2nd ed. New York: Oxford University Press.

Glover, Wil. 1992. "Transformation of an urban squatter settlement in India: Modernism in the margins," in *Traditional Dwellings and Settlements.* Working Paper Series No. 51. Berkeley: Center for Environmental Design Research, University of California.

Grant, William, Ross Bigalow, Tom Mahoney, and Robert Strauss. 1989. "AID microenterprise stocktaking evaluation: Egypt." Washington, D.C.: Development Alternatives Inc.

Grown, Caren, ed. 1989. *Beyond Survival: Expanding Income-earning Opportunities for Women in Developing Countries.* Special issue of *World Development* 17/7.

Guardian [Nigeria]. 1994. Editorial, March 12 (p. 14).

Gugler, Josef, ed. 1988. *The Urbanization of the Third World.* Oxford: Oxford University Press.

Gugler, Josef, and William Flanagan. 1978. *Urbanization and Social Change in West Africa.* Cambridge: Cambridge University Press.

Guiness, Patrick. 1986. *Harmony and Hierarchy in a Javanese Kampung.* New York: Oxford University Press.

Hackenberg, Beverly, and Gerald Barth. 1984. "Growth of the bazaar economy and its significance for women's employment: Trends of the 1970s in Davao City, Philippines," in Gavin Jones, ed. *Women in the Urban and Industrial Workforce: Southeast and East Asia.* Canberra: Australian National University.

Hafkin, Nancy, and Edna Bay, eds. 1976. *Women in Africa: Studies in Social and Economic Changes.* Stanford, Calif.: Stanford University Press.

Hansen, Karen. 1990. "The black market and women traders in Lusaka, Zambia," in Kathleen Staudt and Jane Parpart, eds. Reinner *Women and the State in Africa.* Boulder, Colo.

Hiltzik, M. 1990. "Separatist region tests Senegal on rights issue." *Los Angeles Times,* November 9.

Hotchkiss, Patricia, Haythan Hamdan, and Tom Valentine. 1991. "Minia street food vendors project: MECA internal evaluation." Cairo: Catholic Relief Services.

House, William. 1984. "Nairobi's informal sector: dynamic entrepreneurs or surplus labor?" *Economic Development and Cultural Change* 32/2:277–302.

House, Willaim, Gerrishon K. Ikiara, and Dorothy McCormick. 1993. "Urban self-employment in Kenya: Panacea or viable strategy?" *World Development* 21/7:1205–1223.

Hyden, Goran. 1980. *Beyond Ujamaa in Tanzania: Underdevelopment and an Uncaptured Peasantry.* Berkeley: University of California Press.

ILO. 1972. *Employment, Incomes and Equality: A Strategy for Increasing Employment in Kenya.* Geneva: International Labour Organization.

———. 1995. *International Labor Conference Report V(1): Home Work.* 82nd session. Geneva: International Labour Organization.

INSTRAW. 1990. "Methods of collecting and analysing statistics on women in the informal sector and their contributions to national product." Report of a regional workshop in Zambia. Santo Domingo: INSTRAW.

———. 1991. "Analysis of women's participation in the informal sector." Report of the consultative meeting on macro-economic policy, Rome. Santo Domingo: INSTRAW.

International Life Sciences Institute (ISLI). 1993. "Street foods: epidemiology management and practical approaches." Abstracts of conference presentations in Beijing, China, sponsored by the Chinese Academy of Preventive Medicine and ISLI in cooperation with FAO and WHO.

IURD. 1994. "Women in socio-economic transition in Vietnam, Laos, Cambodia and China." Issue papers from a conference in Bangkok. Irene Tinker, convenor. Berkeley, CA: Institute for Urban and Regional Development.

Jain, Devaki. 1980. *Women's Quest for Power.* New Delhi: Vikas.

Jaquette, Jane. 1993. "The family as a development issue," in Young et al., *Women at the Center,* pp. 45–62.

Jayasuriya, D. C. 1994. "Street food vending in Asia: Some policy and legal aspects." *Food Control* 5/4:222–226.

Jellinek, Lea. 1977. "The Life of a Jakarta Street Trader," in Janet Abu Lughod and Richard Hay, Jr., eds., *Third World Urbanization.* Chicago: Maaroufa Press.

Jhabvala, Renana. 1994. "Self-employed women's association: Organizing women by struggle and development," in Shiela Rowbotham and Swasti Mitter, eds. *Dignity and Daily Bread: New Forms of Economic Organizing among Poor Women in the Third World and the First.* New York: Routledge.

Joseph, Rebecca. 1987. *Worker, Middlewoman, Entrepeneur: Women in the Indonesian Batik Industry.* Bangkok: Population Council Regional Office.

Kandiyoti, Deniz. 1985. *Women in Rural Production Systems: Problems and Policies.* Paris: UNESCO.

———. 1988. "Bargaining with patriarchy." *Gender and Society* 2/3:274–90.

Kennedy, Eileen, and Pauline Peters. 1992. "Household food security and child nutrition: The interaction of income and gender of household head." *World Development* 20/8:1077–85.

Khan, Sahed Anwer. 1994. "Attributes of informal settlements affect their vulnerability to eviction: A study of Bangkok." *Environment and Urbanization* 6/1:25–39.

Kudva, Neema. 1996. "Uneasy partnerships? Government-NGO relations in India." Working paper. Berkeley: Institute for Urban and Regional Development.

Kujore, Olufemi O. 1984a. "Street foods in Ile-Ife interim report: Background information and methodology." Paper submitted to the Ford Foundation, Lagos, and EPOC.

———. 1984b. "The environment in which street foods are prepared and sold in a Yoruba town." Paper presented at the Africa Studies Association meeting, Los Angeles, Calif. 25–28 Oct.

———. 1985. "Street foods and street food vendors in Ile-Ife, Nigeria." Paper presented at the Association for Women in Develoment conference, Washington, D.C., 27 April.

———. 1991. "Nutrition and health implications of street foods." Paper presented at the training workshop for public health superintendents in local government, health technologists, school meal inspectors, Owolowo University, Ile-Ife, 22–26 April.

Kujore, Olufemi O., and Tola Olu Pearce. 1989. *Street Foods in Ile-Ife: Preparation, Marketing, and Health Aspects of a Small-scale Enterprise.* Final report of the Nigerian portion of the Street Foods Project. Ife: Owolowo University.

Kujore, Olufemi O., and Tola Olu Pearce. 1992. "Comprehensive summary and final report on health care of families: The approach of market women in Ile-Ife." Final report of follow-up project, submitted to the Ford Foundation, June. Ile-Ife: Owolowo University.

Kujore, Olufemi O. Tola Olu Pearce, and V. Aina Agboh-Bankole. 1985. "Report of the First Seminar on Street Foods in Ile-Ife." Ile-Ife, Nigeria: Faculty of Health Sciences, University of Ife.

Kusterer, Ken. 1990. "The imminent demise of patriarchy," in Tinker, *Persistent Inequalities*, pp. 239–255.

Lewis, Barbara. 1976. "The limitations of group action among entrepeneurs: the market women of Abidjan," in Hafkin and Bay, *Women in Africa.*

Liang, Y., and X. Yuan. 1991. "Investigation of bacterial contaminants of street-vended foods." *Journal of Milk, Food and Environmental Sanitarians* 11:725–27.

Loza, Sarah. 1985. *Street Foods and Beverages in the City of Minia.* Cairo: Social Planning, Analysis, and Administration Consultants (SPAAC).

Mabogunje, Akin. 1958. "The Yoruba home." *Odu* 5:28–36. As quoted in Pearce, Kujore, and Agboh-Bankole, 1988, "Generating and income in the urban environment," p. 000.

Massiah, J. 1990. "Defining women's work in the Commonwealth Caribbean," in Tinker, *Persistent Inequalities*, pp. 223–238.

Mataya, C., and J. Waudo. 1993. "Improving the status of women in the marketing and distribution of food and food products in sub-Saharan Africa." Project proposal. Edmonton: University of Alberta.

Mathur, O. P., and C. Moser, eds. 1984. Special issue on "The urban informal sector." *Regional Development Dialogue* 5/3.

McGee, Terence, and Yue-man Yeung. 1977. *Hawkers in Southeast Asian Cities: Planning for the Bazaar Economy.* Ottawa: International Development Research Institute.

McKean, Cressida. 1994. "Training and technical assistance for small- and micro-enterprise: A discussion of their effectiveness," in Rakowski, *Contrapunto*, pp. 199–219.

Meis, Maria. 1982. *The Lacemakers of Narsapur: Indian Housewives Produce for the World Market.* London: Zed Press.

Meis, Maria, Veronica Bennholdt-Thomsen, and Claudia von Werlhof. 1988. *Women: The Last Colony*. London: Zed Press.

Mintz, Sidney. 1971. "Men, women and trade." *Comparative Studies in Society and History* 13/3:247–69.

Miraftab, Faranak. 1994. "(Re)production at home: Reconceptualizing home and family." *Journal of Family Issues* 15/3:467–89.

———. 1995. "A misfit between policy and people: The seach for housing by female headed households in Guadalajara, Mexico," Ph.D. diss., Department of Architecture, University of California at Berkeley.

———. 1996. "Old enemies, new rivals, future partners? The case of state-NGO relations in Mexico." Working paper. Berkeley: Institute for Urban and Regional Development.

Moser, Caroline. 1984. "The informal sector reworked: Viability and vulnerability in urban development." *Regional Development Dialogue* 5/3:135–78.

National Agency for Science and Engineering Infrastructure. 1992. *Nigeria Country Report*. Lagos: Government of Nigeria, for the International Conference on Nutrition.

National Economic and Development Authority (NEDA). 1983. *Philippine Statistical Yearbook*. Manila: NEDA.

National Restaurant Association. 1993. *Off-Premises Market*. Washington, D.C.: NRA.

Natrass, N. 1987. "Street trading in Transkei—A struggle against poverty, persecution and prosecution." *World Development* 15:861–75.

New York Times. 1993. "Senegal releases 4 men held in killing of election official." 19 May.

Nicholls, William, and William Dyson. 1983. *The Informal Economy: Where People Are the Bottom Line*. Ottawa: VIF Publications.

Noble, K. 1991. "Senegal scenes: Idyllic beaches, bullets, bombs." *New York Times*, 29 January.

Osei-Opare, Freme. 1991. "Detailed studies of the social characteristics and nature of economic activities of fisherfolks in selected villages in Bendel and Aska Ibom states, Nigeria." FAO: Integrated Rural Fisheries Development Project.

Otero, Maria. 1990. *A Handful of Rice: Savings Mobilization by Micro-enterprise Programs and Perspectives for the Future*. Monograph Series No. 3. Washington, D.C.: Action International.

———. 1994. "The role of governments and private institutions in addressing the informal sector in Latin America," in Rakowski, *Contrapunto*, pp. 177–197.

Owens, Naomi, and Naseem Hussain. 1984. *Street Foods in Bangladesh*. Washington, D.C.: EPOC.

Page, John M., and William F. Steel. 1984. "Small enterprise development: Economic issues from African experience." Technical Ppaper No. 26. Washington, D.C.: World Bank.

Papenek, Hanna. 1991. "The ideal woman and the ideal society: Control and autonomy in the construction of gender," in Valentine Moghadam, ed., *Identity Politics and Women*. Boulder, Colo.: Westview.

Pearce, Tola Olu. 1992. "Perceptions on the availability of social support for childcare among women in Ile-Ife." Report submitted to the Ford Foundation, as part of the final report on "Health care of families."

Pearce, Tola Olu, Olufemi O. Kujore, and V. Aina Agboh-Bankole. 1988. "Generating an income in the urban environment: The experience of street food vendors in Ile-Ife, Nigeria." *Africa* 58/4:385–400.

Peattie, L. 1987. "An idea in good currency and how it grew: The informal sector." *World Development* 15/7:851–60.

Perez Sains, J., and R. Menjivar Larin. 1994. "American men and women in the urban informal sector." *Journal of Latin American Studies* 26/2:431.

Philippines, Government of. 1992. *Philippine Development Plan for Women 1989–1992*. Manila: Government of the Philippines.

———. *Regulations on Selling and Setting up of Stalls in Makati*. Manila: Government of the Philippines.

———. 1993. *GOP Report to CEDAW*. [CEDAW/C/PHI/3]. Manila: Government of the Philippines.

Pongsapich, Amara. 1993. "Defining the nonprofit sector: Thailand." Working paper no. 11. Comparative Nonprofit Sector Project, Baltimore: Johns Hopkins University.

Pongsapich, Amara, and Nitaya Kateleeradabhan. 1994. *Philanthropy, NGO Activities, and Corporate Funding in Thailand*. Bangkok: Chulalengborn University Social Research Institute, (CUSRI).

Pongsapich, Amara, Nitaya Kataleeradabhan, Preeda Sirisawat, and Ratana Jarubenja, 1989. *Women Homeworkers in Thailand*. Bangkok: Chulalengborn University Social Research Institute, (CUSRI).

Population Crisis Committee (PCC). 1990. *Cities: Life in the World's 100 Largest Metropolitan Areas*. Washington D.C.: PCC.

Portes, Alejandro, Silvia Blitzer, and John Curtin. 1986. "The urban informal sector in Uruguay: Its internal structure, characteristics and effects." *World Development* 14/6:727–41.

Portes, Alejandro, Manuel Castells, and Lauren A. Benton, eds. 1989. *The Informal Economy: Studies in Advanced and Less Development Countries*. Baltimore: Johns Hopkins University Press.

Posner, Jill. 1983. *Street Foods in Senegal*. Washington, D.C.: EPOC.

Powell, Dorian, Eleanor Wint, Erna Brodber, and Versada Campbell. 1989. "The Jamaican street foods study." *Cajanus* (Caribbean Food and Nutrition Institute Quarterly) 22/1:13–35.

Powell, Dorian, Eleanor Wint, Erna Brodber, and Versada Campbell. 1990. *Street Foods of Kingston*. Kingston, Jamaica: Institute of Social and Economic Research and the University of West Indies, Mona.

Prügl, Elizabeth, and Irene Tinker. Forthcoming. "Micro-entrepeneurs and home workers: a false dichotomy."

Rahman, Rushidan Islam. 1982. "New technologies in Bangladesh agriculture: Adoption and its impact on rural labor market." Bangkok: International Labour Organization.

Rakodi, Carole. 1991. "Women's work or household strategies?" *Environment and Urbanization* 3/2:39–50.

Rakowski, Cathy, ed. 1994. *Contrapunto: The Informal Sector Debate in Latin America*. Albany: SUNY Press.

Remy, Dorothy. 1975. "Underdevelopment and the experience of women: A Nigerian case study," in Rayna Reiter, ed., *Towards an Anthropology of Women*. New York: Monthly Review Press.

Rhyne, Elizabeth, and Maria Otero. 1992. "Financial services for microenterprises: Principles and institutions." *World Development* 20/11:1561–71.

Richardson, Harry. 1984. "The role of the urban informal sector: An overview." *Regional Development Dialogue* 5/3:3–40.

Roberts, J. Timmons. 1995. "Trickling down and scrambling up: The informal sector, food provisioning and local benefits of the Carajas mining 'growth pole' in the Brazilian Amazon." *World Development* 23/3:385–400.

Robertson, Claire. 1995. "Trade, gender and poverty in the Nairobi area," in Blumberg et al., *Engendering Wealth*, pp. 65–87.

Rose, Kalima. 1992. *Where Women Are Leaders: The SEWA Movement in India.* London: Zed Press.

Safa, Helen. 1995. *The Myth of the Male Breadwinner: Women and Industrialization in the Caribbean.* Boulder, Colo.: Westview.

Savara, Mira. 1981. "Organizing the Annapurna." *Bulletin of the Institute for Development Studies* 12/3:48–53.

Sen, Amartya. 1990. "Gender and cooperative conflicts," in Tinker, *Persistent Inequalities*, pp. 123–149.

Sen, Gita. 1988. "Ethics in Third World development: A feminist perspective." Rama Mehta Lecture. Radcliffe College.

Senauer, Benjamin. 1990. "The impact of the value of women's time on food and nutrition," in Tinker, *Persistent Inequalities*, pp. 150–181.

Sethuraman, S. V., ed. 1981. *The Informal Sector in Developing Countries: Employment, Poverty and Environment.* Geneva: International Labour Organization.

———. 1985. "The informal sector in Indonesia: Politics and prospects." *International Labor Review* 124/6:719–735.

Sharif, Imam. 1983. "BRAC experience in financing small farmers," *ADAB News* special issue on "Rural Credit," Sept.–Oct. Dhaka: Agricultural Development Agencies in Bangladesh.

Silas, Johan. 1989. "Marginal settlements in Surabaya, Indonesia: Problem or potential?" *Environment and Urbanization* 1/2:60–70.

Simmons, Emmy. 1981. "The small-scale rural food-processing Industry in Northern Nigeria." *Food Research Institute Studies* 14:147–161.

Singh, Andrea, and Anita Kelles-Viitanen, eds. 1987. *Invisible Hands: Women in Home-based Production.* New Delhi: Sage.

Sirola, Paula. 1991. "Economic survival alternatives for urban immigrants: informal sector strategies in Los Angeles." Paper presented at the 17th Pacific Science Congress, Honolulu. June.

Sit, V. 1987. "Urban fairs in China." *Economic Geography* 53/4:199–209.

Smale, Melinda. 1980. *Women in Mauritania: The Effects of Drought and Migration on their Economic Status and Implications for Development Programs.* Washington, D.C.: U.S. Agency for International Development.

Smart, J. 1989. *The Political Economy of Street Hawkers in Hong Kong.* Hong Kong: Centre of Asian Studies at the University of Hong Kong.

Smith, Joan, Immanuel Wallerstein, et al. 1992. *Creating and Transforming Households: The Constraints of the World-Economy.* Cambridge: Cambridge University Press.

Splater-Roth, Roberta. 1988. "The sexual political economy of street vending in Washington, D.C.," in Ann Bookman and Sandra Morgen, eds. *Women and the Politics of Empowerment.* Philadelphia: Temple University Press.

Stoler, Ann. 1977. "Class structure and female autonomy in rural Java." *Signs* 3/1:74–89.

Strassman, Paul. 1987. "Home-based enterprises in cities of developing countries." *Economic Development and Cultural Change* 36/1:121–44.

Sudarkasa, Niara. 1973. *Where Women Work: A Study of Yoruba Women in the Market-place and in the Home.* Anthropological Paper No. 53. Ann Arbor, Mich.: Museum of Anthropology, University of Michigan.

Sullerot, Evelyne. 1971. *Women, Society and Change.* New York: McGraw-Hill.

Sullivan, Margaret. 1985. *Can Survive, la! Cottage Industries in High-rise Singapore.* Singapore: Graham Brash.

Szanton, Christina Blanc. 1982. "People in movement: social mobility and leadership in a central Thai town." Ph.D. diss., Columbia University.

Szanton, Christina Blanc. 1985. "Preliminary report for Bangkok seminar, 30 July 1985." Washington, D.C.: EPOC.

Szanton, Christina Blanc, with contributors. 1994. *Urban Children in Distress: Global Predicament and Innovative Strategies.* Langhorne, Penn.: Gordan and Breach for UNICEF.

Szanton, Christina Blanc, and Napat Sirisambhand. 1986. *Thailand's Street Vending: The Urban Informal Sector and Traditional Fast Foods.* Bangkok, Thailand: Chulalongkorn Social Science Research Institute, (CUSRI).

Tendler, Judith. 1987. *What Ever Happened to Poverty Alleviation?* Report to the Ford Foundation, New York. A shorter version appeared in *World Development* 17/7:1033–44.

Thakur, Mina. 1994. "Street food vending in urban Guwahati: An Overview." Unpublished paper, Department of Anthropology, Gauhati University, Guwahati.

Timberg, Thomas. 1992. "Missing research on small and microenterprise promotion programs." *Small Enterprise Development* 3/2:42–7.

———. 1993. "Village banks in Honduras." *Small Enterprise Development* 4/3:52–4

———. 1995. "The poor versus the disenfranchised: Welfare versus empowerment." *Economic Development and Cultural Change* 43/3:651.

Tinker, Irene. 1976. "The adverse impact of development on women," in Tinker, Michelle Bo Bramsen, and Mayra Buvinic, eds., *Women and World Development.* New York: Praeger, for the Overseas Development Council. [Spanish translation: *Las mujeres en el mundo de hoy: Prejuicios y perjuicios.* Buenos Aires: Editorial Fraterna, 1981.]

———. 1983. "Women in development," in Tinker, ed., *Women in Washington: Advocates for Public Policy.* Beverly Hills, Calif.: Sage.

———. 1984. "The real rural energy crisis: Women's time." *Energy Journal* 87/8:125–46.

———. 1987. *Street Foods: Testing Assumptions about Informal Sector Activity by Women and Men.* Entire issues of *Current Sociology* 35/3.

———. 1989. "Credit for poor women: necessary, but not always sufficient for change." *Marga* [Colombo, Sri Lanka] 10/2:31–48.

———. 1990. "A context for the field" and "The making of a field: Advocates, practitioners and scholars," in Tinker, *Persistent Inequalities*, pp. 27–53.

———. 1993a. "The urban street food trade: Regional variations of women's involvement," in Esther Ngan-ling Chow and Catherine White Berheide, eds., *Women, the Family, and Policy: A Global Perspective.* Albany: SUNY Press. pp. 163–187.

———. 1993b. "Women and shelter: Combining women's roles," in Young et al., *Women at the Center*, pp. 63–78.

———. 1993c. "The organization for development and support of street food vendors in the city of Minia: model for empowering the working poor." Cairo: SPAAC for the Ford Foundation.

———. 1993d. "The street food project: using research for planning." *Berkeley Planning Journal* 8:1–20.

————. 1994. "Beyond economics: Sheltering the whole woman," in Blumberg et al., *Engendering Wealth*, pp. 261–283.

————. 1995. "The human economy of microentrepeneurs," in Dignard and Havet, *Women in Micro- and Small-scale Enterprise Development*, pp. 25–39.

Tinker, Irene, ed. 1990. *Persistent Inequalities: Women and World Development*. New York: Oxford University Press.

————, guest ed. 1992. "Urban food production." *Hunger Notes*. Fall.

Tinker, Irene. 1996. "NGOs and international development: Indigenous NGOs promoting sustainable development and democracy—myth and reality." Working paper. Berkeley: Institute for Urban and Regional Development.

Tinker, Irene, and Monique Cohen. 1985. "Street foods as income and food for the poor." *IFDA Dossier* 49:13–23. Geneva: International Foundation for Development Alternatives.

————. 1985a. "Street foods as income and food for the poor." *Ekistics* 52:83–89.

Trager, Lillian. 1981. "Customers and creditors: Variations in economic personalism in a Nigerian market system." *Ethnology* 20/2:133–46.

————. 1985. "From yams to beer in a Nigerian city: expansion and change in informal sector trade activity," in Stuart Platter, ed., *Markets and Marketing*. Lanham, Md.: University Press of America.

————. 1987. "A re-examination of the urban informal sector in West Africa." *Canadian Journal of African Studies* 21/2:238–55.

————. 1992. "The creation of an illegal urban occupation: Street trading in Nigeria," in Hermine G. de Soto, ed., *Culture and Contradiction: Dialects of Wealth, Power and Symbol*. Lewiston, N.Y.: Edwin Mellen Press.

Trager, Lillian, and Clara Osinulu. 1991. "New women's organizations in Nigeria: One response to structural adjustment," in Christine H. Gladwin, ed., *Structural Adjustment and African Women Farmers*. Gainesville: University of Florida Press.

Tyler, Stephen. 1990. "Household energy use in Thai cities: The influences of value of women's time and commercial activity." Report for IENHE/World Bank.

Uchendu, Victor. 1967. "Some principles of haggling in peasant markets." *Economic Development and Cultural Change* 16/1:37–49.

United Nations. 1990. *Methods of Measuring Women's Participation and Production in the Informal Sector*. New York: United Nations.

United Nations Development Program, government of the Netherlands, ILO, and UNIDO. 1988. *Development of Rural Small Industrial Enterprises: Lessons from Experience*. Vienna: United Nations.

UNICEF. 1989. 1988/89 project to imporve school feeding through street foods. Internal memo. Manila: UNICEF regional office.

Urban Edge. 1992. 6/3. March. Washington, D.C.: World Bank.

USAID. 1982. "The community-based project for productivity and family welfare; through the use of SEA Paluwagan and SEA Kalusugan schemes." Project paper.

————. 1989. "The AID microenterprise stocktaking evaluation." AID Evaluation Highlights No. 6. Washington, D.C.: U.S. Agency for International Development.

van de Laar, Irene. 1989. "Why women participate in the informal sector: The case of Ziguinchor, Senegal," in van Gelder and Bijlmer, *About Fringes*, pp. 265–76.

van Gelder, Paul and Joep Bijlmer, eds. 1989. *About Fringes, Margins and Lucky Dips: The*

Informal Sector in Third World Countries—Recent Developments in Research and Policy. Amsterdam: Free University Press.

van Oostrum, Paula. 1989. "Commercialized courtships in a West African city: A device for social mobility?" in van Gelder and Bijlmer, *About Fringes*, pp. 78–88.

Varley, Ann. 1996. "Women heading households: Some more equal than others?" *World Development.* 24/3:505–520.

Walker, Millidge. 1991. "Decentralized planning for sustainable development: The case of Indonesia." *Review of Urban and Regional Development Studies* 3/1:94–102.

———. 1996. "Indonesian NGOs and their relationship to the state." Working paper. Berkeley: Institute for Urban and Regional Development.

Weidemann, Jean, and Zohra Merabetn, 1992. *Egyptian Women and microenterprise: The invisible entrepreneurs.* GEMINI [Growth and Equity through Microenterprise Investiments and Institutions] Technical Report No. 34. Washington, D.C.: Nathan Asso. North South Consultants Exchange of Cairo and Development Alternatives.

Winarno, F. G. 1989. *Streetfoods in West Java. A Base Line Survey.* Streetfood Project Working Report No. 1. Bogor: Food and Technology Development Centre, Bogor Agricultural University, in cooperation with TNO Division of Nutrition and Food Research, Zeist, The Netherlands; and Centre for Development Cooperation Services, Free University, Amsterdam.

———. 1990. *Streetfood Enterprises: Case Studies of Producers and Vendors in Bogor, West Java.* Streetfood Project Working Report No. 4. Bogor: Food and Technology Development Centre, Bogor Agricultural University, in cooperation with TNO Division of Nutrition and Food Research, Zeist, The Netherlands; and Centre for Development Cooperation Services, Free University, Amsterdam.

Winarno, F. G., and A. Allain, 1991. "Street foods in developing countries: Lessons from Asia." *FNA/ANA* 1/1:11–18.

Wipper, Audrey. 1972. "The roles of African women: Past, present and future." *Canadian Journal of African Studies* 6/2.

Wolf, D. 1992. *Factory Daughters: Gender, Household Dynamics and Rural Industrialization in Java.* Berkeley: University of California Press.

World Bank. 1980. *Aspects of Poverty in the Philippines: A Review and Assessment.* Vol. 1. Country Programs Development, East Asia and Pacific Regional Office.

———. 1992. *World Development Report.* New York: Oxford University Press.

World Resources Institute (WRI). 1994. *World Resources 1994–95.* New York: Oxford University Press.

Yasmeen, Gisele. 1990. "Bangkok's restaurant sector: gender, employment, and consumption." *Journal of Social Research* [CUSRI: Bangkok] 15/2:69–81.

———. 1992. "Bangkok's restaurant sector: Gender, employment and consumption." *Journal of Social Research* [Bangkok: CUSRI] 15/2:69–81.

———. 1996. "Bangkok's foodscapes: gendered access to public space in the city." Ph.D. University of British Columbia.

Young, Gay, Vidjamali Samarasinghe, and Ken Kusterer, eds. 1993. *Women at the Center: Development Issues and Practice for the 1990s.* West Hartford, Conn.: Kumarian Press.

Yunus, M. 1983. "Group-based savings and credit for the rural poor." *ADAB News,* special issue on "Rural Credit," Sept.–Oct. Dhaka: Agricultural Development Agencies in Bangladesh.

Index of Recipes

General Index